Helena Gomm & Jon Hird

Inside Out

Teacher's Book

MACMILLAN

Macmillan Education
Between Towns Road, Oxford OX4 3PP, UK
A division of Macmillan Publishers Limited
Companies and representatives throughout the world

ISBN 0 333 92344 8 (International Edition)
ISBN 0 333 96763 1 (Level V)

Text © Ceri Jones, Tania Bastow, Sue Kay and Vaughan Jones 2001
Text by Helena Gomm and Jon Hird
Design and illustration © Macmillan Publishers Limited 2001

First published 2001

Designed by J&L Composition Ltd
Illustrated by Julian Mosedale p 8; Martina Farrow p 8.
Cover design by Andrew Oliver

The authors and publishers would like to thank the following for
permission to reproduce their material:

Anvil Press Poetry for Stealing, taken from Selling Manhattan by
Carol Ann Duffy, published by Anvil Press Poetry in 1987; EMI
Music Publishing Ltd for My Girl, words and music by Michael
Barson © 1979, reproduced by permission of EMI Music Publishing
Ltd, London WC2H 0EA and I'm Going Slightly Mad, words and
music by Freddie Mercury, Brian May, Roger Taylor, John Deacon ©
1991, reproduced by permission of Queen Music Ltd / EMI Music
Publishing Ltd, London WC2H 0EA; David Higham Associates for
extract from The Day of the Triffids by John Wyndham, published
by Penguin Books Ltd; International Music Publications Ltd for
Love in the First Degree, words and music by Sarah Dallin, Keren
Woodward, Siobhan Fahey, Mike Stock, Matt Aitken and Peter
Waterman © 1987 Warner / Chappell Music Ltd, All Boys Music Ltd,
Mike Stock Publishing Ltd and Sids Songs Ltd. (50%)
Warner / Chappell Music Ltd, London W6 8BS.

Printed and bound in Hong Kong

2005
10 9 8 7 6

Introduction

At the heart of 'Inside Out' is the belief that the most effective conditions for language learning come about when students engage in activities on a personal level rather than 'going through the motions'. Engagement can be triggered by anything from understanding and smiling at a cartoon to talking at length to a partner about an important event in your life.

Advanced students have reached a point where they are competent communicators. They can usually cope easily and comfortably in a wide range of situations. They are probably fairly fluent but will see themselves as still lacking in range, of both structures and vocabulary, as well as missing out on many of the finer nuances and subtleties of the language.

- Although they feel comfortable and confident using most of the basic grammar, they tend to 'play safe' and avoid more complex structures.

- They typically have an active lexicon of somewhere between 3,000 and 5,000 words and can recognise many more. They may have an understanding of the basic meaning of a word or lexical item but will not be sure of exactly how it is used in context, its collocations, its register or strength. This means that they often find it hard to reproduce a given effect when necessary.

- When listening or reading, although they will generally be able to follow the gist and understand specific information, they may not always be able to pick up on register or style, which may lead to confusion or misunderstandings, and they often find it difficult to respond appropriately.

As they can already get by fairly well in most situations, there is a great danger at this level that students will allow their language to 'fossilise': ie that their language deficiencies will become permanent features of their competence.

The challenge this poses to the teacher is to create a situation in the classroom where students take risks and push themselves to their limits, learning to express themselves more fully and more precisely, both in speech and in writing. *Inside Out* aims to help you do this as easily and efficiently as possible.

Teaching strategies

All the strategies employed in *Inside Out* aim to promote learning by focusing on personal engagement, both intellectual and emotional.

Accessible topics and texts

Each unit is built around a set of related topics. These have been selected to be meaningful to most students: they are subjects about which most people have something to say.

Grammar awareness/grammar practice

The course covers the main grammar areas you would expect in an advanced course book, but in a way appropriate to the needs of advanced students.

At advanced level, there is little point in teaching the uses of *will* in the same way as at lower levels. Advanced students already know a lot about the uses of *will* – and this applies to most of the structures that are generally taught at this level. But students still want, expect and need grammar to fill gaps in their knowledge and deepen their understanding.

To provide appropriate grammar study, *Inside Out* includes 'Close up' sections. These follow a three stage approach: language analysis; practice; personalisation.

1. The language analysis stage promotes 'noticing' of language features and usage. Working with example sentences and text from the book, students articulate and organise what they know, and incorporate new information.

   This stage will work both as individual study or as pair/groupwork. In general, we recommend pair/groupwork as this provides a forum for students to exchange and test out ideas before presenting them in the more intimidating arena of the whole class.

   Unlike other books which use the 'guided discovery' approach to grammar, we have generally avoided gap fills and multiple choice questions. Research showed us that most students are unenthusiastic about using these techniques to study grammar. This may be because they associate them with practice and testing rather than learning. Instead, we provide questions and discussion points.

2. In the practice activities students manipulate or select structures, testing their theories. As they do this, they also become more comfortable with the grammar point.

   The sentences in this section are designed to be realistic rather than relying on invented scenarios about imaginary people. Many can be applied to the students' own lives, and this facilitates the next stage.

3. The personalisation stage is not a conventional free practice, where students, for example, take part in a role play which 'requires' the target structure. As Michael Lewis has pointed out, very few situations in real life actually require a particular structure. Furthermore, when they are faced with a situation without time to prepare, many students will, naturally, decide to rely on what they know, rather than what they studied half an hour ago.

For these reasons, personalisation is based on actual examples of the target structure. Students apply these examples to their own lives, opinions and feelings. Sentences from the practice stage are often recycled for the personalisation. For example:

- Are any of the sentences true for you or your country?

- Do you know anyone like the people described above? Ask your partner.

All the Close up sections are followed by Language reference boxes, which give accurate, clear explanations backed up with examples. These appear in the unit, right where they're needed, rather than being tucked away at the back of the book.

Personalised speaking tasks

Inside Out is filled with speaking tasks. Their main purpose is to develop fluency. While they are not intended principally as grammar practice, they are linked to the topics, lexis and grammar in the unit so as to include opportunities for students to turn input into output.

The tasks do not require complicated classroom configurations. They are easy to set up and enjoyable to use. Most of them encourage students to talk about things that matter to them, rather than playing roles or exchanging invented information.

Personalised, authentic tasks challenge and engage students, and this encourages linguistic 'risk taking': Can I use this word here? Is this how this structure works? Research into second language acquisition suggests that when students take risks they are experimenting, testing theories about how the language works. This is an essential part of language learning.

Anecdotes

There are also extended speaking tasks, where students tackle a longer piece of discourse. We've called these 'anecdotes' and they are based on personal issues. When you learn a musical instrument, you can't spend all your time playing scales and exercises; you also need to learn whole pieces in order to see how music is organised. Anecdotes give students a chance to get to grips with how discourse is organised.

The anecdotes are set up through evocative questions. Students read or listen to a planned series of questions and choose what specifically they will talk about; shyer students can avoid matters they feel are too personal. As they prepare for the anecdote, students also think about the language they will need. This student preparation is a key stage. Research, by Peter Skehan among others, has shown that learners who plan for tasks attempt more ambitious language, hesitate less and make fewer basic errors.

The simplest way to prepare students for an anecdote is to ask them to read the list of questions in the book and decide which they want to talk about. Ask them to think about the language they will need. Encourage them to use dictionaries and make notes, but not to write out what they will actually say. Finally, put them into pairs to exchange anecdotes.

Alternatively, ask students to close their books – and then to close their eyes. Ask them to listen to the questions as you read them aloud and think about what they evoke. Some classes will find this a more involving process. It also allows you to adapt the questions to your class, adding new ones or missing out ones you think inappropriate. After the reading, give students a couple of minutes to finalise their preparation before starting the speaking task.

Teachers may also want to ask students to produce a written account of the anecdote as a follow-up activity. This allows those students who are slightly more reticent when speaking to push themselves a little further and develop confidence in their abilities, as well as encouraging students to review any new structures or lexical items that have come up in the unit. It also provides practice in writing to prepare for speaking, something students will probably have to do more of as their English advances.

Repeating anecdotes

Consider going back to anecdotes and repeating them in later classes. Let students know that you are going to do this. This will reassure them that you are doing it on purpose, but more importantly, it will mean that they can dedicate some time and thought to preparation. When you repeat the task, mix the class so that each student works with a new partner, ie one who has not previously heard the anecdote.

Repeating complex tasks reflects real interactions. We all have our set pieces and we tend to refine and improve them as we retell them. Many students will appreciate the opportunity to do the same thing in their second language, and research has shown that given this opportunity, they become more adventurous and more precise in the language they use.

You can also repeat the anecdotes as a speaking component to accompany the tests in the Teacher's Book.

In the second half of the book, students are given the opportunity to give a brief presentation in front of the class. The preparatory discussion and thinking time involved in these activities allows students to clarify their ideas and choose what they are going to say and how they are going to say it. Having to speak to an audience pushes students to take more care in how they express themselves and to monitor their own speech more closely. Research suggests that this 'pushed output' helps students develop their awareness of style and register and their understanding of the relationship between form and meaning.

Realistic reading

In theory, no matter how difficult a text may be, the task that accompanies it can be designed to be within the competence of the student, ie 'grade the task not the text'. But conversations with students and teachers have convinced us that this is an insight of only limited value. However easy the task, students are quickly disillusioned by an incomprehensible text.

At the other extreme, many of the texts that have appeared in ELT coursebooks in the past have obviously been written merely in order to include examples of a given grammatical structure. Texts like this are often boring to read and unconvincing as discourse.

The solution adopted in *Inside Out* has been to base all reading texts on authentic modern sources, including magazines, novels, newspapers and personal communications. Where necessary, the source texts have been edited and graded so as to make them challenging without being impossible. The texts have been selected not only for their language content but also for their interest and their appropriacy to students.

Varied listening work

The listenings include texts specially written for language learning, improvisations in the studio and authentic recordings. There are dialogues, conversations, monologues and real pop songs by the original artists. There is a variety of English accents and some examples of non-native speakers. The tasks are designed to develop real life listening skills.

Contemporary lexis in context

Selecting lexis to teach becomes more difficult at higher levels. It is relatively easy to predict the needs of beginners: 'hello', 'please', 'thank you'. As learners progress to higher levels, their vocabulary needs come to depend more and more on their individual situations: jobs, courses of study, exams, personal interests.

In *Inside Out*, lexis is selected to be generally useful and appropriate to the typical student, who is likely to be 17–35 years old and relatively well-educated. It is always presented in some sort of context and is related to the themes and topics in the unit.

Lexis is first of all highlighted in exercises which draw attention to it, then recycled in back up exercises. The Workbook provides further recycling, as do the photocopiable tests in the Teacher's Book. The exercises encourage students to deal with lexis as part of a system, rather than as a list of discrete words, through tasks to focus on collocation, connotation and social register.

Motivating writing practice

The Student's Book contains structured writing tasks which offer students opportunities to get to grips with a variety of formats: newspaper and magazine reviews and articles of varying lengths, letters of varying degrees of formality, guide book excerpts, diary excerpts, short stories and personal profiles.

This is backed up by a self-contained writing course which runs through the Workbook.

Components

Each level of *Inside Out* includes a Student's Book, a Teacher's Book, a Workbook, Class Cassettes and CDs, a Workbook Cassette and CD, and a photocopiable Resource Pack. The course also includes a Video and a Video Teacher's Book.

Student's Book

The Student's Book covers about 90 hours of classroom teaching. It is made up of 12 main units (1–6 and 8–13) and two review units (7 and 14). The units do not follow a rigid template: the flow of each one comes from the texts, tasks and language points in it.

The book includes all the tapescripts, plus a glossary of grammatical terminology, a guide to the phonemic alphabet and an overview of the structures covered in the book.

Class Cassettes/CDs

These have all the listening materials from the Student's Book.

Workbook

The Workbook provides revision of all the main points in the Student's Book, plus extra listening practice, pronunciation work and a complete self-contained writing course.

Workbook Cassette/CD

This contains listening practice and pronunciation work.

Teacher's Book

In this book you'll find step-by-step notes and answers for every exercise. These include closed-book activities to warm the class up before beginning a new set of work. The tapescripts are included in the body of the notes for easy reference.

For every one of the main units there is a one-page photocopiable test, for use as soon as you finish the unit or a couple of weeks later. There are longer mid course and end of course tests which go with the two review units (7 and 14).

At the beginning of the book there is a two-part Zero Unit.

- The first part is a quiz about the Student's Book to help familiarise students with it: how language is described, the kinds of activities they will do, how the list of contents works, what they can find at the back of the book.

- The second part is a Student profile. It aims to discover something about each student's language learning history and reasons for studying English. Students can fill the form out individually or by interviewing each other in pairs. The Student profile is similar to a needs analysis. Knowing about your students' needs and wants will help you to plan lessons, to use the Student's Book more appropriately and to get to know your students better.

Resource Pack

The Resource Pack contains thirty-seven photocopiable worksheets designed to supplement or extend the Student's Book. The worksheets are based on the themes and grammar points in the book and are linked to the book unit by unit. They were written for this project by eleven different ELT teachers. They are very varied, but one thing they have in common is that they provide practical, useful classroom practice. There are full teaching notes for every worksheet.

Video

The video contains one sequence for each main unit of the Student's Book. Each sequence fits exercises and pages in the Student's Book, either using tapescripts to create a visual version of listening exercises, or taking a topic and developing it more fully. For example: video unit 3 develops the reading text about Leicester Square on page 30.

Video Teacher's Book

The Video Teacher's Book provides photocopiable worksheets for the video sequences, as well as full keys and tapescripts.

Over to you

If you have any comments about *Inside Out* you will find a feedback form on our website at: www.insideout.net, where you can also register to receive extra teaching materials free every week by e-mail.

Zero Unit answers:

(Page numbers refer to the Student's Book)

1 a) 14   b) They're review units

2 a) Mind (unit 6)   b) Cyberspace (unit 8)   c) Words (unit 12)
d) Firsts (unit 10)   e) Luck (unit 5)

3 a) clauses (p 142)   b) measure (p 143)   c) anyway (p 151)
d) chance, English (p 140)

4 a) Unreal conditionals (p 48)   b) Word linking (p 62)

5 a) Identity (p 7)   b) Firsts (p 94)

6 a) Britain (p 11)   b) Dr Oliver Sacks (p 54)   c) Climb
each of the world's 14 mountains over 8,000 metres (p 92)
d) Samuel Langhorne Clemens (p 117)

0 Zero unit

Book quiz

Look through your book and find the answers to these questions.

1 a) How many units are there in the book?

   _____

   b) Why are units 7 and 14 different?

   _____

2 Look at the list of contents. In which unit can you:

   a) listen to a song by the group *Queen*?

   _____

   b) study vocabulary of the Internet and e-mail?

   _____

   c) read about suggestions for improving English spelling?

   _____

   d) write some quiz questions?

   _____

   e) play a game called *Wishful thinking*?

   _____

3 a) In the Grammar glossary, what is defined as 'groups of words containing a verb'?

   _____

   b) Which word illustrates /ʒ/ in the table of phonetic symbols?

   _____

   c) What is the last word of tapescript 34?

   _____

   d) This sentence is in the verb structures section. Add the missing words.

   I wish I had more _____ to speak _____ .

4 a) Which grammar structure is dealt with in the first Language reference section in *Luck*?

   _____

   b) What pronunciation area is dealt with in *Mind*?

   _____

5 Look at the list of contents. Decide which units you think these pictures are in and then check in the unit.

   a)

   _____

   b)

   _____

6 a) Where is the pop group *Madness* from?

   _____

   b) Who wrote *The Man Who Mistook His Wife for a Hat*?

   _____

   c) Mountaineer Reinhold Messner was the first to do what?

   _____

   d) What was the writer Mark Twain's real name?

   _____

Student profile

- **Name**

  _____

- **Have you studied English in the past?**

  No ☐   Yes ☐ → When and where? _____

- **Have you got any English language qualifications?**

  No ☐   Yes ☐ → When and where did you take them? _____

  What are they? _____

  _____

- **Do you use English outside the class?**

  No ☐   Yes ☐ → When do you use English and where? _____

  _____

- **Are you studying English, or in English, outside this class?**

  No ☐   Yes ☐ → Please give details _____

  _____

- **Do you speak any other languages?**

  No ☐   Yes ☐ → Which ones? _____

  _____

- **Why are you studying English?**

  I need it for work.

  No ☐   Yes ☐ → What do you do? _____

  _____

  I need it to study.

  No ☐   Yes ☐ → What are you studying? _____

  _____

  Where? _____

  I'm going to take an examination.

  No ☐   Yes ☐ → What examination are you going to take? ___

  _____

  When? _____

  For personal interest.

  No ☐   Yes ☐ → What do you like doing in your free time? ___

  _____

1 Identity Overview

The topic of this unit is identity and this word is interpreted in several ways, from how we describe ourselves to others to the differences between men and women. The main grammatical focus is on adverbials and phrasal verbs with objects.

The unit begins by considering the way we define our own identity. Students discuss their backgrounds and the way they describe themselves to strangers. They listen and make notes as people answer questions about their identity. Students then move on to talk about which factor in their lives (job, home town or family) they identify most strongly with.

Next, students read extracts from the book *Men Are From Mars, Women Are From Venus* and examine the differences in perception and outlook between men and women. The song *My Girl* is used for further discussion of the ways in which differences between men and women can lead to misunderstanding and conflict.

Finally, students read a short text which can be interpreted in different ways. They consider situations that fit all the facts given and discuss the implications of jumping to the wrong conclusion.

Section	Aims	What the students are doing
Introduction page 4	*Conversation skills*: fluency work	Talking about ID cards.
Born & bred page 4	*Listening skills*: listening for detail; making notes on answers to questions	Listening and taking notes on how people describe themselves.
Close up pages 5–6	*Grammar*: adverbials	Identifying different types of adverbials. Studying the implications of the position of adverbials.
I am who I am page 7	*Conversaton skills*: fluency work	Anecdote: talking about what you identify most strongly with.
The gender gap pages 8–9	*Reading skills*: predicting	Reading the blurb from a book cover and predicting what will be in the book.
	reading for detail	Doing a jigsaw reading and discussing extracts from a book.
	Lexis: personal values; wordbuilding	Focusing on vocabulary of personal values from the extract and forming nouns, verbs, adjectives and adverbs from these words.
Close up pages 10–11	*Grammar*: phrasal verbs with objects	Matching phrasal verbs with their meanings. Identifying different types of phrasal verbs. Completing sentences with phrasal verbs.
My girl pages 11–12	*Listening skills*: listening for detail	Predicting the content of a song from expressions taken from the lyrics. Listening to the song and numbering the expressions as they occur.
	Speaking skills: telephone conversations	Practising a conversation between the characters in the song.
	Pronunciation: intonation	Identifying angry tones from the conversation and practising them.
Mistaken identity page 13	*Reading skills*: reading for detail	Reading a short text and deciding exactly what it says. Making up a situation to fit the text.
	Conversation skills: discussing a situation	Discussing the implications of jumping to conclusions.

1 *Identity* *Teacher's notes*

Closed books. Whole class. Before students open their books, ask them to identify some famous people from the following information. (If Elton John and Venus Williams are unknown to your students, use information about famous people they are familiar with.) Pause after each clue to see if anyone can identify the person. The information is arranged so that the clues become easier.

1 He was born in 1947. He was born in Pinner, England. His real name is Reg Dwight. He is a famous singer. He plays the piano. One of his most famous songs is *Candle in the Wind*. (Elton John)

2 She was born in Lynwood, California. She was born in 1980. She has a sister who does the same job. She plays tennis. She won the women's singles at Wimbledon in 2000. (Venus Williams)

1 Groupwork. Students try to identify the people in the ID cards. You may need to point out that the jobs on the cards are not necessarily the ones they are most famous for. They note down as much extra information as they can about each one.

2 Students turn to page 132 and check their answers.

> A Sean Connery (British actor and film star; most famous for his portrayal of British spy James Bond in a series of films in the 1960s)
>
> B Marilyn Monroe (American film star; real name Norma Jean Baker; died of an overdose of barbiturates in 1962; friendly with John F Kennedy; married to baseball star Joe di Maggio and playwright Arthur Miller)
>
> C Margaret Thatcher (First woman leader of a British political party and first woman prime minister of Britain; born Margaret Hilda Roberts; worked as a research chemist and a lawyer before entering politics; longest serving British prime minister in the 20th century (1979–1990); created a life peer in 1992)
>
> D Bill Clinton (42nd President of the United States; served for two terms, despite a number of sex scandals; only the second president to be impeached following the Monica Lewinsky scandal; was acquitted)

3 Pairwork. Students discuss the six questions. They then report back to the class. Invite any students who have their ID with them to show it to the class if they wish.

Born and bred (p 4)

1 Groupwork. Students discuss the three questions and report back to the class.

2 ▭ 01 SB p 143

Play the recording. Students listen and make notes on what the speakers say and identify which questions they answer.

> Steve answers all the questions.
>
> David answers all the questions except: *Were your parents born there too?*
>
> Valeria answers two questions in a, but not *Where is your home town?* She answers question c but she does not answer the questions in b.

▭ 01

Steve

(I = Interviewer; S = Steve)

I: *Steve, what would you say was your home town?*

S: *Um, ah, that's a difficult one because I've travelled around so much. Still, um, Toronto, I suppose. I mean, I've lived there for more than twenty years and that's where I was born.*

I: *Your parents weren't born there, though, were they?*

S: *Oh no, my parents were born in England, in Manchester.*

I: *Both of them?*

S: *Yeah, both of them.*

I: *And what would they say was their home town?*

S: *Well, my Dad's really proud to be English and proud to be from Manchester, but he's also proud to be Canadian – a naturalised Canadian. He's just become Canadian after thirty-five years of living there and he's really proud of that, but I guess it would be difficult for them to answer too.*

I: *And when someone asks you where you're from, what do you say?*

S: *Canada.*

I: *That's because you live abroad?*

S: *Yes, but when I'm back home at my parents' house, they've moved since I left Canada, and someone asks me where I'm from, I say Toronto.*

I: *And what would you say was maybe the most important thing for you in defining yourself, you know, your personal identity?*

S: *Wow! Well that's a big one.*

I: *You know, like is it your town, your country, your language, your job?*

S: *Well, it isn't my home town I don't think. Or my country. Maybe it's language, because Canada has got the two languages and people tend to define themselves according to the language so I'd say I was English-speaking Canadian, I suppose, you know, as opposed to French-speaking Canadian. But it's not really that at all. I mean it's more to do with my attitude. Yeah, you know, my attitude, my opinions about things. I guess that's who I am.*

David

(I = Interviewer; D = David)

I: *If someone asks you where you come from, what do you say?*

D: *I usually say I'm Welsh. Or it depends I suppose depending on who's asking or where I am at the time. Obviously if I'm back home in Wales, then I give the name of my home town – Aberystwyth. Even though I haven't lived there in years.*

I: *Were you born there?*

D: *Yes I was, and spent most of my childhood there as well, until I was eighteen.*

I: *And, if you're not back home, I mean, what if you're on holiday or whatever?*

D: *Yes, sometimes, when I'm abroad people take it for granted that I'm English, or maybe they're just using the word English to mean British. That can be quite annoying, or not that exactly. It's when I explain that I'm from Wales and they say, 'Isn't that in England?' Now that, that's annoying.*

I: *Is it really that important to you?*

D: *Oh, that's a big question. Um, yeah, I suppose it is. I suppose it's kind of a central part of my identity. Part of how I see myself, define who I am.*

I: *Do you speak Welsh?*

D: *Yes, I do. Maybe that's part of the reason why it's so important. I mean, I think the language you speak really defines the way you think sometimes. Or at least I feel like it's another side to me. Like there's my English side and there's my Welsh side. I haven't lived in Wales for years and sometimes I really miss speaking the language like I'm missing a part of myself.*

I: *Do you speak Welsh at all these days?*

D: *Yeah, on the phone to my mum, or my brother. Once or twice a week. But that's about all.*

I: *So, what would you say is your mother tongue, then? Welsh or English?*

D: *Both I suppose. I mean I was brought up speaking both as a kid. It's impossible not to be an English speaker in Wales. You're just*

surrounded by the language everywhere. On the TV, in films. There is a Welsh TV channel and weekly papers and stuff, but it's just not such a strong presence I suppose. I mean, it is possible to ignore it. It is totally possible to live in Wales and not be a Welsh speaker – well, most people aren't.

Valeria

(I = Interviewer; V = Valeria)

I: *So if I asked you to say who you are, I mean like, how you define yourself, what would you say was the most important factor? Your home town? Your job?*

V: *Difficult to say. Both I suppose. I mean, I've lived here all my life, and so have my family. My family have actually lived in the same house for seven generations. Well, OK, that's a bit of an exaggeration. But we do still have a house in a village nearby that we use in the summer, and my grandmother was born there, and her grandparents before her ... I love that house, its big thick stone walls and vaulted ceilings ...*

I: *So maybe the house is what you identify with?*

V: *Oh no, not only the house, the village, the town, the whole region really.*

I: *And what about your job?*

V: *Mmm, yes, well being a notary is kind of a family trade. I mean, again we go back generations and generations ... my father, my grandfather ... I'm actually the first woman in our family to become a notary and I really like the idea that I'm the seventh generation of notaries in the family and that a woman can carry on what was basically a male tradition until very recently.*

I: *And did you always know you were going to follow in your father's footsteps? Or did you resist it at all at any time?*

V: *No, no, there was no question of resisting at all. I'm really happy with my choice. I really love my job. You know, it's such an old tradition, such a, I know this is going to sound a bit pompous, a bit clichéd, but it's such a respected profession and I feel really proud about carrying on the family tradition.*

3 Pairwork. Students compare their answers and discuss the two questions.

Close up (p 5)

Types of adverbials

1 Whole class. Establish that adverbials can be either one word or a phrase which adds information to a sentence.

Elicit some examples of adverbials from the class to check that students understand what they are.

Students then work individually to read the sentences and underline the adverbials. Allow students to compare with a partner before checking answers with the class.

a) always
b) in the North of England
c) there, since I left home
d) there, to study medicine
e) really, there

2 Pairwork. Before students begin, focus attention on the sentences in 1 and elicit that adverbials can be placed in a variety of positions in a sentence. Students look at the extracts from the listening and decide where the adverbials go. Go through the example with them first. Note that the adverbials are listed in the order they appear in the sentences.

3 02 SB p 143

Play the recording. Students listen and check their answers.

02

a) *He's just become Canadian after thirty-five years of living there and he's really proud of that ...*

b) *... sometimes, when I'm abroad people take it for granted that I'm English, or maybe they're just using the word English to mean British.*

c) *There is a Welsh TV channel and weekly papers and stuff, but it's just not such a strong presence I suppose. I mean, it is possible to ignore it. It is totally possible to live in Wales and not be a Welsh speaker ...*

d) *... I've lived here all my life, and so have my family. My family have actually lived in the same house for seven generations.*

e) *... I really like the idea that I'm the seventh generation of notaries in the family and that a woman can carry on what was basically a male tradition until very recently.*

4 Pairwork. Students put the adverbials in the categories. Check answers with the whole class. Students who finish early could check with other pairs whilst waiting for everyone to finish.

a) sometimes
b) really, totally
c) actually, just, really
d) when I'm abroad, in Wales
e) just, after thirty-five years of living there

f) all my life, for seven generations, until very recently
g) just, basically

If necessary, refer to the Language reference section on page 6 and the Grammar glossary on page 142.

Position of adverbials (p 5)

1 Pairwork. Students study the sentences and decide where to put *always* in each one. Encourage them to read the sentences aloud and see what sounds right in each case. Check answers with the class.

These are the normal positions of *always*. Note that for special emphasis it would be possible to place the word in other positions.

• We always define ourselves according to our place of birth.

• We have always defined ourselves according to our place of birth.

• We would always have defined ourselves according to our place of birth.

• We wouldn't always have defined ourselves according to our place of birth.

2 Students work individually to read through the questions and decide on their answers. They can be encouraged to read the sentence aloud, putting the adverbials in different places in order to decide what sounds best.

Pairwork. With a partner, students then check their answers against the Language reference section on page 6. This will get them used to referring to the Language reference section and encourage them to try to find out information for themselves first before coming to you. While they are doing this, write the sentence on the board. Elicit answers to the questions from the class.

a) *Note: some other positions are possible.*
   when we are children: 1
   often: 2
   if we live there: 1, 5
   to some extent: 1, 4
   on the whole: 1
   probably: 2

b) when we are children, if we live there, to some extent, on the whole. This is because the adverbial is a phrase and not a word.

c) Position 3, between the verb and the object.

3 Students modify the sentence with adverbials to make it true for them. Allow them to compare answers with a partner. Elicit a few opinions around the class.

4 Pairwork. Go through the example with the whole class. Students then look at the pairs of sentences in pairs or small groups and discuss how the meaning is changed by moving the adverbials. Check answers with the class.

1A	No-one else, apart from Kate, knows how to look after horses.
1B	Looking after horses is the only thing Kate knows how to do.
2A	If I'm honest I have to say that I'm fed up with her and can't speak to her any more.
2B	I don't feel I can tell her the truth any more.
3A	At an earlier time I had wanted Rich to come to the meeting, but then I changed my mind.
3B	I had wanted Rich to arrive at the meeting earlier than he did.

5 Pairwork. Students take turns to interview each other and make notes on what they hear. They then write their profiles, using at least five adverbials. Encourage them to exchange their profiles and comment on and correct each other's work. Display the finished profiles for the rest of the class to read and enjoy.

Alternative activity

Students write their profiles but don't put their names on them. Display the profiles on the wall. Students circulate and try to identify the student being described. The profiles could stay on the wall in the classroom to help the class gain a sense of group and could be used later on in the course to compare early written work and later work.

I am who I am (p 7)

Anecdote

See Introduction, page 4, for more ideas on how to set up, monitor and repeat Anecdotes.

1 Go through the instructions with the class, making sure they understand that they have to choose just one of the topics to talk about. Give them plenty of time to read the questions and to think about their answers. Direct their attention to the Language toolbox where they will find useful expressions which they can incorporate. Also point out the final question in each section which invites them to add anything else that they would like.

2 Pairwork. Make sure students understand that they have to ask questions when their partner has finished speaking and should note down questions as they listen. This will ensure that they listen attentively to what their partner says. Students take turns to talk and ask questions.

Encourage students to report back to the class anything interesting that they heard in their pairs.

The gender gap (p 8)

Books closed. Tell students that the next section of the unit is called *The gender gap*. Ask them to speculate on what this

means and what they think the section will be about. If they have no ideas, tell them the meaning of *gender*. They should be able to work out that *gender gap* refers to the differences in behaviour and attitude between people of different sexes and they can then speculate on what these are and what problems, if any, they cause. Make sure students don't discuss anything that may come up later in this section.

1 Groupwork. Students read and discuss the questions. One member of the group should take notes of their answers to report back to the class. Remember to ask each group to say which question generated the most discussion. Encourage students to say why they think this was.

2 Whole class. Students look at the book cover. Elicit what Mars and Venus are (two planets) and what the two names mean (Mars was the Roman god of war and Venus the goddess of love). Students then read the blurb and the questions which follow.

If anyone has actually read this book, ask them to tell the class briefly about it and whether they enjoyed it. Elicit answers to the other questions. Make a note of students' predictions on the board and leave them there so they can check them after reading the texts.

3 Pairwork. Students A and B read different texts, one on Mars and one on Venus. You could set this up in various ways according to what you think will work best in your class. If you have a roughly equal number of male and female students, you could assign the Mars text to all the male students and the Venus text to all the female students and then put them in pairs of male and female for discussion. Alternatively, you might want to have the male students read about Venus and the female students about Mars.

Students who have read the same text could compare notes with each other before working with a partner who has read the other text.

4 Pairwork. Students who have read different texts tell their partners about their extracts and discuss the questions.

Whole class. Get feedback from several pairs and allow the rest of the class to comment on what is said. An additional discussion question which you could ask the class is: *Are men and women's roles becoming less defined? If so, give examples.*

Lexis (p 8)

1 Pairwork. Students read the sentences and decide whether they refer to men or women. Make sure students understand that this is in reference to the book *Men Are From Mars, Women Are From Venus*. They are not being asked to say whether they personally think these sentences describe men or women. After they have completed the exercise, you might like to ask them if they agree with the writer on these descriptions.

Whole class. Ask individual students to read out the sentences in turn. The class can then vote on whether they think they refer to men or women.

a) men b) men c) women d) women	
e) men f) women g) men	

2 Pairwork. Allow students time to read the definitions and match them to the words in 1. Allow students to check with a partner before checking answers with the class.

> a) skills   b) achievement   c) competence
> d) efficiency   e) satisfaction   f) fulfilment
> g) considerate   h) value

3 Students work individually to create and complete the table with words from their answers to 2. Allow them to compare notes with a partner before checking answers with the class.

noun	verb	adjective	adverb
skills	–	skilful / skilled	skilfully
achievement	achieve	achievable	–
competence	–	competent	competently
efficiency	–	efficient	efficiently
satisfaction	satisfy	satisfying / satisfied / satisfactory	satisfyingly
fulfilment	fulfil	fulfilling / fulfilled	–
consideration	consider	considerate	considerately
value	value	valuable / valued	valuably

4 Students work individually to complete the gaps in the sentences. Allow them to compare answers with a partner before checking with the class. Note that there could be more than one answer for some of the gaps. Accept any answers that are grammatically correct and make sense.

> a) consideration   b) satisfying / fulfilling   c) value
> d) satisfied   e) achievement   f) efficient
> g) satisfaction   h) skills   i) competent

5 Students work individually to read the completed sentences in 4 again and decide whether or not they agree with them. Allow students time to change any of the sentences that are not true for them.

6 Pairwork. Students compare their answers. It would be good at this stage to get the students to work in pairs of the opposite sex. Pairs report back to the class on what they have learnt. Encourage students to say whether they think any differences between them reflect the fact that they are of a different sex or whether they are just the result of different personalities.

Close up (p 10)

Phrasal verbs with objects

Note: The term *phrasal verbs* is being used here to cover all multi-word verbs, whether they are phrasal verbs or prepositional verbs.

1 ▄▄ **03 SB p 143**

Play the recording. Students listen and answer the questions.

> a) Liz has read it, Martha has only read the first few pages.
> b) Liz liked it and thought it made sense. Martha thought the main idea was a bit contrived.
> c) They discuss the part at the beginning where the author says that men and women are from different planets; the passage on how the different sexes deal with stress and problems; the passage on how men take pride in being able to achieve things alone; and the book's conclusion.

▄▄ **03**

(M = Martha; L = Liz)

M: *Oh, you've got 'Men Are From Mars, Women Are From Venus'. I saw it.*

L: *Yeah, Trish lent it to me. Have you read it?*

M: *No, well not properly. I just saw it in a bookshop and I flicked through it just briefly. I read the first few pages though, the bit ... oh, what was it? The bit about men and women being from different planets. You know. It sounded really funny. I think, um, it's quite a nice idea but maybe just a little bit contrived. A bit obvious, you know. Have you read it?*

L: *Yeah, I've just finished it. I know what you mean about it seeming a bit contrived, but I do think it's actually quite a neat way of putting the idea across. You know, it's very clear. And it's very original and I didn't find it at all patronising.*

M: *That's good. I got the impression that it's very politically correct. What did you think of it? Do you think that men and women are from different planets?*

L: *Well, sort of. I quite liked what it had to say actually. For example, how men and women cope with stress and problems. How we cope differently. How men like to sort things out on their own.*

M: *Oh, that's true.*

L: *Take time to think things through quietly, all on their own.*

M: *Well, actually, that really means just bottling things up, doesn't it?*

L: *Well, it's interesting you should say that because that's exactly what the book predicted that that's how a woman would interpret it.*

M: *Really?*

L: *Because women actually differ from men in that they prefer to talk about problems and vent their feelings, whereas, as I say, men think it's far more efficient to sort things out on their own.*

M: *When I was flicking through, I caught a glimpse, a bit about how men really take pride in being able to do things and achieve things actually without help, totally on their own.*

L: *I think they do. I think they do actually and I think that's the root of some of the problems really because women like to talk things through and express themselves and it really gets them down if they've got a partner who won't join in, won't tell them anything.*

M: *Yeah. So what solution did the book come up with?*

L: *Well, tolerance really. You know, the best thing to do is be aware that we're different. Realise that men and women have a different style of approaching things and then learn to put up with it. Makes sense.*

M: *Yeah.*

2 Pairwork. Students read the statements and discuss whether they are true or false. They should make a note of their answers. Do not check answers at this stage.

3 Pairwork. Play the recording again. Students listen and check their answers, discussing and amending any they wish to change. Check answers with the whole class.

a) false   b) false   c) false   d) true
e) false   f) false   g) true   h) true

4 Students work individually to match the phrasal verbs to the italicised phrases in 2. Allow students to check with a partner before checking answers with the class.

1   c) to find solutions to
2   e) not to show
3   h) to tolerate
4   a) to look at very quickly and superficially
5   d) to reflect on
6   g) to depress
7   f) to discuss
8   b) to communicate
9   h) to propose

5 Pairwork. Students look at the types of phrasal verbs which take objects and answer the questions. Make sure they understand which part of a phrasal verb is the particle. Encourage them to read the sentences aloud to see what sounds right. When they have finished, give them an opportunity to check their answers in the Language reference section on page 12 before checking answers with the class.

Type 1
Sentences a) and c) are not correct.

Type 2
Sentence d) is not correct.

Type 3
a)   We should learn to put up with each others' differences.
b)   What solution did the author come up with?

6 Whole class. Elicit the rules for word order in the first two types of phrasal verbs. Ask students to say whether type 3 verbs are similar to type 1 or type 2.

a)   Type 1 (not separable) verb + particle + object
     Type 2 (separable), either: verb + object + particle, or: verb + particle + object
     If the object is a pronoun, only the first order is possible.
b)   Type 1

7 Pairwork. Allow students to work with a partner to decide what type the other phrasal verbs in 4 are. Tell them that writing an example sentence using each one may help them decide. They should only look at the tapescript on page 143 if they still can't decide. Check answers with the class.

Type 1
No other answers.
Type 2
sort out   bottle up   think through   get down
talk through
Type 3
No other answers.

8 Students work individually to complete the sentences. Allow them to compare their answers in pairs before checking with the class.

a)   I try not to bottle up my feelings, it's always much better to talk about them with a friend. (*bottle my feelings up* is also possible)
b)   I hate asking people for help. I'd much rather sort my problems out on my own. (*sort out my problems* is also possible)
c)   I don't often buy a newspaper, but sometimes I flick through one at the bar.

d) I'm not a very confident speaker. Sometimes I'm not sure I've managed to put my ideas across very effectively. (*put across my ideas* is also possible)

e) My motto is 'if you can't change it, then you'll just have to put up with it'.

f) I tend to be a little too impulsive and don't think things through enough.

g) I hate arguments, I'd much rather talk things through quietly and calmly.

h) My sister's a really happy, positive person, nothing ever gets her down.

9 Pairwork. Students work individually to read the completed sentences again and decide if they are true for them. They make any necessary changes so that they are true and then compare their answers with a partner.

My girl (p 11)

Books closed. Tell students that the title of the next section is *My girl* and that it features a song. Ask them if they know a song called *My Girl*, who it is by and what it is about.

Open books. Whole class. Students look at the photo and read the information about Madness. Find out if anyone has any CDs by Madness or if they know the other songs listed.

1 Pairwork. Students make lists of five common complaints made by girlfriends and boyfriends. They discuss these and decide whether they differ according to sex. In a feedback session with the whole class, find out how many pairs thought of the same complaints and which complaint occurs on the most lists.

2 Whole class. Students read the expressions in the box. Elicit a few ideas on what the song might be about, getting the students to justify their ideas by referring to the expressions. Write up a few good ideas on the board.

3 📼 **04 SB p 144**

Play the recording. Students listen and number the expressions as they hear them. They check their answers in pairs. If the task seems quite easy for them then check answers with the class. If not, check their predictions and then let them listen again to number the expressions.

1 mad at me
2 see the film tonight
3 had enough
4 lovely to me
5 on my own
6 on the telephone
7 why can't I explain
8 doesn't understand
9 we argued just the other night
10 talked it out
11 I don't care

📼 **04**

My Girl by Madness

My girl's mad at me, I didn't want to see the film tonight,
I found it hard to say, she thought I'd had enough of her.
Why can't she see,
She's lovely to me,
But I like to stay in and watch TV on my own every now and then.

My girl's mad at me, been on the telephone for an hour,
We hardly said a word, I tried and tried, but I could not be heard.
Why can't I explain,
Why do I feel this pain?
'Cos everything I say she doesn't understand, she doesn't realise,
She takes it all the wrong way.

My girl's mad at me, we argued just the other night,
I thought we'd got it straight, we talked and talked until it was light.
I thought we'd agreed,
I thought we'd talked it out,
Now when I try to speak she says that I don't care,
She says I'm unaware and now she says I'm weak.

4 Whole class. Go back over the students' predictions noted on the board. Were any of them correct? Elicit from the class what the boy is complaining about and what the girl is upset about.

The boy complains that his girlfriend is angry because he doesn't want to see a film with her tonight. She takes this as a sign that he's not interested in her. He wishes she could understand that he is interested in her but sometimes prefers to spend time on his own watching TV. He has tried to explain, but he isn't very good at expressing his feelings and she takes everything he says the wrong way. He thought they had settled this problem the other night when they had a long argument, but she still doesn't understand and is still angry with him.

The girl is upset because he doesn't want to see her tonight and go to a film. She is exasperated because he can't express his feelings clearly and she feels hurt. She interprets what he says as meaning that he doesn't care about her. She needs to talk the problem over more and can't understand why he thinks the problem has already been solved.

5 Pairwork. Students look at their respective pages. Student A will read a situation from a girl's point of view, Student B the same situation from a boy's point of view. When assigning A and B roles, you could let students take roles at random or make the male students B and the female students A, but it might be interesting to make the male students A (the girl) and the female students B (the boy). Give them plenty of time to read about their roles and to decide what they are going to say.

Pairs then act out a conversation. Go round, offering assistance where necessary. Take note of any particularly interesting conversations and ask those students to perform their conversations again for the whole class. If you assigned the roles to students of the 'wrong' sex, or they decided to take opposite sex roles themselves, ask them to say whether they found it more difficult or easier to put across the point of view of someone of a different sex.

6 ⊟ **05 SB p 144**

Play the recording. Students listen and see how different it is from the conversation they have just had.

⊟ **05**

(B = Brian; S = Suzi)

B: *Hello?*

S: *Hi, it's me!*

B: *Hiya! How are you doing?*

S: *Fine, a bit stressed out, had a hard day at work, you know, the usual.*

B: *Yeah, me too.*

S: *So, what about the film then? I just phoned the cinema to check the times and it's on at 7 o'clock and 9.30. Which do you reckon?*

B: *Listen, love, do you mind if we go another night? I'm tired, I just fancy a quiet night in, you know, bit of a veg on the sofa, watch some footie on TV.*

S: *But it's the last night. You said you really wanted to go!*

B: *Why don't you go with your sister? You said she wanted to see the film ...*

S: *This is the third time you've pulled out. What's going on?*

B: *Nothing. I just don't fancy it tonight, that's all.*

S: *Come on, if there's something wrong you can tell me. I'm not going to fly off the handle.*

B: *There's nothing wrong ...*

S: *Yes, there is. You've been off for days. You don't talk to me, you don't want to see me.*

B: *That's not true.*

S: *Are you bored with me? Is there someone else? Have I done something wrong?*

B: *No, no, of course not.*

S: *You never used to shut yourself away like this, you used to want to spend time with me. What's changed?*

B: *Nothing's changed. Of course I want to see you.*

S: *But not tonight, eh? The football's more interesting I suppose.*

B: *Oh, you know that's not true. It's just that I'm*

---

tired, that's all. It's been a hard day. I just need a quiet night in ...

S: *Alone!*

B: *Look, if it's that important to you, I'll come. What time did you say?*

S: *No, forget it! I wouldn't want you to go out of your way or anything!*

B: *Don't be like that. Come on, shall I come and pick you up?*

S: *No, forget it. I've gone off the idea. Let's just drop it.*

B: *Look, I'd love to do something tomorrow, yeah?*

S: *Whatever. Just please yourself. You always do!*

B: *Suzi, don't ... Suzi. Suzi?*

7 Pairwork. Students should work with the same partners as before. They read the extracts and decide whether it was the boy or the girl who said them. Do not check answers at this stage.

8 Play the recording again for students to check their answers.

---

a) girl b) girl c) boy d) girl e) boy
f) girl g) girl h) boy i) girl j) girl

---

9 Groupwork. Students discuss what the boy should do now and then report back to the class. If possible have single sex groups and see if there is any difference between the solutions proposed by the male students and the female students.

Getting angry (p 12)

1 Pairwork. Students read the two extracts and discuss the questions. Check answers with the class.

---

a) No, not really. She's being sarcastic.

b) By sarcasm and her tone of voice.

---

2 ⊟ **06 SB p 144**

Play the recording. Ask the students to say what the difference is between the two versions. Drill with the whole class, whispered if preferred, and then invite confident students to read the sentences aloud, imitating the angry tone of the second version.

In an angry sentence the stress is more heavily emphasised and the volume is louder.

⊟ **06**

1 *But not tonight, eh? The football's more interesting I suppose.*

2 *But not tonight, eh? The football's more interesting I suppose.*

3   Pairwork. Students look at tapescript 05 on page 144 and
find other phrases where the girl uses an angry tone of
voice. They then read the conversation aloud. Go round
assisting where necessary and ensuring that students' tone
and intonation are correct. Invite any particularly good
pairs to perform the conversation for the class.

Mistaken identity (p 13)

1   Pairwork. Students read the passage and the statements
that follow it carefully. They decide whether the
statements are true, false or unknown.

2   Students check their answers on page 137. Find out by a
show of hands which pair got the most correct answers.

3   Pairwork. Students think of a story that fits all the facts in
the passage. Give them plenty of time to do this and go
around offering assistance where necessary.

Once students have decided on their story, they can split
up and mingle around the class sharing their stories with
other students. They then go back to their original partners
and retell the stories they have heard.

4   Each pair either tells their own story to the class or tells the
class the best story they heard, explaining why they liked
it. The class then vote on which story was the most
original.

5   Groupwork. Students look at the photographs and decide
on an innocent explanation for each situation. One
member of each group should report back to the rest of the
class.

6   Students turn to page 132 to read about the situations and
find out if their explanations were correct.

7   Pairwork. Students discuss the question. Invite some pairs
to tell their stories to the class.

Test

At the end of each unit there is a photocopiable test. Use it at
the end of the unit, or a couple of lessons later. Allow about 30
minutes for it. It scores 40 points: to get a percentage, multiply
the student's score by 2.5. You may not wish to use a grading
system, but if you do this is a possibility.

35–40 = A (excellent);   25–34 = B (good);   20–24 = C (pass)

To make the text more complete, add an oral and/or a written
component. For example, ask students to talk in pairs about the
city where they are from and/or write a profile about a
member of your family.

Scoring: one point per correct answer unless otherwise
indicated.

1   (2 points for each sentence 1–8)
   1   To be honest, I don't think I'll ever go there again.
       OR: I don't think I'll ever go there again to be
       honest.
   2   We usually do our weekly shopping on the way
       home from work on Fridays.
       OR: We usually do our weekly shopping on
       Fridays on the way home from work.
   3   I generally see him once a week at the gym.
       OR: I generally see him at the gym once a
       week.
   4   Things have been incredibly hectic at work for a
       few days now.
       OR: At work things have been incredibly hectic
       for a few days now.
   5   She's worked in Paris on and off for years.
       OR: She's worked in Paris for years on and off.
   6   Unfortunately, they probably won't be able to go.
       OR: They probably won't be able to go,
       unfortunately.
   7   He is always really busy whenever I see him
       these days.
       OR: Whenever I see him these days he is always
       really busy.
   8   Unfortunately, they always try to get away as
       soon as they can whenever they visit me.
       OR: Unfortunately, whenever they visit me, they
       always try to get away as soon as they can.

   9 b)   10 b)   11 a)   12 b)

2   1 through   2 up   3 across   4 out   5 down
       6 through
       7 put   8 talk   9 getting   10 come   11 pick
       12 brought

3   (½ point each)

Noun	Verb	Adjective	Adverb
competence	–	*competent*	*competently*
achievement	*achieve*	achievable	achievably
efficiency	–	efficient	efficiently
satisfaction	satisfy	*satisfactory*	satisfactorily
fulfilment	fulfil	*fulfilling*	–
consideration	*consider*	considerate	*considerately*
value	*value*	valuable / valued	valuably
skill	–	skilful / skilled	skilfully

1 Identity Test

Name: **Total:** _____ /40

1 Position of adverbials *20 points*

Put the adverbs in brackets into an appropriate place in each sentence. In some cases there is more than one possibility.

1 I don't think I'll go again. (there / to be honest / ever)

   _____

2 We do our weekly shopping. (on Fridays / on the way home from work / usually)

   _____

3 I see him. (once a week / at the gym / generally)

   _____

4 Things have been hectic. (incredibly / at work / for a few days now)

   _____

5 She's worked. (for years / in Paris / on and off)

   _____

6 They won't be able to go. (probably / unfortunately)

   _____

7 He is busy. (whenever I see him / these days / always / really)

   _____

8 They try to get away. (as soon as they can / always / whenever they visit me / unfortunately)

   _____

Tick (✓) the sentence, a) or b), which is closest in meaning to the main sentence.

9 Peter went to Paris alone.
   a) Peter only went to Paris.
   b) Only Peter went to Paris.

10 I was in a hurry to do the washing up.
   a) I ate my dinner quickly and washed up.
   b) I ate my dinner and quickly washed up.

11 I do like it – please believe me.
   a) Really, I like it.
   b) I really like it.

12 I don't mind going, but I'd rather not.
   a) I particularly don't want to go.
   b) I don't particularly want to go.

2 Phrasal verbs *12 points*

Choose the correct alternative.

1 I didn't read it all, I just flicked **through/over** it.

2 It's not good to bottle **in/up** your feelings.

3 I didn't put my ideas **through/across** very well.

4 Can you sort **up/out** the mess in the kitchen please?

5 Don't let your boss get you **down/up**.

6 Think it **on/through** before you say anything.

Complete the sentences with verbs from the box. You may need to change the tense of the verb.

bring	come	get	pick	put	talk

7 I can't _____ up with this behaviour any more!

8 I think we should _____ things through together before you make a decision.

9 This awful weather is really _____ me down.

10 Have you _____ up with any new ideas for the meeting?

11 I'll _____ you up at your house at 6.30.

12 He _____ up the subject of your exam results again.

3 Lexis – word building *8 points*

Complete the table.

Noun	Verb	Adjective	Adverb
	–	competent	competently
achievement	achieve		
efficiency	–		
		satisfactory	
fulfilment		fulfilling	–
	consider		considerately
	value		
skill	–		

2 *Taste* Overview

The topic of this unit is taste. The focus is mainly on food, but the unit also looks at the concept of good taste in terms of socially acceptable behaviour. The grammatical focus is on noun phrases, order of adjectives and fronting. There is also an opportunity for students to check their knowledge of past tenses.

Students start by looking at the answers given by people to the question *If you were a food, what food would you be?* They also answer the question for themselves and go on to discuss food likes and dislikes. In the next section they discuss, and listen to other people talking about associations between food and particular situations. They then play a game using noun phrases to make the longest sentences they can.

Students listen to people talking about their experiences of eating foreign food. They practise expressions and intonation for conveying enthusiasm and reservations. They then read about a small Italian restaurant and the changes that have been made to it. In a *Test yourself* section, they can test their knowledge of past tenses. The Anecdote, in which they talk about their favourite restaurant, leads to a writing exercise in which they write a restaurant review.

The focus then turns away from food to a more general interpretation of taste. Students complete a chart with words derived from *taste* and discuss what is meant by *good taste*. They also listen to some definitions on the recording and examine language used for agreeing and disagreeing. Finally, they decide if they consider certain behaviour to be in good taste or not and discuss what has influenced their attitudes to what is or is not socially acceptable.

Section	Aims	What the students are doing
Introduction page 14	*Conversation skills*: fluency work	Matching people with different foods.
		Talking about yourself as if you were a food item.
		Talking about food likes and dislikes.
Food associations page 14	*Listening skills*: listening for gist	Matching foods with situations.
		Listening to people talking about different situations and the foods they associate with them.
		Matching the speakers to the correct situations.
Close up pages 15–16	*Grammar*: describing nouns	Studying the structure and use of noun phrases.
		Completing sentences with noun phrases.
	Order of adjectives	Identifying fact and opinion adjectives and studying the order of adjectives.
A game page 16	*Grammar*: noun phrases	Using noun phrases to play a game.
A taste for travel page 17	*Listening skills*: listening for gist	Listening to people talking about foreign food and finding out if they liked it or not.
	Pronunciation: intonation	Practising using different expressions and tone of voice to convey enthusiasm and reservations.
The demise of a great little restaurant pages 18–19	*Reading skills*: reading for detail	Reading a text to find the answers to questions.
		Doing a jigsaw reading and discussing shared information.
Test yourself page 19	*Grammar*: past tenses	Doing a series of exercises to practise the use of different past tense forms.
Close up page 20	*Grammar*: fronting	Examining the use of different word order to create dramatic effect.
Food for thought pages 20–21	*Conversation skills*: fluency work	Anecdote: talking about your favourite restaurant.
	Writing skills: review	Writing a review of your favourite restaurant.
Taste pages 21–22	*Lexis*: words derived from *taste*	Completing a chart with words derived from *taste*.
		Practising using the correct prepositions with the word *taste*.
A question of taste pages 22–23	*Listening skills*: listening for detail	Discussing the meaning of *good taste* and listening to some definitions.
		Taking notes on what people say.
	Lexis: expressions for agreeing and disagreeing	Examining expressions and intonation used for agreeing and disagreeing.
	Pronunciation: intonation	Practising expressions and intonation for agreeing and disagreeing.
In good taste? page 23	*Conversation skills*: discussion	Discussing the acceptability of certain behaviour and opinions of different generations.
		Deciding what has most influenced your attitudes.

2 *Taste* *Teacher's notes*

Closed books. Invite students to choose one (or two) of the following things and say which they would be and why: an animal, a piece of furniture, a plant, a car, a sport.

1 Students look at the photos of people and food. Read the instructions and the four answers. Give students a few minutes to match the people with the answers. Tell them that you are going to ask for their answers and that you want them to say why they have matched a particular person to an answer. They can share their ideas in pairs first.

2 Students check their answers on page 132. Ask them if they are surprised by the answers.

> a) Nicholas
> b) Melody
> c) Zena
> d) David

3 Pairwork. Students discuss what their answer to the question would be. Go around helping with any vocabulary questions. Encourage them to report any interesting ideas back to the class.

Alternatively, you could get each student, working individually, to write on a piece of paper what food they would be. They should not write their names on the paper. Take the pieces of paper in. You can either display them on the wall and let the students read them and guess who wrote each one or call them out and get the class to make suggestions as to who it might be and then vote on who they think it is. The person named can then either confirm or deny it.

4 Start a discussion by answering the questions yourself. Then elicit answers around the class. Try to find out what was the most loved and the most hated food for the class when they were children and if their tastes changed as they got older. Alternatively, the questions could be discussed in pairs or small groups.

Food associations (p 14)

1 Give students time to think about their answers and make sure they know they have to give reasons for each answer.

2 Pairwork. Students compare and discuss their answers to 1. Encourage them to report back to the class on any similarities or major differences in their answers.

3 🔲 **07 SB p 144**

Go through the questions with the class before you play the recording. Ask students to write the numbers 1–6 on a sheet of paper and make notes for the two questions beside the appropriate numbers.

Allow students to compare their answers in pairs or groups before checking with the class. The speakers don't actually name the situations, but there are clues in each speech that point towards a particular situation. You could ask students to identify what these clues are.

> a) 1 b) 2 d) 3 f) 4 c) 5 a) 6 e)
>
> b) 1 coffee and a burger
>
> 2 (watermelon, strawberries), salad with home-made dressing, cheese, bread, white wine
>
> 3 roast lamb, mashed potatoes, green peas, gravy
>
> 4 milk chocolate biscuits, coffee
>
> 5 nothing, then chocolate and fruit, strawberries and cream
>
> 6 fish and chips, Chinese takeaway, microwaveable convenience food

🔲 **07**

1 *Erm, bitter coffee in a plastic cup and milk in plastic containers. Yeah, either that or a greasy burger on a plastic tray. Looks great in the picture but tastes disgusting and is definitely over-priced.*

2 *Erm ... watermelon maybe, or strawberries ... no, I know, big bowls of fresh salad with home-made dressing, served with cheese, bread and a glass of chilled white wine.*

3 *Roast dinners, you know, huge plates of roast lamb served with mashed potatoes and tiny, sweet green peas, and on top of it all, swimming in it, the best gravy you have ever tasted.*

4 *Crunchy milk chocolate biscuits dipped in coffee, curled up on the sofa watching your favourite film.*

5 *No food really, I mean, I associate it more with not being able to eat anything, well, at first at least ... and later ... maybe chocolate or fruit for some reason ... I don't know, something like strawberries, yes, succulent sweet strawberries with fresh cream.*

6 *I don't know, hot chocolate? Erm, no, fish 'n' chips or a Chinese takeaway – or some kind of microwaveable convenience food that doesn't need any cooking.*

Close up (p 15)

Describing nouns

1 Students complete the sentences. Allow them to compare their answers in pairs or groups, but do not check answers at this stage.

2 Play the recording again for students to check their answers.

> a) bitter coffee in a plastic cup
>
> b) big bowls of fresh salad with home-made dressing
>
> c) huge plates of roast lamb served with mashed potatoes
>
> d) the best gravy you have ever tasted
>
> e) crunchy milk chocolate biscuits dipped in coffee
>
> f) succulent sweet strawberries with fresh cream
>
> g) some kind of microwaveable convenience food that doesn't need any cooking

3 Ensure students know that in its simplest form a noun phrase can be a pronoun or a noun, for example, *it*, *summer*. It can be either the subject or object in a clause or sentence. Note: complex noun phrases must include a head noun and can also include:

1 determiners (*a/the/a bit of/several types of*)

2 some description before the head noun (adjectives or nouns, for example, *warm summer*)

3 some description after the noun (relative clauses, for example, *when the sun shines*, reduced clauses, for example, *followed by long sunny evenings*, prepositional phrases, for example, *of my childhood*).

Do not go into an explanation of a noun phrase yet as it will come up in 4.

Pairwork. Ask students to identify what the subject is in all six noun phrases.

> coffee

Students read and answer the questions in pairs. Check answers with the class.

> a) Students' own answers
>
> b) seven (bitter, strong, black, fresh, hot, milky, iced)
>
> c) vending machine / espresso / filter
>
> d) 1, 3 and 6
>
> e) 2, 3 and 6

> f) 2, 4 and 5; the relative clauses in 4 and 5 are incomplete; the relative pronouns and auxiliary verbs have been omitted.

4 Pairwork. Students work together to find an example of each of the structures listed. Make sure they know they are looking for these in the descriptions in 1. Check answers with the class. Then draw a diagram on the board with the word *NOUN* in the middle. Elicit whether each of the structures listed goes before or after the noun. As the students give their answers, write them up in the diagram on the correct side of the word *NOUN*. Ask early finishers to come to the board and start filling in the diagram.

Refer students to the Language reference section on page 16 for further information or the Grammar glossary on page 142.

> a) milk chocolate, convenience
>
> b) in a plastic cup, with home-made dressing, with fresh cream
>
> c) bitter, plastic, big, fresh, home-made, huge, roast, mashed, best, crunchy, succulent, sweet, microwaveable
>
> d) that doesn't need any cooking
>
> e) served with mashed potatoes, you have ever tasted, dipped in coffee
>
> f) a, the, some kind of
>
> Structures c and f go before the noun. Structures b, d and e go after the noun.

5 Students work individually to complete the descriptions. Do not check answers at this stage. Encourage them to read their sentences aloud to try to find what order of adjectives sounds best. The correct order of adjectives will be addressed in the next section, so don't spend too much time on this here.

6 Pairwork. Students compare their answers and then check with the whole class. They then work in pairs to discuss which of the things they would most like to eat. You could then get the class to vote on the most and least delicious-sounding thing.

> a) a selection of mouth-watering caramelised fruit
>
> b) a tempting multi-layered chocolate gateau
>
> c) a helping of superb home-made apple crumble just like your grandmother used to make
>
> d) a bowl of fabulous fresh-water crayfish served in a white wine sauce
>
> e) an exquisite savoury pancake stuffed with delicious stir-fried vegetables

Order of adjectives (p 16)

Closed books. Ask if students can remember the adjectives they used in the last exercise. As students call them out, write them on the board. Open books and check if they are all there.

1 Whole class. Refer students back to the descriptions they completed in the previous exercise. Ask them to say how they decided in which order to put the adjectives. Then ask them to look at the adjectives in the box and answer the questions below. Allow them to compare their answers in pairs before checking them with the class.

> a) mouth-watering, delicious, exquisite, superb, fabulous, tempting
>
> b) caramelised, savoury, home-made
>
> c) The opinion adjectives tend to come first.

2 Pairwork. Students write out their noun phrases in the wrong order before reading them to their partners. Alternatively, the descriptions can be written out word by word on pieces of paper and partners can then physically reorder the words. Pairs can then circulate reordering each other's descriptions.

A game (p 16)

1 Whole class. Write the sentence *The girl was eating an apple* on the board. Elicit the two noun phrases. To consolidate what students have learnt, elicit also that both noun phrases consist of a noun and a determiner.

> The girl, an apple

2 Groupwork. Teams of students take turns to read out the sentence, adding an element to either of the noun phrases each time. You may like to add them to the sentence on the board. Each team should include the modifications made by the previous teams.

For Round 2, the teams have three minutes to discuss and expand the new sentence in the same way. The teams then read out their sentences and the class votes on the best sentence. Alternatively, the prize goes to the longest coherent sentence.

A taste for travel (p 17)

Closed books. Ask students to think what their favourite foreign food is and to make a list of adjectives which they can use to describe it. They should work individually and not discuss this with a partner. Then invite several students to read their lists out to the class. The class has to guess what kind of food is being described. Alternatively, students can just describe their favourite foreign food and say why they like it.

Whole class. Ask students to open their books and look at the photo at the top of page 17. Ask them to guess which country they think it is and to say if they have been anywhere like this.

1 ▭ 08 SB p 144

Before students listen to the people talking about their experiences of foreign food, make sure they understand that these are not meant to be definitive descriptions of the local cuisine, but subjective opinions which they can disagree with if they wish. The ambiguity is intentional and should add an additional discussion point when students decide whether the speakers liked the local food or not.

Groupwork. Give students a few minutes to discuss what they have heard and decide the answers to the question.

> Anne loved it. Kim didn't like it at first but grew to like it. Bill didn't like much of it, but there were some things, like the bread and the soups that he loved. Steve liked it.

▭ 08

Anne

The food? Mmm, it's superb, really hot and spicy, but quite delicate too. Kind of like a cross between Indian and Chinese food but with its own special flavours too. They use a lot of lemon grass and coconut and a lot of fish. I really liked the soups. You can buy them from stalls on the corner of the street. You choose the meat you want in your soup and the kind of noodles – long thin white rice noodles, or big fat, thick yellowish ones, and there are these tubs of spices too and you choose as much or as little of whatever you want. Then you sit there on the street, or in the market or wherever you are and eat it. I had some for breakfast one day – it was great! Really great!

Kim

The food? Well, it took a bit of getting used to actually. I like hot, spicy food, but this was too much for me at the beginning. I reckon I built up a kind of immunity to it as time went by though and I got to like it by the end. It's nothing like the kind of food we get in restaurants back home. I loved the ritual of it, going to the small street cafés where they serve your food on a banana leaf. They wash the leaf and then serve a huge helping of rice right in the middle and give you generous helpings of all the various different sauces on offer that day. You don't get a knife and a fork. You eat with your right hand, making little balls of rice and then soaking up the sauce with these little balls – it takes quite a long time to get good at it. When you've finished they bundle the banana leaf up with any leftovers and throw it out on the street where the goats and cows eat them. I love that side of it too, nothing goes to waste!

Bill

The food? Well, to tell you the truth, I didn't really like it that much. It isn't the healthiest of diets. Everything is either fried or cooked in pig's fat and mmm, I don't really like cabbage that much and that's a staple part of their diet, like a lot of places in Central Europe. It's usually pickled and served with sour cream – so, no, it isn't really my favourite. Having said that, there were some things I loved – the bread for example, it's really soft and tasty, and so many different kinds, and the scones and pastries too are really good. And some of the soups, the various kinds of goulash – that's their national dish – and the bean soups are really delicious and the paprika makes them quite spicy – great on a cold day.

Steve

The food? It isn't particularly elaborate, but it's good. The seafood is especially good, and there's just such a variety, so many different kinds of shellfish, I wouldn't know the names for half of them in English. Another favourite of mine is the grilled green chilli peppers. They serve them up by the plateful to be shared between friends over a beer or two. There's always one that's so spicy it almost blows your head off. More than anything else I love the eating out culture. It's quite informal, you go to a bar and order huge platefuls of various different specialities and share them, everybody eating off the same plates. It's very sociable – a really nice social eating ritual.

2 Before students listen again, make sure they have paper and pencil ready to note down all the food vocabulary they hear. Emphasise that this is not just the names of foods; they are also listening for adjectives to describe food, ways of cooking, etc. You might like to set this up as a team game. Give the teams a few minutes to discuss strategies for getting the most words, for example by nominating certain students to listen out for the names of dishes, others for adjectives describing food, etc.

3 Pairwork. If students have done the previous exercise individually, allow them to compare their lists with a partner before deciding which countries they are talking about. If you have had a team game, allow the teams to look at their lists and decide. Finally, allow them to check their answers on page 137.

Anne:	Thailand
Kim:	Southern India
Bill:	Hungary
Steve:	Spain

4 Pairwork. Students discuss the questions. Go round listening for any particularly interesting points which can be related to the whole class.

Optional activity

Elicit how easy it is to get foreign food where students live and how popular it is. You can also ask what they think the most typical dish of their own country's cuisine is and how foreigners react to it.

Expressing enthusiasm & reservations
(p 17)

1 Read the title of this section showing the meanings of the two words by your intonation, ie saying *enthusiasm* with a bright cheerful intonation and *reservations* with a certain amount of doubt and distrust reflected in your voice. Elicit that *enthusiasm* is excitement about things you like and *reservations* are doubts about things you don't like or are not sure about.

Students read the extracts and underline the words they think the speakers stress in order to convey their enthusiasm or reservations.

2 🔲 09 SB p 145

Students listen to the extracts and check their answers.

> 🔲 09
>
> a) *Mmm, it's superb, really hot and spicy ...*
>
> b) *Well, it took a bit of getting used to actually.*
>
> c) *Well, to tell you the truth, I didn't really like it that much.*
>
> d) *... and mmm, I don't really like cabbage that much ...*
>
> e) *... no, it isn't really my favourite.*
>
> f) *It isn't particularly elaborate, but it's good.*

3 Students match the words and sounds to the situations. Check answers with the whole class and invite students to read out the words and sounds with appropriate intonation. Elicit that when *Mmm* expresses enthusiasm, the voice tends to go up and when it expresses reservation, it tends to go down. There is also a difference in volume.

> a) 3   b) 1   c) 2

4 Pairwork. Students read the exchanges and use the expressions they have learnt to make the responses more or less enthusiastic. Encourage them to read their exchanges aloud to check the effects of their additions. Go round checking that the correct intonation is being used. Invite some pairs to perform their exchanges for the class.

5 Pairwork. Students take turns to ask and answer the questions. Go round, checking that they are using the expressions to suggest enthusiasm or reservations and offer help where necessary. Take note of any interesting information that can be related to the whole class.

The demise of a great little restaurant (p 18)

Closed books. Ask students to work in pairs and tell their partner about the last time they ate out, where they went, what they ate, and whether it was a special occasion or not. Ask for some brief feedback from a couple of students.

1 Allow the students plenty of time to read the text and the questions. You might like to go through the questions with the whole class first before they read the text. Do not check answers at this stage.

2 Pairwork. Students compare their answers. Then check with the whole class.

> a) Ten years ago.
>
> b) It was on an island. Access was by boat. There were no advance bookings. You had to wait for the owner to come and pick you up. They had a bar on the jetty. There was only one waiter. There were only four tables. The menu was limited. The price was low. You ate the fish or seafood the owner had caught that morning. They grew their own produce.
>
> c) The food was fresh and good. It was cheap. He liked the owners. It was an unusual and pleasant setting.
>
> d) Students; own answers.

3 Pairwork. Students discuss the questions and think of some possible answers. They should make notes of these so they can check later how accurate their guesses were.

4 Pairwork. Students turn to the relevant pages and read different parts of the rest of the review. Each student makes notes on the answers to the questions about their section of text and compares their answers with another student who has read the same text. They then go back to their original partners to complete the exercise, telling their partners what they have learnt and discussing whether their earlier predictions were correct.

> **Student A**
>
> a) The tiny village was now a thriving tourist town.
>
> b) The bar was larger and had tables inside and out. It played pop music. They had a list of bookings. They served beer and the drinks were expensive. It served more than just the restaurant clientele and was much busier.
>
> c) The boat was larger and faster. It had a smartly-dressed crew. You couldn't chat to the owner any more. They played music.
>
> **Student B**
>
> a) There were a lot more tables. The tables were on a concrete terrace exposed to the sun. The tablecloths were made of paper. The bread

> wasn't home-made. There were a lot of waiters. Their waiter spoke English. The service was less personal and more hurried. The kitchen was larger and there were four chefs.
>
> b) The menu had expanded. The ingredients weren't produced on the island. The squid now came in batter with chips. The prices were higher.
>
> c) The gardens had disappeared and been replaced with hotel rooms.

5 Pairwork. Students discuss the questions. Go around offering help and taking note of any interesting answers or information that can be shared with the whole class.

Lexis (p 19)

1 Pairwork. Students who were Student A in the previous exercise should continue to be Student A here. Likewise students who were B in the previous exercise should continue to be B here. Students work with a partner who has read the same text as them. Before they find their words in the text or look them up in a dictionary, encourage students to see if they can remember what the words mean and how they were used by the author.

Students then find the words in their sections of text and discuss their meanings. They decide on the best way to explain them. This could be by putting them in a sentence, explaining the meaning in English, translating them or a combination of all three.

2 Pairwork. Students teach their words to partners who read the other part of the text.

3 Students write sentences containing the words they have just been taught.

4 Pairwork. Partners should check each other's sentences and make corrections. Monitor and check the sentences as the students work in pairs.

Optional activity

Play a game in two groups. Each group has to give the other a word to make a sentence with, for example, *pricey – The dishes were pricey, but delicious.* Each team scores two points for a correct sentence.

Test yourself (p 19)

Past tenses

Note: students do not have to have read all three texts about Le Palmier in order to do these exercises.

1 Students look at the extract and choose the most appropriate verb forms. Allow students to check their answers with a partner before checking with the class.

> 1 ate   2 had caught   3 had
> 4 was barbecued   5 served   6 was singing

2 Students complete the extracts with the correct form of the verbs in brackets. Point out that in some cases more than one answer is correct. Do not check answers at this stage.

3 Pairwork. Students check their answers with the review and discuss any differences. Make sure they realise that sometimes more than one answer is correct.

> **A** 1 catered   2 were looking
>   3 worried   4 were called
> **B** 1 asked   2 had become (became)
>   3 had retired (retired)   4 sold (had sold)
>   5 remained   6 had married
>   7 was managing (managed)

4 Students choose one of the openings. Give them time to think about what they are going to say.

5 Pairwork. Students use the openings to tell a partner about something which has happened to them recently.

Close up (p 20)

Fronting

1 Make sure students do the reordering without looking back at the text. Tell them that they are to put the sentences in the correct order. Do not alert them to the fact that in the text they are ordered differently from standard English word order.

> The answers reflect standard English word order, and are not as the words were ordered in the review.
> a)   The family lived on the upper floors.
> b)   The opportunity to chat with Marianne was gone.
> c)   Waiters ran between the tables.

2 Pairwork. Students look back at the review to check their answers and then answer the questions. They may be surprised to find the order in the review is quite different from what they have written.

> a)   On the upper floors lived the family.
> b)   Gone was the opportunity to chat with Marianne.
> c)   Between the tables ran waiters.
> The order in the review is different from standard word order.
> The reason for this is to emphasise the part of the sentence that is placed first and to create dramatic effect.

Refer students to the Language reference section on page 20 and the Grammar glossary on page 142 and draw attention to the fact that fronting is not commonly used in everyday speech.

3 Students complete the sentences with memories of a place from their past. Go round giving help.

4 Pairwork. Students compare their sentences and explain and discuss the changes that have taken place. Ask a few students to read their sentences to the class.

Food for thought (p 20)

Anecdote

See Introduction, page 4, for more ideas on how to set up, monitor and repeat Anecdotes.

1 Go through the questions with the class and give students time to think about which restaurant they are going to talk about and what they are going to say.

2 Pairwork. Students take turns to tell a partner about their restaurant. To encourage attentive listening, ask students to take notes.

3 Students answer the questions about what their partner has told them and discuss the answers with their partners.

Writing (p 21)

1 The writing of the restaurant review could be done for homework. To get students started, you could talk briefly about your own favourite restaurant, giving some of the information listed in b). Alternatively, you could brainstorm information about the students' ideal restaurant, noting the details they supply on the board.

2 If you have noted information on the students' ideal restaurant on the board, encourage them to decide as a class what order the information should be presented in.

3 Students write their reviews. If this is done in class, you can go round offering help and advice. If it is done for homework, try to find time in a subsequent lesson for students to read and enjoy each other's work. This could be done by displaying the reviews in the classroom, asking students to exchange reviews, read them, and tell another student about it.

Taste (p 21)

Collocations

1 This could be done as a team game with the winning team being the one that comes up with the most words formed from *taste*. After checking answers, students should note down any words they missed from their lists. You may want to do this as a closed book activity on the board.

> Make sure the following words are included in their lists:
> tasteful, tastefully, tasty, tasteless, taster, tasting, tastes

2 Students complete the sentences with *taste* words. Allow students to check with a partner before checking answers with the class.

> a) taste b) taste c) tasty d) tastefully
> e) tasteful f) taster g) tasting h) tastes
> i) taste j) taste k) taste l) tastes m) taste

3 Give students a few minutes to study the sentences in 2 and come up with the two basic meanings of *taste*.

> 1 The feeling that something you eat or drink produces in your mouth.
> 2 A value judgement about the quality of something.

4 Students look at the words and expressions and decide which of the two meanings of *taste* they relate to. Allow students to check with a partner before checking answers with the class.

> a) meaning 1
> b) meaning 1
> c) meaning 2
> d) meaning 2
> e) meaning 1

5 Students work individually to complete the sentences. Check answers with the class.

> a) for b) in

6 Elicit answers from the class.

> Sentence b) talks about choice and sentence a) about preference.

7 Give students a few minutes to choose the correct prepositions in the expressions. Allow students to check with a partner before checking answers with the class.

> a) in b) for c) for d) in e) in

8 Pairwork. Students look at the expressions again and think of people who have each of these tastes. They take turns to tell their partner about these people. Listening partners should ask questions where possible to elicit further details.

A question of taste (p 22)

Closed books. Write *good taste* on one side of the board and *bad taste* on the other. Brainstorm examples of each from the class. If students have difficulty coming up with ideas, suggest one or two of your own. For example, *Italian leather shoes* and *checked shirt and striped tie*. Allow them a few minutes to discuss their ideas in small groups and then write them up on the board.

1 Pairwork. Students discuss what good taste is and try to write a definition in no more than twenty words. This is not an easy thing to do, so go round offering help and encouragement.

2 Give students time to share their definitions with other students in the class. Allow them to mingle around the classroom to do this. If you wish, you could ask the class to vote on which they think is the best definition.

3 ◖▬◗ 10 SB p 145

Before students listen to the tape, establish that there are three speakers and that they are going to discuss good taste. (If you like, you could divide the students into three groups and get each group to make notes on one of the speakers. Then form new groups of three with a member from each of the original groups. Students then pool their information.)

> ◖▬◗ 10
> (S = Sarah; A = Angela; D = David)
> S: ... I can't believe he bought her plastic flowers for her birthday. I mean, that is so tacky. That is such bad taste.
> A: I don't know. It's the thought that counts.
> D: No! Come on! Plastic flowers don't count!
> A: Well, no, it might not be your cup of tea but you know, one man's wine is another man's poison.
> D: Eh?
> S: What?
> A: Well, I mean, I know people who like plastic flowers and they don't necessarily have bad taste.
> D: It depends what you consider bad taste.
> S: Yes, I mean, taste is a very personal thing.
> A: Yes. Beauty is in the eye of the beholder and that sort of thing.
> S: Exactly. Everyone's different and so I suppose everyone has a different idea of what good taste is.
> D: Yes, so it really depends on your own taste, doesn't it?
> S: Well, yeah, but having said that, no-one thinks plastic flowers are in good taste, do they?
> D: No. Good taste is ...

A: *It's really hard to say what good taste is. Bad taste is like being flash, you know what I mean, like wearing a big gold medallion, or something.*

D: *Oh yes, definitely! Things like that are awful, aren't they?*

A: *Socks!*

D: *Socks and sandals, and white socks and black shoes, definitely!*

S: *Not necessarily, some people like them.*

A: *Good taste is really then, I suppose, it might be an ability to judge the beauty or the elegance of things.*

D: *Yes, possibly.*

S: *No. I don't think beauty's got anything to do with it. I think it's knowing what's right for the moment. It's knowing what's appropriate that's good taste.*

D: *Yes, I think you've got a point there. It's also about being able to judge the quality of things. Good quality stuff is usually quite tasteful. And yes, Sarah, you're right – it's about choosing the right thing at the right time too.*

A: *That reminds me of Rebecca the other day at Jo's wedding. Talk about the wrong clothes at the wrong time!*

S: *What, wearing that blue dress thing?*

A: *Yeah, it was obviously expensive, but talk about bad taste.*

D: *Absolutely. She looked completely out of place.*

S: *Well, yes, I suppose you're right. But Rebecca, you know, Rebecca has class, which isn't the same as taste. It's not the same.*

D: *No, but class doesn't excuse her bad taste.*

S: *But it does in a way, because having class means being confident in yourself. You don't worry what other people think, you just do what you want to do and people accept you for what you are.*

A: *But class is about knowing how to behave, not how to dress.*

S: *I don't totally agree there, not these days. Class means being yourself and not caring what other people think.*

D: *Yes, but I think there's more to it than that. I think it's that you know how to behave in every circumstance, no matter how difficult the situation might be and how to deal with it. That's class.*

A: *Yes, yes, I guess it is. That feeling you can take everything in your stride ... you're not fazed by any situation or any group of people, you just carry on being yourself regardless.*

D: *You're cool; you don't get upset, you don't get het up, you know. Yeah.*

4 Pairwork. If your students have made notes on all the speakers, allow them to compare answers in pairs and

discuss how the speakers' ideas on good taste differ from theirs. Alternatively, ask them to work in groups of three as suggested above and pool their information.

Sarah:	taste is a very personal thing; good taste is knowing what is appropriate
Angela:	good taste is an ability to judge the beauty or elegance of things
David:	good taste is the ability to judge the quality of things

5 Elicit the answers to the questions from the whole class. Do not comment on their answers at this stage as they will be asked to listen again in 6.

6 Students listen again and check their answers. Give them time to discuss what they have heard and to decide if they agree with the definitions of class.

The other quality they mention is class. They understand by this: knowing how to behave in all circumstances and not being adversely affected by what is happening around you.

Agreeing & disagreeing (p 22)

1 Make sure the students understand that the missing words all express agreement or disagreement. They read the extracts and decide which type of expression is missing in each gap. Do not check answers at this stage.

2 🔲 **11 SB p 145**

a) 1 disagreement 2 disagreement
b) 3 agreement
c) 4 agreement 5 disagreement
d) 6 agreement 7 agreement 8 agreement
e) 9 disagreement 10 agreement

🔲 **11**

(S = Sarah; A = Angela; D = David)

a

S: *... I can't believe he bought her plastic flowers for her birthday. I mean, that is so tacky. That is such bad taste.*

A: **I don't know.** *It's the thought that counts.*

D: **No! Come on!** *Plastic flowers don't count!*

b

S: *Yes, I mean, taste is a very personal thing.*

A: *Yes. Beauty is in the eye of the beholder and that sort of thing.*

S: **Exactly.** *Everyone's different and so I suppose ...*

c

A: *... wearing a big gold medallion, or something.*

D: **Oh yes, definitely!** *Things like that are awful, aren't they?*

A: *Socks!*

D: *Socks and sandals, and white socks and black shoes, definitely!*

S: **Not necessarily**, *some people like them.*

d

A: *... It's knowing what is appropriate that's good taste.*

D: **Yes, I think you've got a point there**. *It's also about being able to judge the quality of things. Good quality stuff is usually quite tasteful. And yes, Sarah, you're right – it's about choosing the right thing at the right time too.*

A: *That reminds me of Rebecca the other day at Jo's wedding. Talk about the wrong clothes at the wrong time!*

S: *What, wearing that blue dress thing?*

A: *Yeah, it was obviously expensive, but talk about bad taste.*

A: **Absolutely**. *She looked completely out of place.*

S: *Well, **yes, I suppose you're right**. But Rebecca, you know, Rebecca has class ...*

e

A: *But class is about knowing how to behave, not how to dress.*

S: **I don't totally agree there**, *not these days. Class means being yourself and not caring what other people think.*

D: *Yes, but I think there's more to it than that. I think it's that you know how to behave in every circumstance, no matter how difficult the situation might be and how to deal with it. That's class.*

A: **Yes, yes, I guess it is**. *That feeling you can take everything in your stride ...*

Students listen and make a note of the expressions used.

3 Pairwork. With multinational classes, try to arrange pairs of students who speak the same language. Students think of other expressions for agreeing and disagreeing and discuss whether they use similar expressions in their own language. They can then report back to the class.

Intonation (p 23)

1 🔲 12 SB p 145

Students write 1 to 6 on a piece of paper. They listen to the recording and put a) next to the appropriate number if the

speaker is uncertain, b) if he or she is agreeing and c) if he or she is disagreeing. They may need to listen two or three times before you give them the answers. Check answers with the class.

> 1 c) 2 b) 3 b) 4 a) 5 c) 6 a)

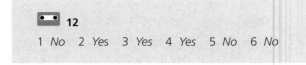
> 🔲 **12**
>
> 1 *No* 2 *Yes* 3 *Yes* 4 *Yes* 5 *No* 6 *No*

2 Invite the students to comment on the way the intonation changes. You may want to ask students to listen and repeat.

3 🔲 **13 SB p 145**

Pairwork. Students listen to the recording and take turns to respond with *yes* or *no*. The listening partners should say if they are agreeing, disagreeing or uncertain. If students want to extend their answers beyond simply *yes* and *no*, they could use some of the expressions from previous exercises.

> 🔲 **13**
>
> a) *The best way to eat fish is raw.*
>
> b) *French cuisine is the best in the world.*
>
> c) *People who smoke in restaurants are inconsiderate.*
>
> d) *If you want to get to the top, you have to start at the bottom.*
>
> e) *Life is too short to waste time worrying about what other people think.*
>
> f) *Travel is the best way of broadening the mind.*

In good taste? (p 23)

Closed books. Ask students to give examples of behaviour that is never acceptable, behaviour that is always acceptable and behaviour that is only acceptable in certain circumstances.

1 Go through the list of actions. Give students time to decide if they would mark them a) unacceptable, b) acceptable in certain circumstances or c) totally acceptable.

2 Pairwork. Students compare their views on the list of actions and discuss the questions. Monitor, making notes of any interesting points you can feed back to the class later.

Test

Scoring: one point per correct answer unless otherwise indicated.

1
1 I'm not going to that awful fast-food place again.
2 He's just bought a fabulous state-of-the-art TV.
3 What a wonderful new building!
4 She's always wanted a sleek red sports car.

2 (2 points for each correct sentence)
1 I had a huge slice of home-made pizza served with chips and salad.
2 There's a fantastic Thai restaurant just round the corner which serves vegetarian food. / There's a fantastic Thai restaurant which serves vegetarian food just round the corner.
3 Can I have a cup of coffee with just a drop of milk and no sugar? / Can I have a cup of coffee with no sugar and just a drop of milk?
4 We stayed in that beautiful old hotel your brother recommended.
5 We're going to see the new play reviewed in the paper last week.

3
1 tasty / tasteless
2 tasteless
3 taste
4 tasteful
5 taste
6 taste
7 tasted
8 tastes
9 taste
10 tastefully

4 1 f) 2 e) 3 b) 4 a) 5 c) or d) 6 c) or d)

5
1 Down poured the rain for hours and hours.
2 Long gone are the days when we could do that.
3 'Kiki's' was the restaurant's name.
4 Banking is what I want to do when I leave school.

6
1 thriving
2 brash
3 chunk
4 sprinkle
5 exquisite
6 totting up

Taste Test

Name: _____ **Total:** _____ /40

---

1 Order of adjectives *4 points*

Put the adjectives in brackets into an appropriate place in each sentence.

1 I'm not going to that place again. (fast-food / awful)

_____

2 He's just bought a TV. (state-of-the-art / fabulous)

_____

3 What a building! (new / wonderful)

_____

4 She's always wanted a car. (red / sleek / sports)

_____

2 Describing nouns *10 points*

Reorder the words and phrases below to form logical sentences.

1 I had ... served with / pizza / a huge slice of / chips and salad / home-made.

_____

2 There's a ... just round the corner / which serves vegetarian food / fantastic / Thai restaurant.

_____

3 Can I have ... just a drop of / a cup of / milk / with / no sugar / coffee / and?

_____

4 We stayed in ... /that / hotel / beautiful/ your brother recommended / old.

_____

5 We're going to see ... reviewed in the paper / play / new / the / last week.

_____

3 Lexis – *taste* *10 points*

Complete the sentences using a form of the word *taste*.

1 The pizza is really _____ .

2 This is awful. The pictures are totally _____ .

3 He's got great _____ in clothes.

4 She wore a lovely dress in a _____ shade of pink.

5 It would _____ better with a bit more sugar in it.

6 That joke is in very poor _____ .

7 You don't like it? It was OK when I _____ it earlier.

8 The city has something to suit all _____ .

9 I've recently developed a real _____ for red wine.

10 Their house is very nice – really _____ decorated.

4 Agreeing and disagreeing *6 points*

Join the two halves to make expressions used for agreeing and disagreeing.

1 Come   a) a point there.

2 Not   b) it is.

3 Yes, I guess c) totally agree.

4 You've got   d) know.

5 I don't   e) necessarily.

6 I don't   f) on!

5 Fronting *4 points*

Rewrite the sentences beginning with the words given.

1 The rain poured down for hours and hours.

Down _____

2 The days when we could do that are long gone.

Long gone _____

3 The restaurant's name was 'Kiki's'.

'Kiki's' _____

4 What I want to do when I leave school is banking.

Banking _____

6 Lexis – general *6 points*

Complete the words by adding the missing letters.

1 The bar is th_ _v_n_ now the tourists have found it.

2 The restaurant's cl_ _nt_l_ is mostly local.

3 Entre_ _ _ _ _ _ _ _ can create employment opportunities.

4 _o_ _r_te is a cheap building material.

5 The food was _x_ _ _ s_t_. I've never tasted better.

6 The British eat fish cooked in b_ _ _er with chips.

3 *City* Overview

The topic of this unit is cities and city life. The grammar focus is on hedging and negative and limiting adverbials.

Students start by doing a quiz about cities around the world, checking their answers by listening to an extract from a radio programme. They use various hedging expressions to talk about cities and then listen to the story behind a newspaper headline. Next, they read sections from city guides and try to identify the cities being described. The guides are also used to expand students' knowledge of useful adjectives for describing cities. Students then practise using negative and limiting adverbials in descriptions and write a short description of a famous town or city in their country.

In the Anecdote, students talk about cities which have made an impression on them. They then read a short text about London's Leicester Square and discuss busy city areas that they know. The focus then changes to city life and the problems and dangers that it brings. Students listen to two friends talking about the dangers of city life and practise using expressions which add emphasis. They then discuss dangers and security in their own cities.

Finally, students read and listen to a poem about a young person who steals a snowman out of boredom with city life. They also look at a picture and discuss how to deal with boredom.

Section	Aims	What the students are doing
Introduction page 24	*Listening skills*: listening for specific information	Doing a quiz on cities and listening for the answers.
Close up pages 24–25	*Grammar*: hedging	Studying extracts from the previous listening to complete hedging expressions.
		Using hedging expressions to talk about cities.
	Listening skills: listening for gist	Listening to people discussing a newspaper story and choosing the correct headline.
		Making notes and using them to write a brief newspaper report.
Where in the world? pages 26–27	*Reading skills*: reading for detail	Reading extracts from city guides and deciding which cities they describe.
	Lexis: city collocations	Matching adjectives with noun phrases.
Close up pages 28–29	*Grammar*: negative & limiting adverbials	Identifying and examining adverbials which have negative or limiting meanings.
		Rewriting sentences using negative or limiting adverbials.
	Writing skills: description	Writing a description of a famous town or city.
	Conversation skills: fluency work	Anecdote: talking about a city which has made an impression on you.
One big party page 30	*Reading skills*: reading for detail	Reading a description of London's Leicester Square and answering questions.
		Inserting extra words into a text.
		Discussing busy places you know.
City life page 31	*Listening skills*: listening for detail	Listening to people talking about the dangers of city life.
	Pronunciation: intonation	Adding emphasis to statements.
	Conversation skills: discussion	Discussing safety in cities.
An urban poem pages 32–33	*Lexis*: informal vocabulary	Identifying and examining informal expressions.
	Reading skills: reading for gist	Reordering a poem and discussing the issues it raises.
	Conversation skills: discussion	Looking at a painting and discussing the issues it raises.

City *Teacher's notes*

Closed books. Whole class. Before students open their books, ask them to call out the names of as many capital cities as they can in one minute. Write them up on the board, emphasising the pronunciation and main stress. Then ask questions about them, for example, *Which of these cities has the biggest population? Which is the most polluted?*

1 Pairwork. Students look at the photo and speculate on which city it is or which country it is in (New York, USA). Give them time to go through the quiz and discuss their answers. Do not check answers with the class at this stage, but you could encourage students to say which answers they are confident about and which questions they found more difficult to answer.

2 📼 **14 SB p 145**

Play the recording. Students listen and check their answers. Find out how many they got right.

> 1 d) 2 c) 3 a) 4 b) 5 a) 6 d)

📼 **14**

(M = Mike; S = Sue)

M: *... Thank you, John, and now it's back to the studio for the answers to last week's quiz. Sue?*

S: *Thanks, Mike. Hello, yes, and there are a few surprises in the answers this week. So let's start with the first question, which I think held the biggest surprise for our contestants.*

According to data collected by the UN, 53% of the world's population lives in cities, whilst 47% live in rural areas. In the EU the percentage of people living in urban centres rises to a staggering 74% and an even higher 76% in the USA. It would appear that there is a steady movement towards urban areas and that the proportion of city dwellers will continue to rise.

Although it may seem a fairly straightforward question to answer, there is still some discussion as to which is the world's largest capital. This is mainly due to the difficulty in deciding where the world's largest cities actually end as they all tend to be surrounded by a mass of satellite towns which all merge into one large agglomeration. If we take 'city' to mean the population which lives within the city limits, then Mexico City, with a population of more than 20,000,000, is the world's largest capital, closely followed by Seoul at 12,000,000 and Tokyo at 8,000,000.

Likewise, it is very difficult to tell which is Europe's noisiest capital, mainly as there don't seem to be any standardised noise pollution measurements across the countries of the EU, and very few exhaustive studies have been carried out. However, it is widely recognised that Athens is the European capital which suffers from the worst noise pollution levels. It's not known whether this information is based on popular opinion or on statistical data from Greek authorities however. Judging from the entries we've received, this will come as quite a surprise to some of our listeners.

On to the fourth question. There is still some debate over this one. The Syrians claim that their capital city, Damascus, is the world's oldest city, though other Middle Eastern inhabitants would claim that their capitals are just as old. Sources seem to suggest that the Syrians are right and that their capital is indeed the oldest in the world, having been continuously inhabited since 5000 BC.

Question five was pretty straightforward. There is no doubt whatsoever about which of the world's capital cities is the highest. La Paz, in the Bolivian Andes, stands four kilometres above sea level.

And finally, the last question, again a fairly straightforward question. The first city to have reached a population of 1,000,000 was Rome which had a population of over a million during the heyday of the Roman Empire in 133 BC. London reached the mark in 1810 and New York in 1875. Today there are over 300 cities in the world that boast a population in excess of one million.

So, the winners this week are, Jane Turbot from Whitstable in Kent, Carol Jackson from St Andrews ...

Close up (p 24)

Hedging

1 Students look at the first gapped sentence. Establish that it is an extract from the listening they have just heard and elicit ways of completing it. Each blank represents one word. The missing words complete expressions which are called *hedges*. They are used to soften opinions and make them less categorical. This style is often used in newspapers.

Students can work in pairs or in groups to complete the remaining sentences. Do not confirm answers yet.

2 ▭ **15 SB p 146**

Play the recording for students to check their answers. Let them check in pairs first and then ask them if they need to listen again. If they do, play the recording again. Then check answers with the whole class. Refer them to the Language reference section on page 25 for more information about hedging.

> Note: answers given here are those from the recording, but there may be other correct answers as it depends on subjective opinion.
>
> a) would appear   b) discussion
> c) widely recognised   d) not known
> e) seem   f) no doubt whatsoever

> ▭ **15**
>
> a) *It would appear that there is a steady movement towards urban areas ...*
>
> b) *... there is still some discussion as to which is the world's largest capital.*
>
> c) *... it is widely recognised that Athens is the European capital which suffers from the worst noise pollution levels.*
>
> d) *It's not known whether this information is based on popular opinion or on statistical data from Greek authorities however.*
>
> e) *Sources seem to suggest that the Syrians are right ...*
>
> f) *There is no doubt whatsoever about which of the world's capital cities is the highest.*

3 Pairwork. Students look at the extracts and discuss how strong the evidence is for each statement. Check answers with the whole class.

> a) Statement f)   b) Statements a), c) and e)
> c) Statement b)   d) Statement d)

4 Pairwork. Students read the data and write sentences based upon it, using the expressions in 1.

> *Possible answers*
>
> It would appear that people enjoy living in cities.
>
> It seems that there are many people who live in a city who would prefer to live in a rural area.
>
> There is no doubt whatsoever that many people under the age of 30 living in rural areas would prefer to live in cities.
>
> There is little evidence that people over the age of 50 living in rural areas would prefer to live in cities.
>
> It is not known how many people were questioned.

5 Pairwork. Students decide which group or groups they would come into and discuss this with their partners. Encourage them to give reasons why they enjoy living in cities or would prefer to live in a rural area, etc.

Optional activity

If possible, bring in an English language newspaper and see if students can find examples of the language featured in the previous section. They can then look at one or two of the newspaper's headlines and try to work out what they mean.

6 Whole class. Read the first newspaper headline and elicit answers from the class as to what the accompanying story might be. Write the ideas on the board.

Pairwork. Students discuss the headlines and think of ideas for the stories behind each of them. Go round offering help and encouragement. Choose a few pairs to tell their ideas to the rest of the class.

7 ▭ **16 SB p 146**

Play the recording. Students listen and decide which story the speakers are talking about. In pairs they discuss how accurate their ideas about the story were.

> Story B

> ▭ **16**
>
> (A = Alison; B = Bart)
>
> A: *Have you seen this? The article about that new survey ...*
>
> B: *Yes, I was reading it earlier. No surprises there I don't think ... seems pretty obvious to me. You don't need a survey to tell you that, do you?*
>
> A: *Yeah, well, I don't know, I mean, it's not that simple is it? I mean, some people like living in the country ...*
>
> B: *Yeah, and you can see why; less stress, less traffic, less smog ... but I don't think it's just a simple question of what you like, you know ...*
>
> A: *No, it's more like ... it seems like it's a question of work and money more than anything else, I mean ...*
>
> B: *Yeah, it said that, didn't it? The main reason was that they couldn't find a job in the country ...*
>
> A: *Well, it doesn't say that exactly, but yes, it says it's er, it's, you know, easier to find work in large cities and I reckon that's true, don't you?*
>
> B: *Yeah, but I don't think that's the main reason. I mean, it might be the main reason for older people ... you know, no jobs, rural unemployment, whatever ...*
>
> A: *Yeah, there's a lot of that ...*
>
> B: *But it seems to be talking more about young people ... I mean, the statistics here are referring*

to people under thirty and you know, I reckon that even if, even if there were plenty of jobs in the rural areas, well, they'd still go to the cities, wouldn't they?

A: *Do you think so? Maybe you're right. Maybe it's more a kind of lure of the bright lights thing ...*

B: *Yeah, you know, nightlife, music, youth culture in general ...*

A: *Yeah, it says something about that, doesn't it? That bit where it talks about, what is it ... 'leisure time activities' or something like that?*

B: *'Free time facilities'.*

A: *Yeah, that was it.*

B: *... pubs and clubs more like!*

A: *Yeah, and cinemas and exhibitions and stuff as well ...*

B: *Nah, discos and the chance to meet other young people more like ...*

A: *Yeah, OK, the social side of things, but it's important, isn't it?*

B: *Yeah, this survey seems to reckon it's the second most important factor in fact after getting a job. You know, if young people decide to leave their homes in the country, then they reckon the social side of things is the second most important thing they consider. What other things do you think they mentioned?*

A: *Oh, I don't know. Maybe they said there were more opportunities for continuing their education, like going to colleges and stuff. They might be thinking about facilities for their families in the future, like being near good schools and stuff. Um, what about better living conditions ... more modern houses which need less work doing to them and stuff?*

B: *Yeah, I suppose they're all things you'd have to think about, aren't they?*

A: *Yeah, the survey makes quite a lot of sense.*

B: *Mmm.*

8 Play the recording again. Students make notes about the facts of the story.

9 Pairwork. Students use their notes to write the newspaper story. Go round offering help where necessary. Encourage students to use the hedging expressions they have been learning. Discourage them from looking at page 133 until they have finished writing, editing and checking their stories. When students compare their texts encourage them to notice any differences in the use of hedging language.

Where in the world? (p 26)

1 Pairwork. Students discuss the questions. When they have finished they can compare their answers with those of another pair. Ask several pairs to present their findings to the class.

2 Whole class. Direct students' attention to the five extracts from guide books and divide them into small groups.

Groupwork. Students read and discuss the five extracts. They decide which city is being described in each of them. You could get them to divide the extracts between them so that each student is responsible for reading one extract (or two of the shorter ones), telling the others about it and finding the clues which point to the identity of the city.

Encourage students not to look at the clues on pages 132 and 138 until they have discussed the texts fully. If they are still having trouble deciding which cities are being described, refer them to the clues to identify the cities.

3 Students discuss the extracts again and make a final decision on which cities they describe, underlining the information in the texts which helped them decide on the answers. Check answers with the whole class.

> 1 Madrid   2 Prague   3 London   4 Tokyo
> 5 New York

4 Pairwork. Students discuss the questions and then report back to the class.

Lexis (p 27)

1 Pairwork. Students first match the definitions to the adjectives. Check answers with the class. Then ask students to decide which adjectives they would use to describe the noun phrases. Some of them are from the extracts, but discourage students from looking for them at this stage.

> a) grubby   b) bustling   c) haphazard   d) soaring
> e) in-your-face   f) tacky   g) awe-inspiring   h) clogged

> ### Possible answers
> grubby: children's hands, old trainers
> bustling: market, coastal resorts
> haphazard: approach to work, collection of people
> soaring: tree tops, tower blocks
> in-your-face: advertising campaigns, action movies
> tacky: plastic souvenirs, seaside postcards
> awe-inspiring: beauty, scenery
> clogged: arteries, waterways

2 Students look back at the extracts to find the adjectives and what they are describing. Check answers with the class.

> grubby: the city (extract 3 – London)
> bustling: restaurants (extract 4 – Tokyo)
> haphazard: modern development (extract 2 – Prague)
> soaring: office blocks (extract 4 – Tokyo)
> in-your-face: the experience of the city
> (extract 5 – New York)

> tacky: tourist trap (extract 2 – Prague)
>
> awe-inspiring: the beauty of the city
> (extract 1 – other European cities)
>
> clogged: traffic (extract 3 – London)

3 Pairwork. Students look at the verbs and match them to the phrases.

4 Pairwork. Students check their answers with the extracts. They then discuss the expressions and try to work out their meaning. Check answers with the class, inviting different pairs to explain the meaning of each expression.

> a) to make way for the new
> b) to work its magic
> c) to get your bearings
> d) to fall prey to (something)
> e) to live on top of one another
> f) to put a finger on (something)

5 Students fill the gaps with the phrases from 3. Do the first one as an example and make sure they realise that changes may have to be made to make the phrases fit the sentences. Allow students to check their answers in pairs before checking with the whole class.

> a) work their magic
> b) live on top of one another
> c) to get your bearings
> d) to put your finger on
> e) to fall prey to
> f) to make way for the new

Alternative activity

An alternative approach to 3, 4 and 5 would be to ask the students to work in pairs and write definitions for three of the expressions in 3. They give their definitions to another pair who have to match them to the correct phrase. Students then write sentences which are true for them using the expressions.

6 Pairwork. Students discuss the question and report back to the class.

Close up (p 28)

Negative & limiting adverbials

1 Pairwork. Students decide which of the adverbials have negative or limiting meanings. Check answers with the class.

> under no circumstances   quite often
> only after a long night   never
> not until he'd finished   seldom   only then

> only after a long wait   not a word
> rarely   on no account

2 Give students a few minutes to answer the questions. Once they have attempted all of them, allow students to compare answers with a partner and then refer them to the Language reference section on page 29 for more information on negative and limiting adverbials. Check the answers with the class.

> a) 1A
> b) The most common position is the B sentences. In the A sentences they have been moved to first position for emphasis.
> c) The Bs
> d) The word order changes so that the auxiliary comes before the subject. Note: it may be worth pointing out to the students that if there is a verb in the adverbial phrase itself, that verb doesn't change and isn't inverted. For example, *Not until I saw the station did I realise ... NOT* ~~Not until did I see the station I realise ...~~

3 Students work in pairs to rewrite the sentences. When they have finished, write the answers on the board. Pairs check their sentences against the answers. The aim is to encourage students to notice any mistakes they've made themselves. You then only need to check the questions they are still having problems with. This speeds up and facilitates the whole feedback stage.

> a) Rarely do I visit a city more than once, but this place is really special.
> b) Never before had I seen anything so breathtakingly beautiful.
> c) Under no circumstances should you go out alone at night.
> d) Only by wandering down its narrow side streets will you be able to see and feel the heart of this beautiful old town.
> e) Only after you have spent an evening there will you begin to understand the special charm of this place.
> f) Not until you climb to the top can you really understand exactly how beautiful the view is.

4 Groupwork. Students discuss the sentences and try to agree on a place to fit each one. In multinational classes, students could take turns to describe a place they know to the other members of the group.

Writing (p 28)

1 Go through the instructions with the class. Make sure students are aware that they should not write the name of the place they are describing but should leave gaps. Nor should they discuss it with other students. The writing task can be set for homework. If you decide to do it in class, go round offering help and encouragement where necessary.

2 Groupwork. Students take turns to read their descriptions to the rest of their group. The other members have to guess which place is being described and say what information helped them to decide. When the activity is over, you might like to display the finished descriptions for everyone to read and enjoy.

Anecdote (p 29)

See Introduction, page 4, for more ideas on how to set up, monitor and repeat Anecdotes.

1 Go through the instructions with the class. To give them an idea of the sort of things they could say, you could describe a city that has impressed you. Allow the students to ask you questions. Use some of the expressions in the Language toolbox and direct students' attention to it. Give them some time to decide which city they are going to describe and to think about what they are going to say. If they like, they could make notes, but discourage them from reading these notes when they start their descriptions.

2 Pairwork. Students take turns to describe the cities they have chosen. Make sure they understand that they should give as much detail as possible.

3 Whole class. Ask several students to answer the questions and tell the class about their partner's descriptions.

One big party (p 30)

Closed books. Brainstorm the names of as many London landmarks as possible. Find out if students have been to London and, if so, which places they would recommend and why.

1 Whole class. Find out if any of the students have heard of Leicester Square or have been there. If so, ask them to tell the class about it. Establish that it is in London. Direct students' attention to the photograph and ask them what they can see and what adjectives they would use to describe Leicester Square.

2 Pairwork. Students match the questions and answers. Check with the class and explain any difficult vocabulary. (*brash* = vulgar, *seething* = busy)

> a) 4   b) 3   c) 2   d) 1

3 Give students time to read the article and look at the questions. Tell them not to worry about the gaps at this stage. Allow students to check with a partner before eliciting answers from the class.

> a) On the street, buskers play music and make political speeches and there are cartoonists. There are also cinemas, nightclubs, restaurants and an ice cream shop. Just watching the people passing by is also entertaining.

> b) Tourists of all nationalities, young people, movie stars, ordinary Londoners.
>
> c) The Prince Charles cinema which is cheaper than the others; the restaurants of Chinatown nearby which are cheaper than the restaurants that are actually on the square itself.

4 Pairwork. Go through the instructions with the class and then give pairs time to decide where to put the missing words and phrases.

> 1 g)   2 a)   3 c)   4 h)   5 d)   6 b)   7 f)   8 e)

5 Pairwork. Students turn to the relevant pages and follow the instructions. Note: the vocabulary in this exercise is colloquial. Make sure students understand that it is only used in informal writing and speech.

6 Groupwork. Students discuss the questions. Go round offering help with vocabulary where necessary.

City life (p 31)

1 Pairwork. Students discuss the question and draw up their lists. Make a class list of the dangers of city life, inviting different pairs to add ideas. Leave the list on the board as you will need it for the following exercise.

2 ▭ **17 SB p 146**

Go through the questions with the class before you play the recording. Give students a chance to see if they can answer any of the questions before you play the recording for a second time, but don't check answers at this stage.

> ▭ **17**
>
> (H = Helen; R = Robert)
>
> H: *Well, I don't really think it's particularly dangerous. Not any more than any other large city. You have to be sensible, take the normal precautions. I mean I wouldn't walk down a street and stare at somebody and I certainly wouldn't walk home alone, and I wouldn't go down unlit alleys, you know, dark alleys at night, and obviously there are certain areas that you just know you wouldn't go into, but I think on the whole it's not a particularly dangerous city.*
>
> R: *Yeah, I think I agree, but, um, actually there have been a couple of stories in the papers recently about this spate of muggings that's been going on.*
>
> H: *Oh yeah, I read about that. Yeah, because they say things are changing and things are getting worse in the city. I did have a friend, actually, she was on the underground, and her wallet*

was snatched from her bag just as the train was coming into the station, and of course they got off straight away and there was absolutely nothing she could do about it.

R: *Well, I sympathise with her. I mean I've seen that happen too, and, er, you've just got to watch it in a place like that, or like the street market. You've got to be really careful there because there is a big crowd and a lot of pickpockets and they can steal something and run away.*

H: *But I don't think it's really dangerous. They're not violent people, you just have to be sensible and keep your eyes open, and ...*

R: *Well, I don't know. This article I read they said that a lot of the thieves were carrying knives, which means if you resist then, er, you could get badly hurt, so that really makes you think, doesn't it?*

H: *Mmm, I said it wasn't violent, maybe it is. I heard about a group of tourists the other day who were mugged. What do you do if you see something like that? You don't really know what's going on and you don't really want to get involved in case you get hurt.*

R: *Yes. I think it's stupid to try and be a hero. I mean you could get very badly hurt and all they want is just money. I mean I know that is a terrible thing to say, but it's just money. It's not worth losing your life for.*

H: *I suppose so. Apparently these guys had a knife and they cut one of the women's handbags from her shoulder. I think she thought they were going to stab her husband actually.*

R: *Did you hear if anybody was hurt at all?*

H: *No, no-one was hurt. Apparently, the woman had had her passport stolen, and her traveller's cheques taken but the sad thing was that they had only just arrived and they didn't want to leave all their stuff in the hotel. They thought it was safer with them.*

R: *Yeah, well that's a problem with tourists though, isn't it? They're easy targets. They stand out in a crowd, thieves know they're probably carrying money and documents around and they don't speak the language, and they're vulnerable, aren't they?*

H: *Well ...*

R: *I mean it happens to locals as well. There is a friend of mine who was jumped from behind, you know, and they got her bag and they ran away, and she tried to run after them but the thieves were too quick obviously.*

H: *Was she hurt at all?*

R: *No, no, but she was really angry.*

H: *Of course.*

R: *She didn't lose anything really valuable so, um, she didn't report it to the police in the end actually.*

H: *I think she should have done that actually. I think it's quite important when something like that happens because it might be mild at the moment but they could get worse. I think they need to know if a crime's happened actually.*

R: *Yeah. Well, I mean, there should be more police around anyway, shouldn't there? There should be more police on the streets at night.*

H: *I think you're right.*

R: *You can be on main streets and there's nobody, just a police car driving up and down every now and again, would ...*

H: *You would feel better protected I think.*

R: *Yeah, and it would put the muggers and thieves off, wouldn't it?*

3 Pairwork. Students compare answers in pairs and discuss the questions.

a) Helen doesn't think the city is particularly dangerous. Neither does Robert, though he has seen newspaper reports about an increase in muggings.

b) and c) Students' own answers

4 Play the recording again. Students check their answers.

a) You shouldn't walk down a street and stare at someone. You shouldn't walk home alone or go down unlit alleys or into certain bad areas.

b) On the underground and in street markets because in big crowds there are often thieves and pickpockets.

c) There seems to have been an increase in muggings (attacking people in the street in order to steal from them).

d) They haven't been victims of crime themselves, though they both have friends who have been victims.

e) They were mugged in the street. The muggers stole one of the women's handbags containing her passport and traveller's cheques by cutting the strap. She thought they were going to stab her husband.

f) They think there should be more police officers patrolling on the streets at night.

Optional activity

Students compare stories of the scariest experiences they've had in a city. This could be a sensitive subject, so don't force those who don't wish to join in.

Adding emphasis (p 31)

1 Establish that the three words in the box are used to add emphasis. *Just* is used in a limiting way and can mean the same as *only*, for example, *I was just standing by the bus stop* (I wasn't doing anything else). It is also used to emphasise a point in time, for example, *Just as I arrived ... Really* can be used in a similar way to *very*, for example, *I was really tired. Actually* is used to emphasise that something is true or correct, or that it actually happened, for example, *I am actually very angry* and sometimes to show surprise, for example, *He looks very young, but he's actually 58*. Students match the words in the box with a–j. Allow students to check their answers in pairs before checking with the whole class.

> a) really   b) actually   c) just   d) really
> e) actually   f) just   g) actually   h) just
> i) just   j) really

2 Students use the words to complete the extracts. Remind them that they heard these phrases on the recording but ask them to do the exercise without looking at the tapescript. Don't check answers at this stage.

3 🔲 18 SB p 147

Play the recording. Ask students to listen and check their answers and also to listen for where the stress falls in these extracts. Check answers with the class and elicit where the stress falls. Play the recording again if necessary.

> a) just   b) actually   c) just   d) really   e) really
> f) just   g) actually   h) just   i) really   j) actually
>
> The stress falls on the emphasising words: *just*, *really* and *actually*. It adds extra emphasis.

> 🔲 18
> a) ... there are certain areas that you just know you wouldn't go into ...
> b) ... actually there have been a couple of stories in the papers recently about this spate of muggings that's been going on.
> c) ... her wallet was snatched from her bag just as the train was coming into the station ...
> d) You've got to be really careful there because there is a big crowd and a lot of pickpockets ...
> e) You don't really know what's going on ...
> f) ... I know that is a terrible thing to say, but it's just money.
> g) I think she thought they were going to stab her husband actually.
> h) ... but the sad thing was that they had only just arrived ...
> i) She didn't lose anything really valuable ...
> j) I think they need to know if a crime's happened actually.

4 Students work individually to write their paragraphs. They then show them to a partner and practise reading their own and their partner's paragraphs aloud, using correct emphasis.

Discussion (p 31)

Groupwork. Students work in groups of three or four to discuss one of the sets of questions. You may like to ask students to report back on their discussion to the whole class. This can be done by nominating a spokesperson or by letting students choose one.

An urban poem (p 32)

Note: if you have a strong class, you might prefer to change the order here and let the students read the poem and decide on the order of the verses and then listen to the poem to check their answers before studying the lexis. Alternatively they could listen to the poem first with their books closed, then rearrange the verses before looking at the new vocabulary.

Lexis

1 Pairwork. Students look at the words in the box and discuss the questions. Encourage them to use a dictionary to find the meanings of any unknown words. Check answers with the class.

> a) a partner: a mate; a person who can't speak: a mute
> b) a gut (stomach)
> c) to pinch something; to nick something
> d) to boot something or someone
> e) to hug someone
> f) to flog something
> g) to joy-ride
> h) stupid: daft; dirty: mucky

2 Pairwork. Students discuss their own answers to the questions.

Reading (p 32)

1 Groupwork. Students read the poem, then they put the poem in order in small groups and answer the question in b). Give them plenty of time to read and discuss. Elicit answers at this stage but don't give definitive answers.

> a) Correct order: d, c, e, a, b
> b) Students may suggest that the character in the poem is male because of the aggression expressed in the poem and the actions which are described: joy-riding, breaking in, selling stolen goods. They may, on the other hand, suggest that the character is female because of the reference to mirrors and the fact that the snowman is a 'mate', not in the sense of being a friend, but a partner. There is no need to offer a definitive answer.

2   ▭ 19 SB p 147

Play the recording for students to check their answers.

▭ 19

An urban poem

*The most unusual thing I ever stole? A snowman.
Midnight. He looked magnificent; a tall, white mute
beneath the winter moon. I wanted him, a mate
with a mind as cold as the slice of ice
within my own brain. I started with the head.*

*Better off dead than giving in, not taking
what you want. He weighed a ton; his torso,
frozen stiff, hugged to my chest, a fierce chill
piercing my gut. Part of the thrill was knowing
that children would cry in the morning. Life's tough.*

*Sometimes I steal things I don't need. I joy-ride cars
to nowhere, break into houses just to have a look.
I'm a mucky ghost, leave a mess, maybe pinch a camera.
I watch my gloved hand twisting the doorknob.
A stranger's bedroom. Mirrors, I sigh like this – Aah.*

*It took some time. Reassembled in the yard,
he didn't look the same. I took a run
and booted him. Again. Again. My breath ripped out
in rags. It seems daft now. Then I was standing
alone amongst lumps of snow, sick of the world.*

*Boredom. Mostly I'm so bored I could eat myself.
One time, I stole a guitar and thought I might
learn to play. I nicked a bust of Shakespeare once,
flogged it, but the snowman was strangest.
You don't understand a word I'm saying, do you?*

3/4 Groupwork. Students discuss the questions. The title of the poem is *Stealing*.

Optional activity

Ask students to write either a paraphrase of the poem or a brief summary of their reactions to it. The choice of which they write should be left to them. This could be done for homework.

Discussion (p 33)

Groupwork. Students look at the painting for a few minutes and then read and discuss the questions. Elicit a few answers to each question from several groups. Encourage each speaker to give as much detail as possible. Other students can be encouraged to ask further questions.

Optional activity

Pairwork. Students think about a painting which had a powerful effect on them (funny, scary, shocking, romantic, relaxing, etc.). They tell their partners why it had such a strong effect on them.

Test

Scoring: one point per correct answer unless otherwise indicated.

1   1   It would seem that he's made his mind up.
      2   She appears to be quite happy about it.
      3   It would seem that he doesn't agree with us.
      4   It is not known whether they will accept the offer.
      5   There are not believed to be any survivors.
      6   There is little doubt that it was Frank who did it.

2   1   in-your-face   2   get their bearings   3   soaring
      4   bustling   5   clogged   6   awe-inspiring

3   (1 point each for 1–4 and 2 points each for 5–8)
      1   Never again will you see such amazing sights.
      2   Only after you've spent a few years there do you/will you really begin to understand the culture.
      3   On no account should you go out at night.
      4   Barely had we left when it started to snow.
      5   Seldom have I seen such amazing architecture.
      6   Never will you see more perfect beaches.
      7   Not until you've been there for a few days will you start to relax.
      8   Only when I went there did I realise how little I knew.

4   1   I'd just got off the bus when I saw them.
      2   Did you really understand what she said?
      3   There are some areas you really shouldn't go to.
      4   What did he actually say?

5   1   friend
      2   stolen
      3   put her arms round me in affection
      4   kicked
      5   sell
      6   stole
      7   dirty
      8   drove the stolen car around just for fun
      9   silly/stupid
    10   looking/staring
    11   dirty
    12   ate greedily

3 City Test

Name: **Total:** _____ /40

1 Hedging *6 points*

Put the words in *italics* into the correct order to complete the sentences.

1 *it would / that / seem* he's made his mind up.

_____

2 *appears / she / quite happy / to be* about it.

_____

3 *he / it / that / seem / would* doesn't agree with us.

_____

4 *whether / it / not / is / known* they will accept the offer.

_____

5 *believed / to be / there / not / are* any survivors.

_____

6 *is / that / doubt / there / little* it was Frank who did it.

_____

2 Lexis – describing places *6 points*

Rearrange the mixed-up words.

As soon as you arrive your senses will be bombarded from all directions. Everything is (1) **ni-uryo-efac** and it will take even the most experienced of travellers a while to (2) **etg hteri bageinrs**. India has got everything – the (3) **saoinrg** Himalayas in the very north, the (4) **bitlsnug** cities where you risk life and limb whenever you cross their (5) **colgegd** roads and of course the (6) **aew-isniginpr** Taj Mahal.

1 _____ 2 _____ 3 _____

4 _____ 5 _____ 6 _____

3 Negative and limiting adverbials *12 points*

Correct the mistakes in these sentences.

1 Never again you will see such amazing sights.

2 Only after you've spent a few years there you really begin to understand the culture.

3 On no account you should go out at night.

4 Barely we had left when it started to snow.

Rewrite the sentences beginning with the words given.

5 I have seldom seen such amazing architecture.

    Seldom _____

6 You'll never see more perfect beaches.

    Never _____

7 You'll only start to relax when you've been there for a few days.

    Not until _____

8 I didn't realise how little I knew until I went there.

    Only when _____

4 Adding emphasis *4 points*

Put the word in brackets into the correct place in the sentences.

1 I'd got off the bus when I saw them.   (just)

2 Did you understand what she said?   (really)

3 There are some areas you shouldn't go to.   (really)

4 What did he say?   (actually)

5 Lexis – informal words *12 points*

What do the words and phrases in *italics* mean?

1 He's a really good *mate* of mine. _____

2 His car was *nicked* last week. _____

3 She *gave me a big hug* to say thanks. _____

4 His car wouldn't start so he *booted* it. _____

5 She's going to *flog* her computer. _____

6 They *pinched* a few sweets. _____

7 He got really *mucky* playing football. _____

8 We stole a car and *went on a joy-ride*. _____

9 That's a really *daft* idea. _____

10 Stop *gawping* at me! _____

11 The coat was really *grubby*. _____

12 We *gorged ourselves* at the new restaurant last night. _____

Talk Overview

The topic of this unit is conversation. The grammar focus is on general and past tendencies, with an opportunity for students to test their knowledge of *wh*- words.

Students start with a mingling activity, finding someone in the class to match each of the given categories. They then define the word *conversation* in small groups and answer questions about the word and its use.

Students listen to people talking about what makes a good conversationalist and discuss their own ideas. They then go on to read a text about different conversational styles and compare the writer's views with their own experiences. Students then talk about conversations they have overheard and eavesdrop on three conversations, deciding where they take place and what they are about.

Students study the use of *will* and *would* to talk about general tendencies and then listen to a woman talking about the habits and characteristics of members of her family. They go on to talk about a member of their own family to a partner.

In the next section, they examine different forms and uses of the word *talk*. They then listen to someone telling a joke and look at the way intonation, pace and timing are used. Finally, students read a series of short jokes and practise telling them to a partner.

Section	Aims	What the students are doing
Introduction page 34	*Conversation skills*: fluency	Mingling and asking questions.
Conversation piece pages 34–35	*Lexis*: conversation and its collocations	Defining *conversation*. Differentiating between different words for talking. Studying collocations with *conversation*.
The art of conversation pages 35–36	*Listening skills*: listening for gist and taking notes	Listening to people talking about what makes a good conversationalist and taking notes.
	Conversation skills: discussion	Discussing conversations you have had.
Conversational styles pages 36–38	*Reading skills*: reading for gist	Matching headings to sections of a text. Deciding whether statements are true or false.
	Lexis: expressions to describe conversational styles	Discussing differences in conversational styles.
Test yourself pages 38–39	*Grammar*: wh-words	Matching *wh*- words to the things they refer to. Completing sentences with *wh*- words.
Eavesdropping pages 39–40	*Listening skills*: listening for gist	Discussing conversations you have overheard. Listening to three conversations and deciding where they take place.
	Lexis: idioms	Reviewing common expressions.
Close up pages 40–41	*Grammar*: general tendencies; tendencies in the past	Identifying the modal verbs used to talk about general tendencies and tendencies in the past. Completing texts.
I love them dearly but ... page 42	*Listening skills*: listening for specific information	Listening to a woman talking about her family and answering questions.
	Conversation skills: fluency work	Anecdote: talking about a member of your family.
Talk pages 42–43	*Lexis*: collocations and meanings of *talk*	Identifying common uses and forms of the word *talk*. Completing expressions with appropriate prepositions.
A tall tale page 43	*Listening skills*: listening for detail	Predicting the content of a story from pictures.
	Pronunciation: stress	Listening to check predictions. Identifying stress and intonation patterns.
Doctor! Doctor! page 43	*Speaking skills*: telling jokes	Matching the parts of three-line jokes. Practising telling jokes using pace and timing.
	Pronunciation: stress	

Talk *Teacher's notes*

Whole class. Direct students' attention to the photographs and ask in which situation they feel most comfortable: an intimate chat or talking in public. Encourage them to give reasons. 'Find someone who ...' can be done as a mingling activity with students moving round the class asking questions and trying to get one name for each item. The first student to find someone for each item should raise their hand.

Conversation piece (p 34)

1 Groupwork. Remind students that dictionary definitions do not have to be whole sentences, but should be phrases explaining the meaning of the word. A list of twenty words associated with *conversation* is not a definition!

2 Students look at the two dictionary definitions on page 136 and discuss the two questions.

3 Give the groups plenty of time to think about and answer the questions. Don't check answers at this stage.

4 Students check their answers with the dictionary definitions on page 136 before you go through them with the class.

> a) both (*I had several conversations with him about the plans. It was very difficult to engage her in conversation.*)
>
> b) on the third syllable
>
> c) If you *have a conversation*, it implies that both parties have something they want to talk about. If you *make conversation*, the implication is that you start talking to someone (often someone you don't know) in order to be polite or to fill an awkward silence.
>
> d) 1 conversationalist   2 conversationally
>   3 Conversational

Whole class. Read the file card about the derivation of the word *conversation*. Ask students if they agree that being sociable is more important than what you talk about.

5 Pairwork. Students discuss the questions, consulting a dictionary if necessary. Check answers with the class.

> a) A *conversation* is an informal exchange of ideas or information; a *chat* is a friendly conversation, usually not about anything very important; a *discussion* involves talking about something from different points of view, perhaps with a view to reaching a conclusion; an *argument* is a disagreement and can involve a degree of hostility.

> b) carry on, come up in, contribute to, end, forget, get into, hear, hold, interrupt, overhear, prolong, remember, start, stop, strike up
>
> c) in

6 Students work individually to think about the meaning of the adjectives and put them into categories. They then add two more adjectives to each category and compare answers with a partner. Check answers with the class.

> *Possible answers*
>
> | positive | negative | neutral |
> | --- | --- | --- |
> | animated | pointless | recent |
> | riveting | lengthy | overheard |
> | memorable | frustrating | in-depth |
> | enjoyable | predictable | |
> | meaningful | boring | |
> | fascinating | one-way | |
> | hilarious | | |

7 Pairwork. You may need to explain *graded adjective*. A graded adjective is one whose meaning can have different degrees or strength. Graded adjectives can be qualified with adverbs which express these different degrees. *Good* is an example of a graded adjective. We can say *very good, quite good, fairly good*. *Unique* is an adjective which is not graded. Something is either unique (there is only one of it) or it is not. It is not possible to say ~~very unique~~. You may want to point out that a good dictionary will tell you whether an adjective is graded or not. Allow the pairs plenty of time to discuss the questions and then check the answers with the class.

> a) Graded adjectives: animated, lengthy, memorable, frustrating, enjoyable, meaningful, predictable, boring, recent, in-depth
>
> b) Non-graded adjectives: pointless, overheard, riveting, one-way, fascinating, hilarious
>
> c) Students' own answers.

8 Pairwork. Students take turns to tell their partners their answers to all the questions. Each time, the listening partners should listen attentively and be prepared to ask questions and discuss what they have heard.

9 Pairwork. Pairs report back to the class on three things their conversations had in common.

The art of conversation (p 35)

1 Groupwork. Students discuss the questions. Go round, offering help and encouragement where necessary.

2 Whole class. Students compare their answers.

3 📼 **20 SB p 147**

Students make notes as you play the recording. Encourage them first to make a three-column table as in the Student's Book and to fill in the number of the speaker, their notes on what is said and the letter of the question each speaker is answering in the appropriate places. See if students can match speakers and questions before you play the recording for a second time.

> 1 a) 2 c) 3 b) 4 b) 5 a) 6 b)

📼 **20**

1

Well, I like to be able to take an active part, so it helps if there aren't some people who hog the conversation all the time and also people need to have a sense of humour about things, I think, not to take things too seriously and you need a conversation that flows, so that you can ... well, you don't get stuck on one point.

2

Um, a good conversationalist. I'd say it's someone who's got a point that they want to put across during the conversation. Someone with something to say as opposed to someone who just talks endlessly about various subjects and doesn't engage in one particular subject and I'd say it was someone who listens to other people as well, um, that's what I'd say.

3

When people aren't really interested in what you're saying, um, that's very annoying indeed. Also people who interrupt you continually with grunts or opinions of their own or whatever, and also some people don't care about whose turn it is to talk, so they just, you know, butt in when you're in the middle of a thought and obviously, you know, when the topic's boring. That's very irritating. And sometimes, you know, the conversation goes nowhere, it's going nowhere, and that is also extremely irritating.

4

I really hate it when I'm with someone who just drones on and on in a conversation, and who doesn't give you a chance to speak at all. Oh, and I also really hate it when they just carry on and they don't care whether or not you are interested at all

in what they're saying. They seem oblivious to how you are reacting to them. I hate that.

5

It's good when you're talking about things which you've got in common with the person you are talking to, like you're on the same wavelength and you can share the same tastes or experiences so you know where the other person's coming from. It's also nice if you can share a joke or a personal story or an anecdote or something like that.

6

I can't stand it when you have to do all the talking yourself, when the other person's not responding, or when they are responding but it's with monosyllabic answers, you know, just going yeah, er, um, and that's all you're getting back, and when you have to work to keep the conversation going, that's really bad, when you're having to hunt around for things to say, because you're just not getting anything back.

4 Pairwork. Students compare notes and discuss the question.

Lexis (p 36)

1 Students work individually to complete the sentences. You may like to point out that most of the gaps need more than one word. Do not check answers at this stage.

2 Play the recording again. Students listen and check their work in pairs, amending it as necessary. Be prepared to play the recording again if necessary. Check answers with the class and elicit or explain the meaning of any difficult items. Students should be able to guess the meaning of some of them, for example, *hog the conversation*, from the context. You can help by saying things like: *If someone is unable to take an active part in a conversation, what is the other person doing wrong?*

> a) 1 hog   2 flows
> b) 3 put across   4 something to say
> c) 5 turn   6 butt in
> d) 7 drones on and on
> e) 8 the same wavelength
> f) 9 do all the talking
>   10 monosyllabic answers
>   11 keep the conversation going
>   12 hunt around

3 Groupwork. Students should work in different groups from those they formed in *The art of conversation* 1 as the questions are quite similar. When they have finished, you might like to ask them to reflect on whether their discussion was better in this new group or not. Students choose one question to discuss. Remind them to try to use some of the expressions from 1.

Note: there is a Test yourself section on question words on page 38. This would be an alternative place to do this test.

Conversational styles (p 36)

1 Whole class. Give students time to read the title and the first paragraph. Elicit suggestions as to what *Hold your horses* and *What are you waiting for?* might mean. (*Hold your horses* is said to someone who is always rushing ahead to do or say something; it means 'Slow down!'. *What are you waiting for?* is said to someone who is hesitating about doing or saying something; it means 'Hurry up!'.)

Point out that these are references to two conversational styles. Before students decide if they identify with either one, ask them to say what the differences between Sara and Betty are. (Sara is very talkative and tends to dominate the conversation; Betty is quieter and tends to say nothing if she is with someone who talks a lot. Sara is frustrated because Betty doesn't contribute to the conversation, making her do all the work. Betty is frustrated because she feels that Sara doesn't allow her room to say anything.) Encourage students to tell the class if they have ever been in either Sara or Betty's situation.

2 Students read the rest of the article and match the headings to the sections. Allow them to compare answers in pairs before checking with the class.

> a) 5 b) 1 c) 3 d) 2 e) 4

3 Students answer these questions individually.

4 Pairwork. Students compare answers in pairs. Then check answers with the class.

> *Possible answers*
>
> a) Their expectations of how the other would signal turn-taking in conversation were different. Betty was waiting for Sara to pause so that she could speak. Sara saw pauses as awkward silences, so she didn't provide any. When she did speak, Betty used lots of pauses, which Sara misinterpreted as signals that she had finished.
>
> b) Betty was from Britain and Sara from the United States. Conversational styles between the two countries are different (people from Britain expect longer pauses between turns) and this made the problem between the two women worse.
>
> c) The writer explains the communication problems encountered by two women with differing conversational styles. She says that conversation is a matter of taking turns to speak. When two people have similar conversational styles, there is no problem. However, factors such as nationality, gender and age can have a negative effect on a conversation and lead to frustration and misunderstanding.

5 Whole class. Allow students a few minutes to read through the statements and decide whether they are true or false. Go through the statements and have a show of hands on whether they are true or false. Put the results on the board.

6 Give students time to read the article again and decide whether the answers on the board are correct or not. Allow students to compare with a partner before checking answers with the class. Encourage them to provide evidence to support any changes they wish to make.

> a) false (She did, but she felt she didn't have the opportunity to speak because Sara never stopped talking.)
>
> b) true (At least they leave longer pauses, which may be interpreted as being quieter.)
>
> c) true (If Sara is taken as a typical example of a North American.)
>
> d) true (In Scandinavia they have a reputation for being slow and dull.)
>
> e) true (The text says New York is a 'faster-speaking region'.)
>
> f) false (They speak faster than those from the south west.)
>
> g) true (For example, the British think Scandinavians are taciturn.)

Pairwork. Students discuss the three questions.

Whole class. Invite students to say what is happening in the cartoon in the margin.

Lexis (p 38)

1 Encourage students to try this first without looking back at the article. When they have matched as many as they can, they can use the article to help.

2 Pairwork. Students compare answers before you check with the class. Note: in h) the expression *get a word in edgewise* is American English. British people tend to say *edgeways*.

> a) 10 b) 4 c) 6 d) 9 e) 1 f) 3
> g) 5 h) 8 i) 2 j) 7

3 Pairwork. Students discuss the questions. Check answers with the class.

Test yourself (p 38)

wh- words

1 Pairwork. Students match the words in the box with a–g. Check answers with the class.

> a) when b) where c) why d) whose
> e) how f) who g) what, which

2 Pairwork. Students use the question words from the box in 1 to complete the gaps. Check answers with the class.

> **A** 1 When 2 who 3 what 4 who 5 whose
> **B** 6 When 7 how 8 which 9 why

3 Pairwork. Students look back at the completed text in 2 and decide where they could have used *that*. Check answers with the class.

> You could have used *that* in 2, 4 and 8.

4 Pairwork. Students use the words in the box in 1 to complete the questions. Check answers with the class.

> a) Whose b) what c) Who d) when / where
> e) When; why f) How

5 Pairwork. Students discuss their own answers to the questions in 4.

Eavesdropping (p 39)

Books closed. Whole class. Ask students if they have ever intentionally or accidentally overheard someone else's conversation. Find out what are the most interesting / funniest / worst things they have overheard.

Listening (p 39)

1 ▭ **21 SB p 147**

Before you play the recording, go through the instructions with the class so that they know exactly what they are listening for.

> a) Conversation 2   b) Conversation 3
> c) Conversation 1

▭ **21**

1

(H = Helen; K = Kate)

H: *He can be a bit difficult at times. You know sometimes he'll just get really angry about something really trivial like, I don't know, not collecting the dirty glasses quickly enough or something like that, but he'll shout and rant for a while and then half an hour later he'll have forgotten all about it. And then he'll be all sweetness and light after that.*

K: *The woman I used to work for, she was exactly the same. Do you know, she'd complain about everything, and no matter how clean the bar top was, she'd make us clean it over and over again, like three or four times. She'd complain if*

we were milliseconds late for work, she'd complain if we didn't look smart enough and no matter how late it got she would make us stay until all the cleaning up was finished.

H: *Oh, no, no, he's not that bad actually. No, really not, and sometimes he can be really nice, really generous. Like sometimes after we've shut, he'll buy everybody a drink at the end of the night, um, and he'll order in some pizza for everybody and then we'll all sit round and have a nice drink, and a chat, and a bite to eat.*

K: *Oh, that sounds really nice.*

H: *Mmm, it is, yeah.*

2

(B = Bob; J = Jack)

B: *I know, I know exactly what you mean. I mean, sometimes, you know, what I do is, I'll, I'll sit down, you know, I'll get myself all sorted out, get everything ready, and then something catches my eye in the room, like, I mean, I've got the telly on, you know, in the corner, you know, I have the sound turned down, but I just notice the picture – and I'm like, well, I've got to see what that, I mean I've got to see that programme, you know, it'll only take twenty minutes, and then of course, then I'm off and I'm away and I'm here. Oh! It's terrible!*

J: *I know, just before I start, I'll go and make a cup of coffee and then I'll just have a sit down with my cup of coffee rather than work ...*

B: *And you've got to make yourself, you know, a jam sandwich or something to go with it ...*

J: *Absolutely.*

B: *To go with the coffee. Yeah, yeah, you can look around and think 'Well, actually it's more important that I tidy the flat'.*

J: *Yeah, and you've got to wash up your cup of coffee.*

3

(A = Adam; F = Fiona; N = Nick)

A: *... Apparently it's doubled in the last two years. It's absolutely extraordinary.*

F: *Really? That's amazing. Oh, hang on, hang on, er, I'd like you to meet Nick, actually. He ... Nick, hi, I'd like you to meet Adam. Adam ... Nick.*

A: *Nick! Nick Watkins! How are you?*

N: *I don't believe it!*

A: *We were at school together.*

F: *No. Really?*

N: *Gosh! What, twenty years ago?*

F: *That's a long time.*

N: *Oh my goodness me!*

A: *Gosh! Yeah, we used to live next door to each other.*

N: *That's right. That's right. And you always used to be late to the bus stop.*

A: *That's right, every morning!*

F: *I can believe that.*

A: *Yes, the bus would wait for me because he knew I'd always be a minute late.*

N: *And we would sit at the back of the bus.*

A: *We would.*

N: *We had our little club for two.*

A: *That's right. And you, you'd always forget to do your homework and you'd have to crib off mine.*

N: *Yes. Got me where I am today! And do you remember you started me off smoking? Remember we'd go down by the river and smoke at lunchtimes?*

A: *No, you smoked long before then.*

N: *I didn't.*

A: *You did.*

2 Ask students if they think they can answer the questions without listening to the recording a second time. Give them some time to think about their answers. Then play the recording again. Do not check answers at this stage.

3 Pairwork. Students compare their answers and discuss further details from the conversations that they noted. Check answers with the class.

> a) Conversation 3   b) Conversation 1
> c) Conversation 2

Lexis (p 39)

1 Pairwork. Students match the phrases and definitions. Check answers with the class.

> a) 6   b) 5   c) 2   d) 1   e) 4   f) 3

2 Encourage students to discuss and do this first without listening to the recording again. When they have matched as many as they can to the conversations, play the recording again and check answers with the class.

> a) Conversation 1   b) Conversation 2
> c) Conversation 2   d) Conversation 1
> e) Conversation 1   f) Conversation 3

3 Give students a few minutes to complete the sentences, pointing out that they may have to make slight changes to make the phrases fit. Allow them to compare answers in pairs before checking with the class.

> a) a bite to eat
> b) all sweetness and light

c) live next door

d) have a sit down

e) shout and rant

f) catches your eye

4 Pairwork. Students each choose three questions to ask a partner. They take turns asking and answering.

Close up (p 40)

General tendencies

1 Give students a few minutes to write out the full forms of the verbs. Do not check answers yet.

2 Pairwork. Students compare their answers. Do not check answers with the class yet.

3   ▭ **22 SB p 148**

Play the recording. Students listen and compare their answers to the recording. Ask them if they differed and if they think their answers are also correct.

> See tapescript below for the answers on the recording.
>
> *Other possibilities:*
>
> a) ... he shouted and ranted / shouts and rants for a while and then half an hour later he had forgotten / forgot / forgets all about it. And then he was / is all sweetness and light after that.
>
> b) ... he bought / buys everybody a drink at the end of the night and he ordered / orders in some pizza for everybody and then we all sat round / all sit round and have a nice drink and a chat, and a bite to eat.
>
> c) ... I go and make a cup of coffee and then I just have a sit down with my cup of coffee rather than work ...

> ▭ **22**
>
> a) *... he'll shout and rant for a while and then half an hour later he'll have forgotten all about it. And then he'll be all sweetness and light after that.*
>
> b) *... he'll buy everybody a drink at the end of the night, um, and he'll order in some pizza for everybody and then we'll all sit round and have a nice drink and a chat, and a bite to eat.*
>
> c) *... I'll go and make a cup of coffee and then I'll just have a sit down with my cup of coffee rather than work ...*

4 Elicit answers from the class.

will

It is normally associated with the future.

5 Go through the sentences with the class. Then allow students time to read them individually and think about their answers before checking with the class.

> a) The sentences do not refer to any particular time (though they are definitely present and future rather than past).
>
> b) A presents a fact; B mentions a tendency.

6 Students work individually to complete the text. Allow them to compare answers with a partner before checking with the class.

> 1 have   2 'll find   3 'll decide   4 'll start
> 5 'll do   6 'll actually save   7 'll spend

7 Pairwork. Students discuss the questions. As you go around the class, you may like to make a note of any interesting answers to share with the class at the end of the discussion in a whole class feedback session.

Tendencies in the past (p 41)

1 Whole class. Point out 'short answer' after gap (4) is not the verb they must use to complete the gap, but a hint that their answer should be a short form. Give students a few minutes to write out the full forms of the verbs. Do not check answers at this stage.

2 Pairwork. Students compare their answers. Do not check with the class.

3 ▭ **23 SB p 148**

Play the recording for students to listen and check their answers. As before, there may be differences between the students' answers and what is on the recording. This doesn't mean the students' answers are wrong. Ask them to find any differences.

> See tapescript below for the answers on the tape.
> *Other possibilities*
> 1 waited / used to wait   2 was always / always used to be   3 sat / used to sit   4 did   5 always forgot / always used to forget / had always forgotten   6 had to / used to have to   7 went / used to go

▭ **23**

(A = Adam; N = Nick)

A: *Yes, the bus would wait for me because he knew I'd always be a minute late.*

N: *And we would sit at the back of the bus.*

A: *We would.*

N: *We had our little club for two.*

A: *That's right. And you, you'd always forget to do your homework and you'd have to crib off mine.*

N: *Yes. Got me where I am today! And do you remember you started me off smoking? Remember we'd go down by the river and smoke at lunchtimes?*

4 Pairwork. Students discuss the questions and report back to the class.

> a) and b) Students' own answers.
> c) It refers to the past.
> d) It refers to general tendencies.

5 Give students a few minutes to look at the sentences and decide if the past simple can be substituted for *would*. Allow them to discuss this in pairs if they wish before checking with the whole class. The aim of the exercise is to help students recognise the difference between *would* for temporal meanings as opposed to modal / conditional meanings. Refer students to the Language reference section on this page for more information about tendencies.

> Generally *would* can be replaced with the past simple when it is used to talk about a general tendency. It cannot be changed when it is part of a conditional structure.
>
> a) The first *would* can be replaced with the past simple provided *talk* is also changed to the past simple. The second *would* is part of a conditional sentence and cannot be changed.
>
> b) The first *would* can be replaced with the past simple. The second *would* is part of a conditional sentence and cannot be changed.
>
> c) *Would* can be replaced with the past simple.
>
> d) The first *would* can be replaced with the past simple. The second *would* is part of a conditional sentence and cannot be changed.

6 Pairwork. Students discuss whether they know anyone like the people described in the sentences in 5.

I love them dearly but ... (p 42)

Closed books. Write down the names of some members of your family and explain to the class how they are related to each other and to you. For example: *Will, my nephew, is my eldest sister's son and Layla, my niece, is my youngest sister's daughter. They are cousins.* Students then work in pairs, write down names of members of their family and explain how they are related to each other.

Books open. Whole class. Students look at the photograph of Ann and predict what kind of person she might be. Elicit some adjectives to describe her. Ask if anyone has a family member around the same age as Ann and encourage them to tell the class something about this person. Do they feel that the age gap between them and this person makes it easier or harder to get on well with them? Do they share the same values as this older person?

1 🔲 **24 SB p 148**

Tell students they are going to listen to Ann, the woman in the photograph, talking about some of the members of her family. Go through the questions with them before you play the recording so they know what they are listening for. Don't check answers at this stage.

🔲 **24**

The children? All grown up and left the nest. Timothy, my eldest, got married fifteen years ago to a girl he met outside an ice-cream kiosk. Her name's Kate, she was, and still is, a very docile sort of person and was just right for Timothy. Timothy's very highly-strung and always has been. When I think back to his childhood the picture that always springs to mind is that of him sitting at the piano playing brilliantly and being so involved. But that's what he's like. Whatever he's doing he'll do it with total commitment and concentration. I suppose you could say he's a perfectionist, which must be tiring for Kate sometimes. He's been looking particularly run-down of late but that's because he will work all hours. I tell him it's ruining his health but will he listen to me? Of course not! Anyway, they have just the one child, David. He's twelve now and absolutely wild. Though I don't like to criticise my own son, the fault nevertheless lies with him. He appears indifferent to David's behaviour and though I've heard Kate talk to him about it he won't listen to her. They really should have been stricter with him from the beginning. They wouldn't listen to me when I told them that a little discipline would go a long way and now they're paying the price.

My second, Rebecca, got married the same year as Timothy and is now in the middle of extremely bitter divorce proceedings. I knew it would end up this way but there's no use trying to change the minds of two people in love. Fortunately there were no children. Poor Rebecca, she was never very good at making the right decisions but her eternal optimism will get her through this period, I'm sure.

Now Sam, ahhh Sam, my youngest daughter and without a doubt my favourite, though of course I never let it show. A real rascal when she was young, who would charm everyone. She had us all wound round her little finger – real bundle of joy. A little on the lazy side, but good at heart with her head screwed on properly. She married Anthony – a real marriage of hearts and they're still as much in love now as they were twelve years ago. They have three adorable children, Nicholas, Peter and Sarah, who are well-mannered and not too noisy.

2 Pairwork. Students compare their answers. Be prepared to play the recording again if necessary. Check with the class.

> a) Ann mentions her children (Timothy, Rebecca and Sam), her daughter-in-law (Kate), her grandchildren (David, Nicholas, Peter and Sarah) and her son-in-law (Anthony). She also mentions another son-in-law, but she doesn't name him.
>
> b) Ann describes her daughter-in-law Kate as docile and her son Timothy as highly-strung, with great concentration and commitment to everything he does – a perfectionist. She says their son David is absolutely wild and undisciplined. She describes her daughter Rebecca as an eternal optimist, but poor at decision making. Her youngest daughter, Sam, is described as charming and sensible, but a little lazy. She says that Sam's children are adorable, well-mannered and not too noisy.

Students then discuss the questions in pairs. Go round offering help with vocabulary where necessary. Get several pairs to report back to the class and see how much agreement there is.

Anecdote (p 42)

See Introduction, page 4, for more ideas on how to set up, monitor and repeat Anecdotes.

1 Go through the instructions with the class. Allow plenty of time for students to read the questions and think about what they are going to say. Give help with language if asked.

2 Pairwork. Students tell each other about their person.

3 Pairwork. Students look back at the list of questions and see which ones their partner answered. Encourage several students to report back to the class on what their partner told them and to say whether there was anything in common between their two descriptions. Alternatively, put students in new pairs and ask them to tell their new partner about their conversation with their first partner.

Talk (p 42)

Books closed. Whole class. Ask which parts of speech *talk* can be used as (for example, noun: *She gave a talk on her experiences in China.*; verb: *We talked all afternoon.*).

Lexis

1 Pairwork. Students read the sentences and note down the parts of speech.

> A verb   B verb   C noun (countable)   D noun
> (uncountable)   E verb   F noun (countable)
> G adjective   H noun (uncountable)   I verb
> J verb   K noun (countable)   L noun (countable)
> M adjective   N verb   O noun (uncountable)
> P noun (uncountable)

2 Students answer the questions. You might like to ask them to try this first without looking back at the sentences in 1. They can then look back and check their work and complete the ones they didn't know. This may be done in pairs.

> a) 1 to; about 2 on / about (We tend to use *on* to refer to the specific title or topic of a talk and *about* to refer to general themes.)
>
> b) It means she was the subject of gossip. Everyone was talking about her.
>
> c) If a person criticises someone else's behaviour when they themselves are also guilty of that behaviour.
>
> d) 1 talks 2 talk 3 talkative 4 talking
>
> e) *talks* (a plural noun) means a formal exchange of opinions, as in *peace talks*
>
> *a talk* is an informal speech or lecture
>
> *talk* is public discussion of something that everyone is interested in; it can mean rumour or gossip

3 Pairwork. Students discuss the questions and report back to the class.

A tall tale (p 43)

Stress

1 Whole class. Students look at the pictures and say what they can see in them.

Pairwork. Students discuss how the four items could be linked in a story.

2 ▄▄ **25 SB p 148**

Play the recording for students to listen to the story. Elicit whether or not they found it funny.

> ▄▄ **25**
>
> A rich lady returned home from a <u>ball</u>. // She rang the <u>bell</u> for her <u>butler</u> // and when he ap<u>pear</u>ed she <u>said</u>, // 'Edward, take off my <u>shoes</u>,' // and he <u>did</u>. // Then she <u>said</u>, // 'Edward, take off my <u>coat</u>,' // and he <u>did</u>. // 'Take off my <u>dress</u>,' // and he <u>did</u>. // 'And <u>now</u> take off my <u>underwear</u>,' // and he <u>did</u>. // 'And now, <u>Edward</u>,' // she <u>said</u>, // 'if you wish to re<u>main</u> in my <u>service</u>, // you are <u>never</u> to wear any of my clothes a<u>gain</u>.'

3 Note: students who are doing this for the first time might find it quite difficult and so it is important to follow the steps slowly and carefully.

Students turn to page 133. They first mark the main stresses and the places where they think the speaker should pause. Then they compare answers with a partner.

Before playing the recording again for students to check their answers, make sure they understand that they should mark any differences between the speaker's stresses and pauses and theirs. You might like to do this on the board with the first sentence as an example.

Students follow the instructions and shadow the speaker on the tape. At the end, you might like to ask confident students to tell the story to the class without the recording.

Doctor! Doctor! (p 43)

Whole class. Elicit some of the things that make a joke funny (puns, unusual situations, punchlines, timing, delivery, etc.).

1 Students match the beginnings, middles and endings of these three-line jokes.

2 Pairwork. Students compare answers with a partner and then practise reading the jokes aloud.

> a) 5 and 2   b) 6 and 3   c) 4 and 1

3 Pairwork. Students discuss the questions. Encourage them to tell some jokes, in English if possible.

Test

> Scoring: one point per correct answer unless otherwise indicated.
>
> **1** 1 conversationalist 2 conversational
> 3 conversations 4 conversationally
> 5 animated 6 predictable 7 in-depth
> 8 lengthy 9 meaningful 10 pointless
> 11 boring 12 one-way
> 13 hogging 14 say 15 drones 16 wavelength
> 17 across 18 butting 19 talking 20 ranting
>
> **2** 1 She'll always be the last to join in the conversation.
> 2 When I was little I would play on my own for hours.
> 3 As a child my parents would read me a story in bed every night.
> 4 They'll go on for hours if you let them.
> 5 ✓
> 6 –
> 7 –
> 8 ✓
> 9 ✗ I lived in Paris for two years when I was younger.
> 10 ✓
> 11 ✗ He really hates opera – he always has.
> 12 ✓
>
> **3** 1 talkative 2 talk 3 talking 4 talk 5 talks
> 6 talked 7 talk 8 talking

4 *Talk* Test

Name: _____   **Total:** _____ /40

---

1 Lexis – conversation *20 points*

Add the correct ending to the word *conversation*.

1 He's a brilliant story-teller and conversation_____.

2 I only want to learn conversation_____ Spanish.

3 We had several long conversation_____ about it.

4 She writes her novels very conversation_____ .

Complete these words. They can all be used to describe a conversation.

5 an_m_ _ed   6 pr_d_ _t_ _le   7 i_d _p _ h

8 l_ng_ _ y   9 me_n_ng_ _l   10 po_ _tl_ _s

11 b_r_ _ g   12 o_e-w_y

Complete the sentences with words from the box.

> across   butting   drones   hogging
> ranting   say   talking   wavelength

13 She's always _____ the conversation. You can never get a word in edgeways.

14 He's always got something to _____ .

15 He just _____ on and on and on.

16 We've always been on the same _____ .

17 She never puts her ideas _____ very well.

18 Aargh! She's always _____ in when you're talking.

19 He didn't say a word. I had to do all the _____ .

20 He was shouting and _____ at them all evening.

2 Tendencies *12 points*

Put the words in *italics* into the correct order to complete the sentences.

1 *always / be / the last / 'll / she* to join in the conversation.

_____

2 *play / would / when I was little / I* on my own for hours.

_____

3 *my parents / read / would / as a child* me a story in bed every night.

_____

4 *go on / for hours / 'll / they* if you let them.

_____

Tick (✔) the sentences in which *would* + infinitive can be replaced with the past simple.

5 I'd always be the last to hear any new gossip.

6 I'd really love to go there one day.

7 Had I had the time, I would have learnt Spanish.

8 When we were young we'd go to the beach every summer.

Two of the sentences are wrong. Mark the sentences ✔ or ✗. Correct the ones which are wrong.

9 I would live in Paris for two years when I was younger.

10 She'll always go out of her way to help you.

11 He'll really hate opera – he always has.

12 As a child, I'd love going to fun-fairs.

3 Lexis – talk *8 points*

Complete the sentences using a form of the word *talk*.

1 He's a very _____ person. He won't shut up!

2 She gave a really interesting _____ on publishing.

3 Will he or won't he? It's a real _____ point.

4 All that _____ of food has made me really hungry.

5 The peace _____ began in New York yesterday.

6 Nice to meet you at last. She's _____ of you often.

7 There's already a lot of _____ about the new boss.

8 She's not _____ to her sister at the moment.

5

Luck *Overview*

The topic of this unit is luck. It starts by examining the things that people consider lucky and moves on to people who have had lucky experiences. The main grammar focus is on unreal conditions and expressing wishes and regrets.

The first section is about lucky charms. Students match pictures of charms to different countries and listen to people discussing them. They then talk about what is considered lucky in their own countries.

Students read an article about a woman who won money on the national lottery and discuss how she reacted to her win and what type of person she is. They go on to do a cultural quiz before examining descriptive verbs from the article. Students then listen to two people discussing the article and identify and practise unreal conditionals.

Next, students look at a series of pictures telling the story of someone who had a lucky break. They predict what happens in the story before listening to it and discussing what happened. They then practise the language of wishes and regrets.

In the last two sections, students listen to extracts from John Wyndham's book *The Day of the Triffids*. A man who initially seems to have had bad luck by being in hospital with his eyes bandaged when everyone else is enjoying a fantastic meteor shower, turns out to have had incredible good luck because he is now one of the very few people in the world who is not blind. Students discuss the implications of the story and then write entries for the man's diary for three months after the initial events.

Section	Aims	What the students are doing
Introduction page 44	*Conversation skills:* fluency work	Matching lucky charms and countries.
		Discussing lucky charms around the world.
	Listening skills: listening for specific information	Listening to people discussing lucky charms.
Winning the big one pages 44–46	*Reading skills:* reading for gist and specific information	Reading an article about a woman who won the lottery.
	Lexis: cultural items;	Answering a quiz testing knowledge of cultural information.
	descriptive verbs	Identifying descriptive verbs used in the article and completing sentences with these verbs.
Close up pages 47–48	*Grammar:* unreal conditions	Studying the structure and use of unreal conditions.
		Completing sentences using unreal conditions.
A lucky break pages 48–49	*Listening skills:* listening for detail	Predicting the content of a story from pictures.
		Listening to the story to check predictions and answering questions about it.
Close up pages 49–50	*Grammar:* wishes & regrets	Practising using the correct verb forms to talk about wishes and regrets.
		Playing a game about wishes and regrets.
Wish fulfilment pages 51–52	*Lexis:* collocations of *wish*	Discussing song titles that include the word *wish*.
		Practising words derived from *wish* and collocations with *wish*.
	Conversation skills: fluency work	Anecdote: talking about an event or period of your life that has influenced the way you are today.
The day of the triffids pages 52–53	*Listening skills:* listening for detail	Predicting the content of a story from a picture.
		Listening to extracts from a story and identifying true and false statements.
	Conversation skills: discussion	Discussing issues raised by the story.
Three months on ... page 53	*Writing skills:* diary entries	Writing diary entries for the narrator of *The Day of the Triffids* one, two and three months after the 'end of the world'.

5 *Luck* Teacher's notes

Books closed. Whole class. Draw a picture of a black cat on the board and ask students what they associate it with. Elicit that it means bad luck in most countries (in the UK it means good luck). Ask them what other things they consider to be lucky or unlucky.

1 Open books. Students look at the photographs and the countries in the box. Establish that the photos show lucky charms, things which people have (and often carry around with them) to bring them luck. Give students a few minutes to try to match the countries with the charms. Do not reveal the answers at this stage.

2 26 SB p 148

Tell students to listen and check their answers. Play the recording. Ask students to compare answers in pairs. If they are still not sure, let them listen again before checking the answers.

> beckoning cat – Japan
> scarab – Egypt
> dragon – China
> blue eye – Turkey
> horn – Italy
> peacock feathers – India

26

(M = Mary; S = Sarah; D = Dave; B = Bob)

M: ... here are your keys back, thanks. What's that horn on your keyring for?

S: It's a souvenir from Italy. I got it last year when we were there on holiday. It's supposed to bring good luck, but it doesn't seem to be working so far! I suppose I did win a tenner on the lottery a couple of weeks ago, but that's about it!

D: Gullible tourists! It's all a racket to make money! You make your own luck in this world.

S: Well, how come people have been carrying round lucky charms with them for so long then? I mean, the Egyptians have been carrying scarabs around and wearing them as jewellery for thousands of years. I think the ancient Egyptians believed that they'd protect them from death and people who died were buried with them.

D: How come you know so much?

S: I'm interested in things like that. Did you know that people in India wear peacock feathers on their clothes to keep evil away?

M: That's interesting because here peacock feathers are supposed to bring bad luck and you shouldn't have any in your house. The eye pattern on them is supposed to be the evil eye. I remember my brother picking one up once and bringing it home and my mum wouldn't let him keep it because it was unlucky.

B: Hmm. I've never heard about that but I know that the eye thing is quite popular in Turkey. You see them all over the place there. People hang them in their houses and in their cars and they're supposed to protect you from the evil eye and bad luck.

S: I've seen them – they're really pretty, aren't they?

D: It's all a load of mumbo jumbo. My mate went out with a Japanese girl when we were at university and she had this little cat statue which went everywhere with her. It had one arm up in the air which was supposed to attract good luck but she dropped it one day and the arm came off. You should have seen the state she got into over it! Just a silly little thing like that! What's the point?

S: Well, everyone's allowed to have their own beliefs, aren't they? I bet you've got a lucky pair of socks or something you wear if you've got a special date or an interview or something!

D: I haven't!

M: I've got a little dragon brooch that I wear sometimes. A Chinese friend of mine gave it to me years ago and told me it would protect me against unhappiness and the loss of love. I should have been wearing it the night Phil told me he didn't want to see me any more!

D: There you are, you see – not a very lucky charm, is it?

M: I wasn't wearing it though. If I had been things might have worked out differently.

D: Rubbish! You believe what you like, but I'm sticking to my theory that life's what you make it, and having lucky rabbits' feet, plastic pigs or Egyptian beetles isn't going to make the slightest bit of difference to whether I get married, make a million or get the job of my dreams.

S: You do that!

3 Pairwork. Students discuss and answer the questions.

Winning the big one (p 44)

1 Whole class. Set the context by reading the side panel about *Tatler*. Then go through the questions so students know what information they are looking for when they read the article. Give them plenty of time to read as the article is quite long.

2 Pairwork. Students compare their answers. Then check with the class.

You may want to explain that in the British national lottery, participants choose six numbers from between 1 and 49. Six main numbers and a bonus number are then chosen at random by the lottery machine. To win the jackpot (usually several million pounds) you have to have the six main numbers correct. If you get five main numbers correct and your sixth number is the same as the bonus number, you win a very large prize. If you get four numbers correct you win around one or two thousand pounds, and if you get three numbers correct you get around ten pounds. Getting the bonus number correct is only valuable if your other five numbers are correct. So, although Carinthia got five numbers correct, one was the bonus number, so in effect she only got four numbers correct.

> a) She usually waits for the numbers to come into her head as if by divine inspiration or she uses numbers that feature in her life such as her birthday, the ideal age for a partner, her bra size, the number of her godchildren, etc.
>
> b) She is from London. She had been to the Isle of Wight for the weekend.
>
> c) Students' own choice, but the original article had *Life's a bitch* as its subtitle. A *bitch* is a female dog but it is sometimes used to mean something unpleasant. Ultimately the writer was disappointed with her win.

3 Pairwork. Students discuss the questions. Allow them to compare answers with another pair before checking with the class.

> a) When she found out that she had won, at first she didn't believe it, then she became very excited. When she found out how much she had won, she was very disappointed.
>
> b) The things she mentions are: going on a spending spree in Harvey Nicks (Harvey Nichols, a big London department store), buying clothes in Hermes and Gucci (designer clothes shops), taking a trip to Rio, buying a Lear jet, a top of the range Mercedes, a summer home in Sardinia, a BMW car and a diamond-encrusted dog collar.
>
> c) Students' own answers.
>
> d) There are clues suggesting that Carinthia is from an upper middle class or upper class background. She seems familiar with one of

London's most expensive department stores and a range of designer shops. She clearly has expensive tastes. Most people would be delighted to win £1,700 but this doesn't seem like a lot of money to Carinthia and although she is disappointed because she was expecting a much bigger amount, she is rather dismissive of the £1,700 she has won.

Lexis (p 46)

1 Encourage students to do the quiz individually and compare results later.

2 Students check their answers on page 132. Have a show of hands to see who are the Carinthias of the class!

> 1 c)   2 b)   3 b)   4 a)   5 a)   6 b)   7 c)   8 b)

3 Students go through the text to find the verbs. Ask them to give the infinitive in each case.

> a) peer
> b) clench
> c) scrabble about
> d) tail off
> e) slink
> f) flit
> g) slip off

4 Whole class. Elicit answers to the questions.

> a) peer
> b) clench, scrabble about
> c) slink, flit, slip off
> d) tail off

5 Students work individually to complete the sentences. Make sure they use appropriate forms of the verbs. Allow them to compare their answers in pairs before checking with the whole class.

> a) slunk
> b) scrabbled about
> c) slipped off
> d) clenched
> e) tailed off
> f) peering
> g) flitted

6 Pairwork. Students each choose two of the actions in 5 and tell their partner about the last time they did them. Encourage the listening partner to ask questions eliciting more details.

Optional activity

If students need more follow-up practice, give them the following list of questions. Working in pairs, students choose two or three of them and discuss their answers.

a) When leaving a party, do you prefer to slip off or make sure you say goodbye to everyone?

b) When was the last time you clenched your fist? Were you angry, nervous or was it some other emotion?

c) Do people peering out of their windows irritate you? Why or why not?

d) When was the last time you scrabbled about?

e) Have you ever seen anyone trying to slink away? Where were you? Who or what were they trying to avoid?

f) Which would be a perfect lifestyle: flitting about from city to city and travelling the world, or settling down in a beautiful spot, far away from the hustle and bustle of modern life?

g) When was the last time your voice tailed off? What made you stop talking?

Close up (p 47)

Unreal conditionals

1 ▭ 27 SB p 149

Go through the instructions and the questions with the class. Then play the recording.

> ▭ 27
>
> (A = Angela; S = Sarah)
>
> A: *Have you read this article about the lottery in the 'Tatler'?*
>
> S: *Yeah, it's fun, isn't it?*
>
> A: *Do you think it's true?*
>
> S: *I don't know, it might be ... but even if it isn't, it's a good story.*
>
> A: *Yeah, and all that stuff about what she'd have done if she'd actually won 'the Big One'.*
>
> S: *Yeah, I really like that bit about how it would have changed her dog's life, like he'd be wearing a diamond-encrusted collar right now ...*
>
> A: *Nah, I think it's more likely that she'd be driving a snazzy little red sports car!*
>
> S: *And I like that bit about how she usually picks her numbers ...*
>
> A: *Yeah, that bit about the birthdays and stuff.*
>
> S: *And the ideal partner ...*
>
> A: *And the bra! I think I should try that!*
>
> S: *Do you think she'd have got the jackpot if she'd been playing her usual numbers?*

> A: *I don't know, I don't think it actually says anything about that ...*
>
> S: *I got really close to winning once. If I'd played my brother's birthday instead of mine, I'd have won.*
>
> A: *How much would you have won if you had?*
>
> S: *Oh, millions no doubt! I would have bought a new house, a car, a luxury yacht and I wouldn't be working as a secretary any more, I can tell you! I still got fifty quid mind you, but I wish I'd chosen a 17 instead of a 19 ... I certainly wouldn't be sitting here having this conversation if I had!*
>
> A: *I never even buy a ticket – it's just a waste of money.*
>
> S: *How boring! If you're not in it, you can't win it!*

2 Pairwork. Students compare their answers. Then check answers with the whole class.

> a) They enjoyed the parts about what Carinthia would have done if she had won the jackpot and the way in which she chooses her numbers.
>
> b) Sarah plays the lottery but Angela doesn't.
>
> c) Sarah has won £50.

3 Students complete the sentences in the extracts from the conversation. Allow them to compare with a partner, but do not check answers at this stage.

4 Play the recording again for students to listen and check their answers.

> **Extract 1**
> Angela: 1 she'd have done   2 she'd actually won
> Sarah: 3 it would have changed
>   4 he'd be wearing
> Angela: 5 she'd be driving
> **Extract 2**
> Sarah: 6 I'd played   7 I'd have won.
> Angela: 8 would you have won   9 you had?
> Sarah: 10 would have bought
>   11 wouldn't be working

5 Pairwork. Students discuss and answer the questions. Check answers with the whole class. Refer students to the Language reference section on page 48.

> **Extract 1**
> a) unreal
> b) It would have changed her dog's life.

c) Her dog would be wearing a diamond-encrusted collar. She would be driving a little red sports car.

Extract 2

a) unreal

b) She would have bought a new house / a car / a luxury yacht.

c) She wouldn't be working as a secretary.

6 Give students a few minutes to write out the correct verb forms. Allow them to compare with a partner before checking answers with the class.

a) had stayed in; wouldn't be / Wouldn't have been

b) hadn't worked / hadn't been working; would have gone

c) had gone; wouldn't have got up / went; wouldn't get up

d) had slept; would not be yawning

7 Whole class. Read the sentences in 6 again and invite students to discuss with a partner which other modal verbs could be substituted. Meanwhile write the answers on the board and then discuss any queries with the class.

Possible answers

a) might not be

b) could have gone / might have gone

c) might not have got up

d) might not be yawning

8 Students work individually to decide if the sentences in 6 are true for them and to amend them if not. They then compare with a partner.

9 Read the sentences with the class and elicit answers to the questions.

a) The sentences begin with the auxiliary *had* rather than *if*.

b) The structure beginning with the auxiliary is more formal.

Refer students to the Language reference section on this page for more information about unreal past situations and consequences.

10 Give students a few minutes to complete the sentences. Then invite them to read their sentences to the class. Alternatively, with a large class, students can compare their sentences in small groups while you go around the class monitoring and helping where necessary.

A lucky break (p 48)

1 Focus attention on the pictures. Invite students to say what they can see and to predict the story that connects them. Do not confirm or deny any of the predictions.

2 ▭ 28 SB p 149

Play the recording. Students listen and see how similar the story is to the ones they suggested.

▭ 28

Did I tell you about what happened to us last week? No? Well, we were out in a bar in town, quite a crowd of us, and of course Kelly had her mobile phone with her. Anyway, while we were in the bar Kelly left her mobile in her coat pocket and we were chatting and laughing and having a good time. It was some time later when Kelly noticed this couple rummaging around in the pile of coats and then getting ready to leave. Well, Kelly was a bit suspicious, so she went over to check if her phone was still there and of course it wasn't! So she went to follow the couple outside to ask them if they'd taken her phone and a couple of the others went with her. They were just approaching the couple when Hannah had a brainwave. She had her mobile on her too, so she phoned Kelly's number and just as Kelly was asking the couple whether or not they'd got her phone, it started ringing in one of their pockets! They couldn't very well deny having it and handed it over very sheepishly! Lucky, eh?

3 Whole class. Ask students to volunteer answers to the questions. If there is disagreement, encourage discussion, but do not provide answers at this stage. When the class have agreed on the answers, play the recording again for them to check.

a) Kelly noticed them rummaging in the coats and then preparing to leave.

b) Kelly went up to them to ask them if they'd taken her phone and at the same moment Hannah phoned Kelly's number so that the stolen phone would ring. The thieves were thus unable to deny that they had taken it.

c) It was Hannah's idea to ring Kelly's number.

d) They were embarrassed (sheepish).

Close up (p 49)

Wishes & regrets

1 Students match the sentence beginnings with their endings.

a) 3 b) 1 c) 2

Elicit that wishes and regrets about the past expressed by *I wish ...* are followed by the past perfect.

2 Groupwork. See which group can come up with the most wishes or regrets that the people in the story might have had. Accept any reasonable answers and give particular praise for ingenuity.

> *Some possible answers*
>
> The thieves might have wished that they had stolen someone else's phone.
>
> The thieves might have wished that they had run away before Kelly approached them.
>
> Kelly might have wished that she had left her mobile phone at home.
>
> Kelly might have wished that she had kept her coat on.

3 Students match the two halves of the sentences. Allow students to compare with a partner before checking answers with the class.

> **1**
> a 2   b 3   c 1
> **2**
> a 3   b 1   c 2
> **3**
> a 3   b 1   c 2

4 Students work individually to decide their answers to the questions. Give them plenty of time to do this. Then allow them to compare in pairs before checking with the whole class.

> a)   2a, 3a, 3c
> b)   1a, 1b
> c)   1c, 2b, 2c, 3b

5 Whole class. Elicit answers to the questions. The Language reference section on page 50 gives more information about backshifting of tenses after *wish* to express unreal and wished for situations. You might like to point out to students that the present continuous is used both for present and future meanings, so when it is backshifted, the past continuous is used for both meanings.

> a)   past perfect
> b)   past simple
> c)   *could* is used to express an inability to change a situation in the present or the future.
>
>   *would* is also used but emphasises a sense of longing or irritation
>
>   past continuous – present continuous backshifted

6 Students work individually to complete the sentences. Allow them to compare with a partner, then invite some students to read their sentences to the class.

Regrets (p 50)

1 Pairwork. Give students a few minutes to read the sentences, discuss them and decide which are correct.

> Sentences a), d), f), g) and i) are correct.
>   b)   If only I hadn't spent so much money at the weekend.
>   c)   I regret having had that argument with my best friend. / I regret having that argument with my best friend.
>   e)   If only I hadn't got up so late this morning.
>   h)   I regret not taking my driving test. / I regret not having taken my driving test.

2 Pairwork. Students discuss the regrets in 1 and say if any are true for them. Encourage them to ask each other questions to elicit more details. Refer the students to the Language reference section on this page for more information.

Game (p 50)

Groupwork. Students follow the instructions and play the game. Award points for teams who guess correctly and teams who think of people and wishes / regrets that the others can't guess. To keep things moving, you might want to allow, say, five incorrect guesses before the team gets a point and has to reveal the answer.

Wish fulfilment (p 51)

Lexis

1 Whole class. Ask students to look at the song titles and artists and answer the questions. Invite discussion on which the most romantic title is and which the saddest.

2 Pairwork. Students refer to the list again and answer the questions. Allow them to compare answers with another pair before checking with the class.

Note: you might want to point out that the adjectives *wishful* and *wishing* are generally only used with these collocations: *wishful thinking, wishing well*.

> a)   *wish* is either a verb in the present simple, for example, *I wish it would rain*, or a noun, for example, *my wish came true*, or an adjective, for example, *wishful thinking*.
> b)   *wishful* (thinking) and *wishing* (well)
> c)   *wish fulfilment* and *wish list*
> d)   Examples: I wish I didn't love you so.
>   I wish you well.
>   I wish you peace / love.

3 Students could do this individually or in pairs. Allow them to compare answers and to present their titles to the class. Ask the class to choose the best one for each.

4 Pairwork. Students work individually to complete the questions, then compare and discuss them with a partner.

> *Possible answers*
> a) make
> b) have / make
> c) come

Anecdote (p 52)

See Introduction, page 4, for more ideas on how to set up, monitor and repeat Anecdotes.

1 Go through the instructions with the class. Give students time to think about what they are going to say.

2 Pairwork. Students take turns to tell their stories. Encourage active listening by asking the listening partner to think of some questions to ask at the end of the story.

3 Pairwork. Students decide if their anecdotes had any features in common.

The day of the triffids (p 52)

The Day of the Triffids is a novel by John Wyndham. It has been made into a film and it is possible that some of your students will have seen the film or read the book in translation. If so, encourage the students who haven't seen the film and don't know what the story is about to do the first exercise. Students who are familiar with it should be discouraged from revealing the story at this stage.

1 Pairwork. Focus attention on the illustration and elicit comments on what the students can see and guesses as to what the story is about.

2 ▭ 29 SB p 149

Before you play the recording, go through the sentences with the class so they know what kind of information they are listening for. You can take this opportunity to explain any unknown vocabulary, or, if you have students who are familiar with the story, encourage them to explain it.

Play the recording, more than once if necessary. Allow students to compare with a partner before checking answers with the class.

> a) false (Only his head was bandaged.)
> b) true
> c) false (He was in an ordinary hospital.)
> d) false (Someone was screaming.)
> e) true
> f) false (He didn't see them.)
> g) true
> h) false (It is a carnivorous plant.)

▭ 29

The way I came to miss the end of the world – well, the end of the world I had known for close on thirty years – was sheer accident: like a lot of survival, when you come to think of it. In the nature of things a good many somebodies are always in hospital, and the law of averages had picked on me to be one of them a week or so before ... my eyes and indeed my whole head was wreathed in bandages.

Customarily the west-bound buses thundered along trying to beat the lights at the corner; as often as not a pig-squeal of brakes and a salvo of shots from the silencer would tell that they hadn't.

But this morning was different. Disturbingly because mysteriously different. No wheels rumbled, no buses roared, no sound of a car of any kind, in fact, was to be heard. No brakes, no horns, not even the clopping of the few rare horses that still occasionally passed. Nor, as there should be at such an hour, the composite tramp of work-bound feet.

... 'Hey!' I shouted. 'I want some breakfast. Room forty-eight!'

For a moment nothing happened. Then came voices all shouting together. It sounded like hundreds of them, and not a word coming through clearly. It was as though I'd put on a record of crowd noises – and an ill-disposed crowd at that. I had a nightmarish flash wondering whether I had been transferred to a mental home while I was sleeping, and that this was not St Merryn's Hospital at all. Those voices simply didn't sound normal to me. At that moment bed seemed to be the one safe, comforting thing in my whole baffling environment. As if to underline that there came a sound which checked me in the act of pulling up the sheets. From the street below rose a scream, wildly distraught and contagiously terrifying. It came three times, and when it had died away it seemed still to tingle in the air.

You'll find it in the records that on Tuesday, 7 May, the Earth's orbit passed through a cloud of comet debris. All that I actually know of the occasion is that I had to spend the evening in my bed listening to eye-witness accounts of what was constantly claimed to be the most remarkable celestial spectacle on record.

... The nurse who brought me my supper had to tell me all about it.

'The sky's simply full of shooting stars,' she said. 'All bright green. They make people's faces look frightfully ghastly. Everybody's out watching them, and sometimes it's almost as light as day – only all the wrong colour. Every now and then there's a big one so bright that it hurts to look at it. It's a marvellous sight. They say there's never been anything like it before. It is such a pity you can't see it, isn't it?'

'It is,' I agreed somewhat shortly.

'Oooh!'

'Why "oooh"?' I inquired.

'That was such a brilliant one then – it made the whole room look green. What a pity you couldn't see it.'

'Isn't it. Now do go away, there's a good girl.'

Was I more scared of endangering my sight by taking off the bandages, or of staying in the dark? ... I had the sense and the self-control to get out of bed and pull the blind down before I started on the safety-pins. Once I had the coverings off, and had found out that I could see in the dimness, I felt a relief that I'd never known before ... I discovered a pair of dark glasses thoughtfully put ready ... Cautiously I put them on before I went right close to the window.

... At the far end of the wide corridor were the doors of a ward ... I opened the door. It was pretty dark in there. The curtains had evidently been drawn after the previous night's display was over – and they were still drawn.

'Sister?' I inquired.

'She ain't 'ere,' a man's voice said. 'What's more,' it went on, 'she ain't been 'ere for ruddy hours, neither. Can't you pull them ruddy curtains, mate, and let's 'ave some flippin' light? Don't know what's come over the bloody place this morning.'

'Okay,' I agreed.

Even if the whole place were disorganised, there didn't seem to be any good reason why the unfortunate patients should have to lie in the dark.

I pulled back the curtains on the nearest window, and let in a shaft of bright sunlight. It was a surgical ward with about twenty patients, all bedridden. Leg injuries mostly, several amputations, by the look of it.

'Stop fooling about with 'em, mate, and pull 'em back,' said the same voice.

I turned and looked at the man who spoke. He was a dark, burly fellow with a weather-beaten skin. He was sitting up in bed, facing directly at me – and at the light. His eyes seemed to be gazing into my own, so did his neighbour's, and the next man's ...

For a few moments I stared back at them. It took that long to register. Then: 'I – they – they seem to be stuck,' I said. 'I'll find someone to see to them.' And with that I fled the ward.

... A Triffid is certainly distinctive ... a height of seven feet or more, here was a plant that had learned to walk ... People were surprised and a little disgusted to learn that the species was carnivorous ... but actually alarming was the discovery that the whorl topping a Triffid's stem could lash out as a slender stinging weapon ten feet long, capable of discharging enough poison to kill a man if it struck squarely on his unprotected skin.

3 Groupwork. Students discuss the questions. Give them plenty of time for this. If they are having trouble, play the recording again or allow them to read the tapescript on page 149.

4 Play the recording again for students to check their answers.

> a) Almost everyone in the world watched the lights caused by the comet debris. This made them go blind. (Although this fact is not included in the sections on tape, students may be able to infer that the Triffids were able to take over the world because people were helpless without their sight.)
>
> b) He didn't go blind because he didn't watch the lights. He was in hospital and his eyes were bandaged that night.
>
> c) He heard a lot of people shouting. They were all shouting together and he couldn't make out any of the words. The shouting didn't sound normal.
>
> d) When he opened the curtains in the surgical ward and the patients couldn't tell that he had opened them even though they were looking directly at the light.
>
> e) They could walk; they were carnivorous (meat-eating); they had a stinging weapon that could attack and kill a man.

5 Pairwork. Students discuss the questions. These questions involve quite a lot of imagination and, given time, students can come up with some interesting answers, so allow plenty of time for the discussion and feedback to the class.

You might also like to ask students to discuss how the narrator's apparent bad luck turned out to be good luck and also whether the narrator and anyone else who kept their sight were really lucky or whether those who lost their sight and died quickly were the lucky ones.

Optional activity

If your students are interested in drama, this listening might make a good starting point for a short dramatic presentation. Working in groups, students could take roles such as the narrator, the nurse and the patient in the surgical ward, and the whole group together could provide the sound effects. In situations where video and audio recording facilities are available, these could be employed to enhance students' motivation and enjoyment.

Three months on ... (p 53)

Pairwork. Students work together to write the narrator's diary. The questions here are just guidelines. Students don't have to answer them all and they may include other information. As with the previous exercise, it is worth allowing plenty of time for this as the results can be extremely good. Make time in class for students to read and enjoy each other's work and display the diaries if possible. Encourage students to illustrate their work where appropriate.

For students who are unfamiliar with the story but would like to know what happens, here is a summary.

A strange new plant is developed for the oil it can produce, but when a plane carrying specimens is shot down, the seeds are scattered across the world. When the weird plants begin to grow everywhere, they attract considerable attention. They have a long, poisonous sting, walk upright on a tripod of three roots, and are carnivorous. They are called Triffids by the newspapers, and although they are dangerous, people learn to live with them by cutting out the sting every year. Companies begin to cultivate the plant. Bill Masen, a man who works for one such company, is put in hospital when a Triffid lashes him across the face. Whilst he is in hospital with his eyes wrapped in bandages, the whole world witnesses a bright meteor shower. When Bill wakes from his operation the next day, he finds that everyone who watched the meteor shower is now blind. Over the coming days he realises the extent of the disaster, and how valuable it is to be able to see. Bill rescues a woman from a gang who are using her to find food because she can also see. Together they struggle to find a way to live in a world in which the blind fight the blind, the people who can see fight amongst themselves for control … and where growing numbers of Triffids follow both, their deadly stings fully grown again.

Test

Scoring: one point per correct answer unless otherwise indicated.

1 (1 point for each correct identification and 1 point for each correction for 1–8. 1 point for each verb in questions 9–12)

1 ✗ If I won the lottery, I'd leave work the next day. / If I'd won the lottery, I'd have left work the next day.

2 ✓

3 ✓

4 ✓

5 ✗ If I hadn't forgotten to invite her, she would be here now.

6 ✗ I would be sitting on a beach in Greece right now if I had gone there with them.

7 ✓

8 ✗ Had you arrived earlier, you wouldn't have missed the flight. / If you had arrived earlier you wouldn't have missed the flight.

9 If I had stayed in last night, I wouldn't be feeling so tired now.

10 If she really didn't like him, she wouldn't have gone to his party last night.

11 If he had worked harder last term, he wouldn't have failed his exams so badly.

12 If I had paid attention in class, I wouldn't be doing extra work now.

2 1 flitted

2 peering

3 scrabbling

4 clenched

5 tailed off

6 slipped off

3 1 b) 2 c) 3 d) 4 a)

5 If only I hadn't come here.

6 I wish I could speak French.

7 I wish they would tell me.

8 If only I had seen him.

9 I wish there was some chocolate left.

10 I regret not paying / having paid attention.

11 I wish I wasn't / weren't feeling ill.

12 I now regret buying / having bought this coat.

13 We regret to announce that Jim is leaving the firm.

14 We wish to congratulate you on your promotion.

Luck Test

Name: _____   **Total:** _____ /40

1 Unreal conditionals *20 points*

Four of the sentences are wrong. Mark the sentences ✓ or ✗. Correct the ones which are wrong.

1   If I'd win the lottery, I'd leave work the next day.

2   If she hadn't liked it, she wouldn't have bought it.

3   If she wasn't so busy, she'd have come with us.

4   I'd have seen it for myself if I'd been there.

5   If I hadn't forgotten to invite her, she is here now.

6   I would be sitting on a beach in Greece right now if I went there with them.

7   She wouldn't be coming with us tonight if she didn't want to see him.

8   You had arrived earlier, you wouldn't have missed the flight.

Put the verbs in brackets into an appropriate form.

9   If I _____ (stay in) last night, I _____ (not/feel) so tired now.

10 If she really _____ (not/like) him, she _____ (not/go) to his party last night.

11 If he _____ (work) harder last term, he _____ (not/fail) his exams so badly.

12 If I _____ (pay) attention in class, I _____ (not/do) extra work now.

2 Lexis – descriptive verbs *6 points*

Complete the text with an appropriate form of the verbs in the box. Use each verb once.

> clench   flit   peer   scrabble   slip off   tail off

When we first arrived at the party we quickly (1) _____ from one room to another to see who was there. We ended up in the kitchen, as you often do at parties, when I suddenly saw this manic face (2) _____ through the window. The face disappeared and when we opened the door we saw this figure frantically (3) _____ around on the floor looking for something. It was Tom – it was his party, to celebrate winning a few thousand pounds on the lottery the week before. I could see the remains of a burnt bit of paper (4) _____ in his hand and he was repeating the words 'My ticket, my ticket.' As he turned round and saw us his voice (5) _____ in desperation. Apparently, he'd

hidden the winning ticket in a magazine and someone had used it to light a fire in the garden. Suddenly Tom was in no mood to party, so we (6) _____ quietly and went home.

3 Wishes and regrets *14 points*

Match the beginnings of these sentences with an appropriate ending.

1   If only I'd said something   a) soon.

2   I wish I could see them   b) last night.

3   I wish I was lying on a beach   c) more often.

4   I wish he'd get here   d) right now.

Complete the wishes and regrets using the verbs in *italics*.

5   I regret *coming* here.

    If only _____

6   I don't *speak* French.

    I wish _____

7   They won't *tell* me.

    I wish _____

8   I didn't *see* him.

    If only _____

9   There *isn't* any chocolate left.

    I wish _____

10 I wasn't *paying* attention.

    I regret _____

11 I'm *feeling* ill.

    I wish _____

12 I *bought* this coat.

    I now regret _____

Put the words in *italics* into the correct order to complete the sentences.

13 We *to announce regret is that Jim* leaving the firm.

    _____

14 We *congratulate you wish to* on your promotion.

    _____

6 *Mind* *Overview*

The topic of this unit is the workings of the mind. The grammar focus is on verbs of the senses (stative and dynamic verbs) and participle clauses.

Students start by reading an article about an interesting medical case in which a man is unable to recognise everyday objects. They examine various verbs used to describe ways of seeing. This leads into a discussion and a listening on the five senses and work on verbs of the senses, differentiating between stative and dynamic verbs.

Students then read the humorous story of a destructive dog which destroys its owner's new van. They examine the style of the story and practise using participle clauses. This is followed by a section on the word *mind* and its collocations.

Finally, students listen to the song *I'm Going Slightly Mad* by Queen and discuss the images and metaphors used in it.

Section	Aims	What the students are doing
Introduction page 54	*Reading skills:* quiz	Answering a quiz on the brain.
Mind matters pages 54–56	*Reading skills:* reading for gist; reading for detail	Matching headings to sections of text. Answering questions on the text.
	Lexis: verbs about seeing	Studying different verbs about seeing.
The five senses page 56	*Conversation skills:* fluency work	Discussing the five senses.
	Listening skills: listening for detail	Listening to people discussing the senses.
Close up pages 57–58	*Grammar:* verbs of the senses	Differentiating between verbs of the senses describing actions and ability. Completing sentences with appropriate verb forms.
Pet psychology page 59	*Conversation skills:* discussion	Talking about owning a pet.
	Reading skills: reading for detail; examining style	Reading a humorous story and discussing expressions used in it.
	Writing skills: summary	Writing a short summary of the story.
Close up pages 60–61	*Grammar:* participle clauses	Identifying and using participle clauses.
Mind pages 61–62	*Lexis: mind* & its collocations	Practising using expressions with *mind*.
	Pronunciation: word linking	Practising word linking.
I'm going slightly mad page 62	*Listening skills:* listening for detail	Listening to a song by Queen and noting the images and metaphors used in it.

Mind Teacher's notes

Closed books. Ask students to work in pairs and write down five facts they know about the human brain. Ask them to put these aside and then come back to them after the quiz. Ask students how many of their facts were mentioned in the quiz and if any were wrong.

1 Students work individually to do the true/false quiz.

2 Allow students to compare and discuss their answers with a partner before they check on page 133. Ask students to say which of the answers they found most surprising.

a) false (The average male brain weighs 1.4kg and the average female brain weighs 1.3kg.)

b) true

c) false (80% of the average human brain is water.)

d) false (The brain is pinkish grey on the surface and white inside.)

e) true

f) false (We use 100% of our brains in everyday life.)

g) true

h) false (The brain is very active during sleep, but the activity is of a different type to waking activity.)

i) false (We yawn more when the brain is being stimulated to allow more oxygen to the brain.)

j) true

Mind matters (p 54)

1 Pairwork. Students look at the information in the file card and discuss the questions. They may be interested to know that Dr Sacks's book, which contains case histories of strange neurological conditions affecting people's perceptions of the world, has been turned into an opera and a subsequent and similar book, *Awakenings,* was turned into a successful film starring Robert De Niro and Robin Williams.

2 Students read the four extracts and match them with the headings. Allow students to check their answers with a partner before checking with the whole class and give help with any difficult vocabulary. Do not explain any vocabulary that comes up in the Lexis section on page 56.

a) 3   b) 2   c) 4   d) 1

3 Pairwork. Students read and discuss the questions. Allow them to compare answers with another pair before

checking with the class. Give them plenty of time to use their imaginations in answering the last question before going to the file cards on page 134 for information. You might like to ask students to say which they think is the strangest case and whether the truth was any stranger than the ideas they came up with.

a) He failed to recognise people by sight, though he could recognise their voices. Then he started seeing faces where there weren't any and started mistaking everyday objects for people.

b) He developed diabetes (a disease which can affect the eyes). The ophthalmologist was unable to help him because there was nothing wrong with his eyes.

c) He didn't look straight at Dr Sacks and when his eyes were turned towards him, they seemed to be focusing on individual features of his face rather than the whole face.

d) He wasn't aware that he didn't see normally, except for the fact that other people told him there was something wrong. He was aware that he sometimes made mistakes connected to vision.

e) He didn't see things as a whole, just parts of them. This meant that he was unable to identify what things were, though he could describe the elements they were made up of.

f) Students' own answers.

g) Dr Sacks advised him to spend his whole life enjoying music. This was unusual advice from a doctor as we generally expect doctors to tell us to do something which will improve our condition. Dr Sacks realised that nothing could be done to change Dr P's condition and that since it didn't really upset him or cause him pain, there was no point in distressing him by telling him there was a problem or trying to cure it. It was better to leave things as they were and help him to concentrate on the one thing in life that he could enjoy totally without making mistakes.

h) Students' own answers.

Lexis (p 56)

1 Students find words in the sentences which match the meanings a–h. This can either be done individually and then checked in pairs before doing a whole class checking activity, or as pairwork.

a) 3 gazing b) 1 observed c) 6 dart
d) 8 perceive e) 2 recognise f) 4 scanned
g) 7 examine h) 5 see

2 Go through the sentences and the verbs in the box. Then do the first one as an example. Allow students to compare answers in pairs before checking with the class.

a) to admit
b) to understand
c) to acknowledge
d) to follow or obey a law / rule
e) to meet someone socially or date someone
f) to comment / remark
g) to watch
h) to have an opinion on something

3 Whole class. With multilingual classes, elicit several replies.

4 Pairwork. Students work individually on their paragraphs and then exchange them with a partner. Allow plenty of time for this.

The five senses (p 56)

1 Pairwork. Students discuss the questions. Allow them to compare notes with another pair.

a) sight, taste, touch, hearing, smell
b) – f) Students' own answers.

2 30 SB p 149

Before playing the recording, go through the instructions with the class so they know what they are listening for. Suggest that they write the speakers' names on a piece of paper with space underneath for notes.

Mike is talking about sight, Maria about hearing, Helen about smell (she also mentions seeing, tasting and feeling), Nick about touch (he also mentions sight, smell and hearing), Petra about smell and taste.

Mike – b)   Maria – e) (indirectly)   Helen – d)
Nick – b)   Petra – e) and f)

30
Mike

Mmm ... sight I suppose. Yes, the most important one is sight I suppose ... I mean, if you're blind, if you can't see, then although you can lead a full life and all that, I think it does make you more

vulnerable, more dependent on other people, I don't know, for silly little things like, for example, like shopping in a supermarket or whatever and I would really hate it if I couldn't see what things or people looked like ... or the expression on a person's face when they're talking to you. I mean, you wouldn't even know if they were looking at you or whether they looked interested in what you were saying.

Maria

No, I haven't, but I read this article about a man who'd gone deaf and then his hearing was restored to him, and he spoke about how isolating it can be if you can't hear. He said that you miss out on a lot of things, that although you can communicate fine when you need to, you miss out on the subtleties of a conversation, and the thing he missed most was humour ... the humour in spontaneous conversation ... because it all gets slowed down when you're signing. And he really missed listening to music, that was the worst part he said. That and not being able to hear his wife's voice. And he said that it was really strange to start with when he regained his hearing. Everything sounded much louder. He said he actually misses total silence sometimes, just not hearing anything, and that it can be really relaxing.

Helen

Umm, I don't know ... but maybe smell I suppose ... like someone can just walk past you on the street and you catch the smell of their perfume and it reminds you really strongly of someone ... or food ... I can't remember where I was the other day, but I suddenly smelt the most wonderful cooking smells; coconut oil and eastern spices and it reminded me so strongly of my holidays in Thailand ... I could see the palm trees, taste the food, feel the sun on my skin ... yes, I think smell triggers the strongest, most vivid memories.

Nick

This may seem like a strange answer, but maybe touch ... you know, the sense of touch ... I think it's probably the one we take most for granted, being able to feel things and it's not, it's not, you know, a sense that's limited to one part of your body either – it's everything, every single pore, every single bit of your skin. I remember seeing a documentary about a man who'd been born deaf and mute and had later lost his sight in an accident – he lived a full life – he was eighty something and he still worked and even travelled. He just lived his life totally through his sense of touch. In this programme they showed him visiting other people like him in Japan. It was amazing – they used an international signing language which was based on touch – they would touch each other and sign on each other's palms, and they could feel each other talking – and it showed them going to a drum concert too – like a traditional Japanese drum concert – and they could feel the music, I mean they could feel the vibrations of the drums, even though they couldn't hear them. It was just totally amazing.

Petra

Well, usually I'm renowned for my sense of smell! Sometimes I can smell things that no-one else notices. That can be good because I'm really sensitive to things like gas leaks and anything that smells bad ... things like food that's gone off. My mum often asks me to smell meat or fish or milk or whatever to see if it's OK ... but recently I've had quite a heavy cold and it's really affected my sense of smell. I mean, I can smell really strong things, like coffee or if something's burning in the kitchen, but I can't smell other things like perfume so I don't know how much to put on. And I really miss the subtler smells in the kitchen. It affects my taste too. Everything tastes so bland.

3 Pairwork. Students compare their notes.

Close up (p 57)

Verbs of the senses

1 Pairwork. Students discuss and categorise the words. The aim here is to encourage the students to distinguish between stative (ability) and dynamic (action) verbs. Check answers with the class.

ability	action	both
see	look	smell
hear	listen	feel
	touch	taste

2 Go through the instructions with the class, then give them time to complete the extracts. Do not check answers at this stage.

3 📼 **31 SB p 150**

Play the recording for students to check their answers.

a) 1 can't see
b) 2 couldn't see 3 were looking
c) 4 can't hear
d) 5 listening 6 hear
e) 7 could see 8 taste 9 feel
f) 10 touch 11 could feel 12 could feel
   13 could feel 14 couldn't hear
g) 15 smells
h) 16 can smell 17 can't smell 18 tastes

📼 **31**

a) *Yes, the most important one is sight I suppose ... I mean, if you're blind, if you can't see, then although you can lead a full life and all that, I think it does make you more vulnerable, more dependent on other people ...*

b) *... I would really hate it if I couldn't see what things or people looked like ... or the expression on a person's face when they're talking to you. I mean, you wouldn't even know if they were looking at you or whether they looked interested in what you were saying.*

c) *... I read this article about a man who'd gone deaf and then his hearing was restored to him, and he spoke about how isolating it can be if you can't hear.*

d) *... he really missed listening to music, that was the worst part he said. That and not being able to hear his wife's voice.*

e) *... I could see the palm trees, taste the food, feel the sun on my skin ...*

f) *... they used an international signing language which was based on touch – they would touch each other and sign on each other's palms, and they could feel each other talking – and it showed them going to a drum concert too – like a traditional Japanese drum concert – and they could feel the music, I mean they could feel the vibrations of the drums, even though they couldn't hear them.*

g) *... I'm really sensitive to things like gas leaks and anything that smells bad ...*

h) *... I can smell really strong things, like coffee or if something's burning in the kitchen, but I can't smell other things like perfume so I don't know how much to put on. And I really miss the subtler smells in the kitchen. It affects my taste too. Everything tastes so bland.*

4 Whole class. Find out if anyone had answers that were different from the recording. Ask them if they think their answers are also correct. Alternatively, this could be done as pairwork, allowing you time to monitor and then write any interesting / relevant differences on the board in a whole class feedback stage.

5 Whole class. Students work individually to go through the sentences and decide whether the *italicised* verbs describe an ability / sensation or an action. Give them plenty of time to do this and then allow them to compare answers in pairs before checking with the class.

a) ability / sensation
b) action; ability / sensation
c) ability / sensation

d) ability / sensation

e) action

f) action

g) ability / sensation; ability / sensation

h) action; action

i) ability / sensation

j) action

6 Pairwork. Students read the sentences again and discuss the questions. Check answers with the class.

a) hear, see, taste, feel, smell

b) watch, touch, listen, smell, taste, look (*feel* is also used to describe an action)

c) can (can't), could, be able to. They are used with descriptions of ability.

7 Students work individually to complete the sentences. Give them plenty of time to do this and allow them to compare answers in pairs before checking with the class.

Possible answers

a) look; didn't listen   b) can't hear   c) could see
d) see   e) smell   f) could taste   g) be able to
see   h) can feel

8 Pairwork. Students discuss whether the sentences are true for them.

9 Whole class. Go through the explanations of dynamic and stative verbs with the class and refer them to the Language reference section on this page for more information on verbs of the senses.

Pairwork. Students read the pairs of sentences and discuss the questions. Check answers with the class.

1A *see* is a stative verb referring to ability to see

1B *see* is a dynamic verb meaning to meet someone socially (Here it is not a verb of the senses.)

2A *hear* is a stative verb referring to ability to hear

2B *hear* is a dynamic verb meaning that people have been telling the speaker things about the other person (Here it is not a verb of the senses.)

3A *feel* is a dynamic verb referring to a consciousness of one's state of health

3B *feel* is a stative verb referring to ability to feel

4A *taste* is a dynamic verb referring to the action of tasting

4B *taste* is a stative verb referring to ability to taste

5A *smell* is a dynamic verb referring to the action of smelling

5B *smell* is a stative verb referring to ability to smell

Pet psychology (p 59)

Discussion

Groupwork. Students discuss the questions and report back to the class on any interesting information that comes up.

Reading (p 59)

1 Explain that items a–e are the names psychologists give to problems. Students have to try to match the problems with the definitions. Encourage them to try to work them out without resorting to dictionaries. When you have checked answers, ask students if they think these problems are confined to humans or whether they think animals can suffer from them too.

a) 3   b) 2   c) 4   d) 5   e) 1

2 Give students plenty of time to read the case history and make their 'diagnosis'. They may decide that it is not appropriate to ascribe any of these conditions to Willy and that he is just a destructive dog! You might also elicit that it is not a good idea to leave a dog in a car as bored dogs can become destructive because they need something to do.

If anything, Willy may have been suffering from separation anxiety, made uneasy by the absence of his owner.

3 Pairwork. Students discuss the meanings of the expressions. Check answers with the class.

a) a gentle, quiet animal

b) torn

c) a short sleep

d) people say

e) a small gift to say thank you for something

4 Students can work on their summaries in pairs. You might want to have a competition to find who can get all the facts of the story in the least number of words.

Possible answer

Mr X left his dog in his new delivery van while he had lunch. The dog destroyed the van and then fell asleep. When Mr X returned it ran away. Mr X chased after it but didn't catch it. Mr X drives the ruined van around town looking for his dog, and it is rumoured that he will shoot it if he ever finds it.

Optional activity

The facts of the story are quite simple and part of the humour of the story lies in the exaggerated style. Ask students to work in groups and to give examples of things that contribute to the humour.

Close up (p 60)

Participle clauses

1 Pairwork. Tell students not to look back at the article as they try to make their sentences. Encourage them to use correct punctuation.

2 Students look back at the text and check their answers.

> a) Having left his trusty companion to keep an eye on the smart new van, Mr X returned from lunch to find that his new mode of transport had been completely remodelled.
>
> b) Waking up with a jump, Willy sat up to greet his owner and barked with excitement.
>
> c) Numbed by the efficiency of his new air-conditioning system, he's often spotted scouring the streets between deliveries, under the protection of a warm blanket.

3 Whole class. Refer students to the Language reference section on page 61 for information about participle clauses. Give students time to think about the questions and allow them to compare answers in pairs before checking with the class.

> a) The participle clauses are the clauses at the beginning (*Having left his trusty companion to keep an eye on the smart new van, Waking up with a jump* and *Numbed by the efficiency of his new air conditioning system*).
>
> present participle: *Waking up*
>
> past participle: *Numbed*
>
> perfect participle: *Having left*
>
> b) present participle subject: Willy
>
> past participle subject: he
>
> perfect participle subject: Mr X
>
> c) The subject comes immediately after the participle clause.

4 Students look at the pair of sentences and answer the questions.

> a) B is more likely to be spoken. A is used in the text.
>
> b) subject, auxiliary and linker

5 Give students plenty of time to rewrite the sentences with participle clauses and allow them to compare answers in pairs before you check with the class.

> a) Having finished university, I took a year out to travel and give myself time to decide what to do next. / Giving myself time to decide what to do next, I took a year out to travel when I finished university.
>
> b) Being totally exhausted, I went straight to bed after my last English exam. / Having finished my last English exam I went straight to bed because I was totally exhausted.
>
> c) Living on my own, I don't really do a lot of cooking.
>
> d) Having a large car, I'm often the driver when I go out with friends in the evening. / Going out with friends in the evening, I'm often the driver because I have a large car.
>
> e) Being tired after a long week at work, I like to spend the weekends relaxing.

6 Whole class. Ask if the sentences in 5 are true for anyone.

7 Pairwork. Students add *not* where necessary. Check answers with the class.

> a) Not wanting to offend people ...
>
> b) Not discouraged by the long climb ...
>
> d) ... but not having spoken English ...
>
> e) Knowing that not arriving on time ...

8 Whole class. Ask what students notice about the position of *not* in the sentences in 7.

> It goes immediately before the participle.

9 As the transformation is from written style to spoken language, it would be best to do this exercise orally, either selecting students to do each one or calling for volunteers. Alternatively, this could be done as pairwork followed by a whole class check.

> Possible answers
>
> b) They were not discouraged by the long climb ahead of them and they set off at dawn, chatting happily.
>
> c) When you have completed the form, please send it, with a photograph, to the address below.

d) Jean has a clear grasp of the grammar, but as he hasn't spoken English for quite a few years, he lacks confidence in conversation.

e) Because he knew that it would make a very bad impression not to arrive on time, he left with plenty of time to spare.

f) Sandra was relieved to hear that she had passed, and immediately phoned her parents.

Mind (p 61)

Collocations

1 Whole class. Read each sentence in turn and ask students just to say whether *mind* is a verb or a noun. The meanings of the expressions will be explored in the next exercise.

> a) verb b) verb c) noun d) noun e) noun
> f) noun g) verb h) verb i) noun j) noun

2 Students match the expressions in 1 with the meanings. Check answers with the class.

> 1 i) 2 b) 3 c) 4 g) 5 d) 6 h) 7 j)
> 8 a) 9 e) 10 f)

3 Whole class. Elicit any other expressions the students know with *mind*. Give them a couple of examples of your own to start them off.

> *Possible answers*
> at the back of my mind   frame of mind
> have half a mind to   set your mind on something
> slip your mind   cross your mind
> have an open mind   blow your mind
> mind your own business   don't mind me

4 Pairwork. Students discuss the questions and report back to the class.

Optional activity

In pairs, students write dialogues using as many of the expressions in 1 as they can and read them to the class. The class can then vote on the best.

Word linking (p 62)

1 ▭ **32 SB p 150**

Go through the instructions with the class to ensure they know what they are listening for. Play the recording for students to listen and note their answers.

> They are in an office. Sue is the boss. Clues: She sends John out of the room. John asks her for

permission to go out for something to eat. Pete asks Sue for permission to smoke. Sue's reply 'If you must', would only be said to someone lower down in a hierarchy, and would be seen as very rude if said to a boss.

▭ **32**

(S = Sue; J = John; P = Pete)

S: *Look John, would you mind leaving the room for a minute? There's something I need to discuss with Pete here.*

J: *No, of course not. I'm feeling a bit peckish anyway. Would you mind if I popped out for something to eat?*

S: *No, go ahead.*

P: *Well, what is it, Sue?*

S: *I've got some bad news I'm afraid.*

P: *Oh, dear. I think I know what you're going to say. Do you mind if I smoke?*

S: *If you must.*

P: *So what is it?*

S: *We've lost the contract.*

P: *Hmm. I thought as much. Mind you, it doesn't come as much of a surprise. Not after last year's fiasco.*

S: *Yes, I suppose so ...*

2 Students complete the sentences with *mind*. Don't check answers at this stage.

3 Play the recording again for students to check their answers.

> a) would you mind   b) Do you mind
> c) Mind you

4 Ask several students to read the phrases before you play the recording again. If they don't use the /dʒuː/ sound, ask them to say the phrases quicker. Ask other students to say whether they think their pronunciation matches the recording or not. Then play the recording. Explain that native English speakers often run sounds together rather than pronouncing each one separately. Get the whole class to practise saying the phrases.

> dʒuː

5 Pairwork. Students discuss the questions and practise saying them out loud. Go round listening and encouraging them to run the underlined sounds together.

I'm going slightly mad (p 62)

Books closed. Whole class. The title of this section is a song by the rock group Queen. Find out how many students are familiar with their music and if they can name any of the members of the band and any of their songs.

1 Students read the information about Queen in the file card and look at the pictures. Give them time to study them and decide what is wrong with each one. Elicit answers from the whole class.

> There is one knitting needle missing.
>
> There is a screw missing from the door.
>
> There is a wheel missing from the car.

2 ▭ **33 SB p 150**

Go through the instructions with the class before you play the recording. Students then listen and decide in which order the images in the pictures appear.

> picture 2, picture 1, picture 3

▭ **33**

I'm Going Slightly Mad by Queen

*When the outside temperature rises
And the meaning is oh so clear,
One thousand and one yellow daffodils
Begin to dance in front of you, oh dear.
Are they trying to tell you something?
You're missing that one final screw,
You're simply not in the pink my dear,
To be honest you haven't got a clue.
I'm going slightly mad,
I'm going slightly mad,
It finally happened, happened,
It finally happened, ooh oh,
It finally happened.
I'm slightly mad. (Oh dear!)
I'm one card short of a full deck,
I'm not quite the shilling,
One wave short of a shipwreck,
I'm not my usual top billing,
I'm coming down with a fever,
I'm really out to sea,
This kettle is boiling over
I think I'm a banana tree.
Oh dear, I'm going slightly mad
I'm going slightly mad
It finally happened, happened
It finally happened uh huh
It finally happened.
I'm slightly mad (Oh dear!)
I'm knitting with only one needle,
Unravelling fast it's true,*

*I'm driving only three wheels these days,
But my dear how about you?
I'm going slightly mad,
I'm going slightly mad,
It finally happened,
It finally happened, oh yes,
It finally happened.
I'm slightly mad!
Just very slightly mad!
And there you have it!*

3 Play the recording again. Students listen and make notes on other images and metaphors used to describe the singer's state of mind. Encourage them to try to do this just by listening to the recording. They should turn to the tapescript on page 150 for help only when they have done as much as they can by listening.

4 Whole class. Start a discussion by finding out what the students know about Freddie Mercury and why they think he wrote this song.

Test

Scoring: one point per correct answer unless otherwise indicated.

1 1 two   2 bear   3 speak   4 Never   5 make
   6 change   7 come   8 go

2 1 Not having been there before, she got lost.
   2 Being the smallest, he climbed through the window.
   3 Worried about his exams, he stayed up all night.
   4 Not feeling tired, they stayed up chatting all night.
   5 Not feeling in the mood for a party, he stayed at home.
   6 Having been told / Told he wouldn't pass his exams, he worked day and night for the next two weeks.
   7 Having been there before, I knew what to do.

3 (1 point for 1–5. 1 point for each recognition in 6–10 and 1 point for each correction)
   1 hear   2 'm listening   3 smells   4 feels
   5 see
   6 ✗ Suddenly I felt something touch my hand.
   7 ✗ Look at that house over there. Can you see it?
   8 ✓
   9 ✗ This fish doesn't taste very fresh.
   10 ✗ I see what you mean, but I don't agree.

4 1 e)   2 f)   3 b)   4 g)   5 a)   6 d)   7 c)
   8 Rumour   9 docile   10 scanned   11 tattered

6 *Mind* Test

Name: _____   **Total:** _____ /40

---

1 Lexis – mind *8 points*

Complete the sentences with the words from the box.

> bear change come go make never speak two

1 I can't decide. I really am in _____ minds about it.

2 Thanks for your suggestion. I'll _____ it in mind.

3 If you're not happy about it, you should _____ your mind and let them know.

4 _____ mind! I'm sure you'll do better next time.

5 Quick, _____ your mind up. I can't wait any longer.

6 I give up! First it's this, then it's that and I'm sure he's going to _____ his mind yet again!

7 Don't worry. Something will _____ to mind. We'll sort it out.

8 Mind how you _____ . The roads are very icy today.

2 Participle clauses *7 points*

Put the words in *italics* into the correct order to complete the sentences.

1 *been having before not there*, she got lost.

_____

2 *smallest being the*, he climbed through the window.

_____

3 *about worried exams his*, he stayed up all night.

_____

4 *feeling not tired*, they stayed up chatting all night.

_____

Rewrite the sentences beginning with the verb in italics and changing it to a present, past or perfect participle. You may need to add a negative.

5 He stayed at home as he wasn't *feeling* in the mood for a party.

_____

6 Because he was *told* he wouldn't pass his exams, he worked day and night for the next two weeks.

_____

7 I knew what to do because I had *been* there before.

_____

3 Verbs of the senses *14 points*

Choose the correct alternative.

1 I **hear / 'm hearing** they're going to get married.

2 Ssssh! I **listen / 'm listening** to the radio.

3 This coffee **smells / is smelling** great!

4 Is he OK? He **feels / is feeling** very hot.

5 I **see / 'm seeing** that the date has been changed.

Some of the sentences are wrong. Mark them ✓ or ✗. Correct the sentences which are wrong.

6 Suddenly I was feeling something touch my hand.

7 Look at that house over there. Are you seeing it?

8 He's tasting it to see if it needs more salt.

9 This fish isn't tasting very fresh.

10 I'm seeing what you mean, but I don't agree.

4 Lexis – general *11 points*

Match the words on the left with their definitions on the right.

1	docile	a) a short sleep
2	rumour	b) old and torn
3	tattered	c) look at something quickly in order to find information
4	dart	d) look steadily at something for a long time
5	nap	e) quiet and gentle / easily controlled
6	gaze	f) news that is perhaps not true
7	scan	g) move suddenly and quickly

Use four of the words to complete the sentences. You may need to change the tense of any verbs you use.

8 _____ has it that they're going to get married.

9 Their dog's very _____ . He spends most of the day asleep in front of the fire.

10 We quickly _____ the paper for the football results.

11 The book was pretty _____ after years of use.

News in brief

Relative & participle clauses (p 63)

1 3 which caught fire / had caught fire   4 stealing
5 eating out   6 entitled / which was entitled
7 who take part / taking part   8 who accompanied /
accompanying   9 wrapped   10 who met

2 Deeply in love: the tank was full of sharks, not
tropical fish!

Verb forms (p 63)

2 to find   3 was marrying / was getting married
4 could not move   5 shout out   6 believing
7 would result   8 Lying   9 remained
10 came   11 went   12 was eventually rescued
13 broke into   14 emerged   15 had been put
16 not having spoken   17 told   18 have always
been   19 wouldn't find   20 don't think
21 will ever be able   22 to forgive   23 Had it not
been   24 would today be celebrating

Words of wisdom (p 64)

Negative & limiting adverbials

1 1 e)   2 c)   3 b)   4 f)   5 d)   6 h)   7 a)
8 g)

2 b) Quote 5   c) Quote 4   d) Quote 6   e) Quote 8
f) Quote 7   g) Quote 2   h) Quote 3

3 Students' own answers

Discussion bingo (p 64)

Students' own answers

All change (p 65)

Position of adverbials

1 a) In A the speaker doesn't mind whether they go
or not. In B they definitely don't want to go.

b) In A the speaker thinks John has his phone
number and nothing else (not his address or

e-mail address, for example). In B the speaker
thinks John is the only person who has his
phone number.

c) In A the speaker knows that she isn't going. In B
the speaker thinks she is going, but she isn't
sure.

d) In A it was the work that the speaker did
quickly. In B it was the preparation for going out
that the speaker did quickly.

e) In A the speaker likes the T-shirt very much. In B
the speaker may have said something negative
about the T-shirt and is now reassuring the
owner of the T-shirt that he or she does like it in
spite of what has been said.

f) In A the other person has been there, but the
speaker didn't know this. In B the other person
has never been there and the speaker knows
this.

g) In A it is the speaker's opinion that he won't
apologise. In B the speaker implies that he may
apologise but not in person (he might send a
letter).

h) In A the speaker had a moment of doubt before
finally believing him. In B the speaker absolutely
does not believe him.

i) In A the speaker thinks he will stay here until
the morning. In B the speaker continues to be
sure that he will come in the morning.

j) In A the only people who went for a drink were
the speaker and Sam. In B the only thing the
speaker and Sam did was to go for a drink.

2 ▭▭ **34 SB p 150**
a) A   b) B   c) B   d) B   e) A   f) A   g) A
h) B   i) A   j) B

▭▭ **34**
(I = Ian; H = Helena; J = John; A = Angela; T = Tom)

a

I: *You haven't forgotten it's Sara's party this evening,
have you Helena? You are coming, aren't you?*

H: *Well, I'm a bit tired actually and I'm not that
bothered to be honest, Ian ... I think I might just stay
here if you don't mind and ... er, ... OK, if that's
what everyone's doing, why not? Yeah, yeah, I'll
come along, but just for a while.*

b

I: *I'll give Tom a ring to see if he fancies coming along to the party. We haven't seen him for ages, have we? Have you got his new phone number?*

H: *Er, no, er, I haven't I'm afraid. I don't know if anyone's got it actually. Oh, hang on, I think John might have. I think he's got it. Give him a ring and ask him.*

c

H: *Do you know if Angela's going to be at the party tonight? I need to, er, speak to her about something.*

I: *Well, I think she is. I think I overheard her saying she was going, but I could be wrong.*

d

H: *This isn't like you John! Jeans and a T-shirt!*

J: *Yeah, I know – work took longer than I expected, so, as you can see, I had to get ready in a bit of a hurry.*

e

J: *Hi Ian, haven't seen you for ages. How's it going?*

I: *Fine, really good. Hey, I love the T-shirt. Snazzy!*

f

J: *Sorry, ... what? ... Oh, this T-shirt? Yeah, I bought it in Ibiza a few years ago.*

I: *You've been to Ibiza? I didn't know that! How was it?*

g

H: *Hi Angela. Hey, how are things with you and Tom? Has he said sorry yet for the other night? Do you know who he was with?*

A: *No, and I don't think he will apologise. He doesn't seem to think he's done anything wrong. Can you believe it?*

h

H: *You'd have thought he'd offer some explanation! I mean, he must have some excuse or something.*

A: *He's certainly tried, but I didn't believe a single word of it. Wait 'til I find out what he was up to! And I don't know where he is tonight. Aaaargh!*

i

A: *You're going home? OK, see you soon Helena. What about Ian? Is he going with you?*

H: *No, I'm going on my own. I'm a bit tired. He'll be dancing all night. I think you'll find he'll be here for breakfast. See ya!*

j

T: *Hello?*

J: *Hi Tom. I didn't see you at the party last night. Where were you?*

T: *Oh, hi John. Well, I didn't quite make it actually. I was all set to go ... my flatmate Sam and I were on our way to the party and we stopped in a bar for a quick drink. We ended up staying there for something to eat and by the time we'd finished it was a bit late to go to the party so we just went home. How was it anyway?*

3 and **4** Students' own answers

Ready, steady, go! (p 65)

Phrasal verbs

Greetings from down under (p 66)

General revision

1 As I haven't written for so long ...
I dropped you all ...
Unfortunately, the weather ...
Never mind, it'll give me ...
I've just found a job working in a friendly little café ...
... recommended by your friend.
It is only a few hours ...
... there are some great people working there.
Most of them are ...
... I met someone who thought he met you ...
Anyway, I have been here in Australia ...
... decided to stay for a while ...
... buses, trains and planes I took to get here ...
... for what felt like hours!
... I wished I had flown ...
Consequently, when I first arrived I spent ...
... the Blue Mountains for a few days.
... are absolutely incredible ...
By the way, have you heard ... ('did you hear' would be correct in American English)
... you should check it out ...
It was at their concert where you first met, wasn't it?
.... if only you were all here ...

2 Students' own answers.

The word game (p 67)

Lexis

1 haphazard 3 talkative 5 slip 6 edgeways /
edgewise 9 mumbler 11 achievement 13 bad /
poor 14 flicked 16 joy-ride 17 in
19 recognised 20 depth 22 clogged / blocked
23 exquisite 24 put / got 26 Rumour 27 nick,
pinch 28 addiction 30 scrabble 31 clenched
33 daft 35 bottle

Mid Course Test

Scoring: one point per correct answer unless otherwise
indicated.

1 (2 points for questions 1–6)

1 We usually go to a restaurant near to where we
   live every weekend.
2 I generally try to get to the cinema once a week.
   / Generally I try to get to the cinema once a
   week.
3 Thankfully they finally arrived at the party at
   midnight. / They finally arrived at the party at
   midnight thankfully.
4 I read something about it in a magazine at the
   dentist only yesterday. / I read something about
   it only yesterday in a magazine at the dentist.
5 To be honest, I was completely exhausted when
   I got home. / I was completely exhausted when I
   got home, to be honest.
6 Quite frankly, he is very often the last person to
   get to work. / He is very often the last person to
   get to work, quite frankly.
7 a)   8 b)   9 a)

2 1 He's just bought a wonderful big flat in London.
2 They brought me a disgusting cold cup of coffee.
3 She was wearing awful huge, bright red earrings.
4 They've got two lovely teenage children.

3 (2 points each sentence)

1 We stayed in a lovely little village near the sea.
2 I've just found a pair of old jeans I had when I
   was a student.
3 I had a huge bowl of strawberries with cream.
4 Have you had any of that Belgian beer your
   brother gave you?
5 I bought them in that little shop just round the
   corner.
6 Can I have a large cup of coffee with milk and
   no sugar, please?

4 (2 points each sentence)

1 Patiently they waited for hours and hours.
2 Long gone are the days when we stayed up all
   night listening to music.
3 The weather was the only thing she didn't like.
4 Chips with cheese was his favourite food.

5 (2 points each sentence)

1 They seem to have left already.
2 It seems that they have left already.
3 There appears to be no-one left.
4 It is not known whether they have left.

6 (2 points each sentence)

1 Never before have I seen anything quite like that.
2 Rarely do you see such a wonderful example as
   this.
3 Not until it was too late did she realise what
   would happen.
4 Not a word did they say to anyone.
5 Only when you're told it's OK can you leave.

7 (1 point each adverb)

1 Did he actually see it or did he just hear about it?
2 It's not actually raining at the moment. It's just
   very dark.
3 I just want to say that I really enjoyed it.
4 Could you just help me for a few minutes? /
   Could you help me just for a few minutes? This
   English homework is really difficult.

8 1 Whenever I went abroad, I would always try to
   learn a few phrases of the language.
2 She'll usually be the first to tell you if there's
   something wrong.
3 When I was a child, I would visit my
   grandparents every weekend.
4 They'll go on for hours if you're not careful.

9 1 on   2 point   3 not

10 (1 point each for 1–8 and 1 point per verb for 9–12)

1 ✓
2 ✓
3 ✓
4 ✗ If she'd got here earlier, we could've gone out.
5 ✗ If she'd got here earlier, we'd have been able
   to go out.
6 ✗ I'd have given you some, if I'd had some. / I'd
   give you some if I had some.
7 ✗ What would you have done if you were in my
   position? / What would you do if you were in
   my position?
8 ✗ If I could, I'd go there right now.
9 If I had followed my instincts, I would be a rich
   woman by now and I would be living in
   Hollywood.

10 We wouldn't have met and, of course, wouldn't be together now if I hadn't gone clubbing that night.

11 Would you have done the same as I did if you had been there?

12 If I had had a nap earlier, I wouldn't have slept through the film!

11 (2 points for each verb)

1 wasn't / weren't raining
2 would get
3 not speaking / not having spoken
4 to inform
5 had listened
6 to notify
7 wasn't / weren't
8 was living / lived   coming / having come
9 would stop;   had never bought

12 (2 points each)

1 Having realised / Realising they had seen the film before, they went to a restaurant instead.
2 Having missed the bus, we decided to take a taxi.
3 Knowing they would be late, they made up an excuse about the car breaking down.
4 Saddened by the news, they decided to call off the holiday.
5 Not having been there before, they got lost and didn't arrive back here until midnight.
6 Kept awake by the noise from next door, they got up and had a party of their own.

13 1 hear
2 see
3 smell
4 'm just tasting / 'll just taste
5 feel
6 're seeing

14 1 out
2 up
3 tastefully
4 in-your-face
5 awe-inspiring
6 hug
7 mucky
8 conversational
9 in-depth
10 one-way
11 butting
12 talkative
13 slipped
14 off
15 peering
16 in
17 speak
18 come
19 tired
20 of

7 *Mid Course* Test

Name: _____   **Total:** _____ /150

---

1 Position of adverbials *15 points*

Reorder the words and phrases below to form logical sentences.

1 near to where we live / we / every weekend / go / to a restaurant / usually.

_____

2 once a week / try to get / I / to the cinema / generally.

_____

3 at midnight / they / at the party / arrived / finally / thankfully.

_____

4 I / only / at the dentist / read something / in a magazine / about it / yesterday.

_____

5 was / to be honest / when I got home / I / exhausted / completely.

_____

6 to get to work / he / quite frankly / very / is / often / the last person.

_____

Tick (✓) the sentence, a) or b), which is closest in meaning to the main sentence.

7 Everyone else was late.
   a) Just Peter arrived in time.
   b) Peter just arrived in time.

8 I didn't realise you'd seen it.
   a) I knew you'd never seen it
   b) I never knew you'd seen it

9 Nobody else knows where they work.
   a) Only he knows where they work.
   b) He only knows where they work.

2 Order of adjectives *4 points*

Put the adjectives in brackets into the correct place in each sentence.

1 He's just bought a big flat in London. (wonderful)

_____

2 They brought me a cold cup of coffee. (disgusting)

_____

3 She was wearing awful huge earrings. (bright red)

_____

4 They've got two teenage children. (lovely)

_____

3 Describing nouns *12 points*

Put the words in brackets into an appropriate place in each sentence.

1 We stayed in a lovely village. (near the sea / little)

_____

2 I've just found old jeans. (a pair of / I had when I was a student)

_____

3 I had a bowl of strawberries. (with cream / huge)

_____

4 Have you had any of that beer? (your brother gave you / Belgian)

_____

5 I bought them. (in that little shop / just round the corner)

_____

6 Can I have a cup of coffee, please? (with milk and no sugar / large)

_____

4 Fronting *8 points*

Look at the example and then rewrite sentences 1–4 in a similar way.

Example: The rain came down for days and days.
           Down came the rain for days and days.

1 They waited patiently for hours and hours.

_____

2 The days when we stayed up all night listening to music are long gone.

_____

   © Ceri Jones, Tania Bastow, Sue Kay & Vaughan Jones, 2001. Published by Macmillan Publishers Limited. This sheet may be photocopied and used within the class.

3   The only thing she didn't like was the weather.

    _____

4   His favourite food was chips with cheese.

    _____

5   Hedging *8 points*

Join words from each column to make four sentences.

They	not known	to be no-one left.
It	seem	to have left already.
There	seems that	whether they have left.
It is	appears	they have left already.

6   Negative and limiting adverbials *10 points*

Rewrite the sentences beginning with the word or words given.

1   I've never seen anything quite like that before.

    Never before _____

2   You rarely see such a wonderful example as this.

    Rarely _____

3   She didn't realise what would happen until it was too late.

    Not until _____

4   They didn't say a word to anyone.

    Not a word _____

5   You can leave only when you're told it's OK.

    Only _____

7   Adding emphasis *8 points*

Put the words in brackets into the correct place in the sentences.

1   Did he see it or did he hear about it? (actually / just)

    _____

2   It's not raining at the moment. It's very dark. (actually / just)

    _____

3   I want to say that I enjoyed it. (just / really)

    _____

4   Could you help me for a few minutes? This English homework is difficult. (just / really)

    _____

8   Tendencies *4 points*

Put the words in *italics* into the correct order to complete the sentences.

1   Whenever I went abroad, *always / would / try / I /* to learn a few phrases of the language.

    _____

2   *be / she / usually / 'll* the first to tell you if there's something wrong.

    _____

3   When I was a child *my grandparents / every weekend / would / I / visit.*

    _____

4   *go on / for hours / 'll / they* if you're not careful.

    _____

9   Agreeing and disagreeing *3 points*

Choose the correct alternative.

1   Come **on** / **off**! You can't be serious.

2   OK, you've got a **view** / **point** there.

3   Well, that's **not** / **no** necessarily always the case.

10   Unreal conditionals *18 points*

Some of the sentences are wrong. Mark them ✓ or ✗. Correct the sentences which are wrong.

1   If he'd been listening, he would've known what to do.

2   I wouldn't be asking for it if I didn't want it.

3   Had I not seen it for myself, I wouldn't believe it.

4   If she gets here earlier, we could've gone out.

5   If she'd got here earlier, we'd be able to go out.

6   I'd give you some, if I'd had some.

7   What do you do if you were in my position?

8   If I could, I'll go there right now.

Put the verbs in brackets into an appropriate form.

9   If I _____ (follow) my instincts, I _____ (be) a rich woman by now and I _____ (live) in Hollywood.

10 We _____ (not/meet) and, of course, _____ (not/be) together now if I _____ (go) clubbing that night.

11 _____ (you/do) the same as I did if you _____ (be) there?

12 If I _____ (have) a nap earlier, I _____ (not/sleep) through the film!

11 Wishes and regrets *22 points*

Complete the wishes by putting the verbs into an appropriate form.

1   I wish it _____ (not/rain). I want to go home and I haven't got my umbrella with me.

2   I've waited long enough. I wish he _____ (get) here soon.

3   He really regrets _____ (not/speak) to her when he had the chance.

4   We regret _____ (inform) you that your application has been unsuccessful on this occasion.

5   If only I _____ (listen) to the advice. Well, I guess it's too late to change anything now.

6   We wish _____ (notify) you of our latest special offer.

7   I bet she wishes she _____ (not/be) here right now.

8   I often wish I _____ (live) back home again with my parents. I sometimes really regret ever _____ (come) here.

9   I really wish you _____ (stop) playing that computer game for one minute. I wish we _____ (never/buy) it for you in the first place.

12 Participle clauses *12 points*

Put the verb in brackets into the correct form – either a present, past or perfect participle.

1   _____ (realise) they had seen the film before, they went to a restaurant instead.

2   _____ (miss) the bus, we decided to take a taxi.

3   _____ (know) they would be late, they made up an excuse about the car breaking down.

4   _____ (sadden) by the news, they decided to call off the holiday.

5   _____ (not/be) there before, they got lost and didn't arrive back here until midnight.

6   _____ (keep) awake by the noise from next door, they got up and had a party of their own.

13 Verbs of the senses *6 points*

Put the verbs in brackets into the correct form.

1   I _____ (hear) they're moving to France.

2   As I _____ (see) it, he's the best person for the job.

3   You _____ (smell) great – is it a new perfume?

4   I _____ (just/taste) it to see if it needs more sugar.

5   Are you OK? You _____ (feel) quite hot.

6   We _____ (see) each other again on Friday.

14 Lexis – general *20 points*

Choose the correct alternative.

1   We need to sort **out / up** the mess in the classroom.

2   I'm sorry, but I won't put **up / on** with this anymore.

3   The house is very **tastily / tastefully** decorated.

4   Everything is very **in-your-head / in-your-face** from the moment you get off the plane.

5   The views were **awe-inspiring / awe-provoking**.

6   He gave me a big kiss and a **hog / hug** to say thanks.

7   I got really **mucky / tacky** playing rugby.

8   I can speak **conversation / conversational** Spanish.

9   We had a very **in-depth / in-deep** discussion.

10/11   The conversation was very **one-directional / one-way**. I didn't say much at all and whenever I started speaking she kept **pushing / butting** in all the time.

12   He's a very **talkative / talking** person.

13   We were tired so we **slipped / slid** off quietly.

14   His voice tailed **out / off** as he realised no-one was listening.

15   I saw him **peering / flitting** at us through the window.

16   I really am **with / in** two minds about it.

17   You should **talk / speak** your mind more.

18   Don't worry. Something will **come / arrive** to mind.

19   If you're **tired / hungry**, have a quick nap.

20   Please accept this as a token **for / of** our gratitude.

8 Cyberspace *Overview*

The topic of this unit is technology and the future. The grammar focus is on *will* for predictions and assumptions, and using discourse markers.

Students start by looking at pictures of gadgets and putting them into categories. They then read and discuss an article on Stephen Hawking's predictions about the future. They also look at prepositional phrases taken from the article.

Students study the use of *will* for predictions and assumptions and make some predictions about their partner. They continue by discussing in groups their own predictions about the future of the world and give a presentation to the rest of the class.

Students then discuss video games and listen to a journalist who has written a book about them. They make notes in preparation for writing an article. Next students study the use of discourse markers and practise using them to complete texts. They then write the article they prepared for earlier.

Students then discuss the Internet and listen to some people talking about e-mail and the Internet. They go on to examine the vocabulary associated with e-mail and the Internet. Finally, students read and talk about the popular TV show *Big Brother*. They discuss what qualities a contestant needs to be accepted by the producers of the show and they write a letter of application from an ideal candidate.

Section	Aims	What the students are doing
Introduction page 68	*Lexis:* gadgets	Categorising a series of gadgets.
Future perfect pages 68–70	*Reading skills:* reading for gist	Reading an article about Stephen Hawking's predictions for the future.
	Lexis: words from the reading text	Using words from the reading text with correct prepositions to complete sentences.
Close up pages 70–72	*Grammar: will* for predictions & assumptions	Matching verb patterns with sentences using *will*.
		Adding *probably* in the correct place in sentences.
		Using *will* to make assumptions and predictions about a partner.
Future worlds pages 72–73	*Conversation skills:* discussion	Making predictions about the future of the world.
	Speaking skills: presentation	Giving a presentation to the class.
🔲 **Video games: a new art form?** pages 73–74	*Conversation skills:* discussion	Talking about video games.
	Listening skills: listening for detail	Listening to an interview with the author of a book on video games.
		Making notes in preparation for writing an article.
🔲 **Close up** pages 74–75	*Grammar:* using discourse markers	Completing a text with appropriate discourse markers.
		Differentiating between types of discourse markers.
		Studying the correct position of discourse markers.
	Writing skills: article	Writing an article using notes made earlier.
🔲 **Net work** page 76	*Conversation skills:* fluency work	Talking about the Internet.
	Listening skills: listening for gist	Listening to people talking about e-mail and the Internet and identifying with the speakers.
	Lexis: vocabulary of e-mail & the Internet	Studying words associated with computers and the Internet.
Big brother is watching you! page 77	*Reading skills:* reading for gist	Reading a text about the TV programme *Big Brother* and discussing it.
	Writing skills: application letter	Writing an application letter to become a contestant on *Big Brother*.

1 Whole class. Before looking at the pictures, establish the meaning of *gadget* (small tool, machine or piece of equipment). Perhaps you could bring some to the class, for example a mobile phone, TV remote control, etc. Then ask students if they can identify the gadgets in the photographs. (The photographs show: a wrist phone with visual display unit, a robot, a palmtop computer and a portable computerised office.)

Students then put the listed items into the categories.

2 Pairwork. Students compare their answers and then add two items to each category. Ask students to report some of their ideas to the class. They could then vote for their favourite idea, for example, the most useful, the most luxurious, etc.

Future perfect (p 68)

Closed books. Ask students if they have read any books or articles or seen anything on TV recently that predicts the future. Either ask students to discuss this in small groups or pairs or, if anyone has, ask one or two of them to tell the rest of the class about the book/article/programme and the predictions.

1 Pairwork. Students look at the photographs of Stephen Hawking and his book. They discuss the questions.

2 Students turn to page 139 and read the information about Stephen Hawking. Ask them if it has any facts they didn't already know.

3 Whole class. Go through points a–d with the class. Students then work in pairs or small groups to make their own predictions. They then report back to the class and find out how much agreement there is about their predictions. Students could decide which of these are the most and least likely. These predictions could be written in two columns on the board to establish any new or complex vocabulary and to refer back to after the first reading.

4 Give students plenty of time to read the article. If students have problems with vocabulary, they should be encouraged to make a note of the problem words/phrases, or underline them so they can come back to them later, after doing the lexis activities. Then ask students to discuss in pairs what Stephen Hawking's predictions are for the topics in 3. Check answers with a brief class discussion.

a) Hawking thinks it is unlikely that we will make contact with life forms from other planets. Even if there is life on other planets, the chances of it being recognisably human are small. Any alien life encountered will be either much more primitive or more advanced than us. If there is a more advanced alien life form

out there, Hawking wonders why it hasn't already visited Earth.

b) Hawking believes that computers will continue to double in speed and complexity every 18 months and this will continue until computers are almost as complex as the human brain. He thinks that electronic circuits will develop enough to make computers act intelligently, and if computers become intelligent they will be able to design even more intelligent computers in turn.

c) He thinks that genetic engineering on plants and animals will be allowed for economic reasons and it will eventually be done on humans too. He believes that in the next 1,000 years our DNA will be able to be increased in complexity which will allow for increased brain size.

d) Hawking thinks that within the next 100 years babies will be grown outside the womb, which will allow for increased brain size. However, an increase in brain size will not mean increased speed in chemical messages responsible for mental activity, which are fairly slow-moving, so humans will either become very intelligent or extremely quick-witted, but not both.

5 Pairwork. Students discuss the questions. Encourage them to report back to the class and move to a class discussion of the questions.

Lexis (p 70)

1 Students work individually or in pairs to complete the sentences without looking back at the text. If they have been working individually, allow them to compare their answers in pairs.

2 Students look back at the text and check their answers.

a) of, for b) by c) to d) By e) for f) of
g) against, at, of h) of

3 Students work individually to complete the sentences with suitable italicised expressions and prepositions from 1. Do not check answers at this stage.

4 Pairwork. Allow students to compare their answers with a partner before checking the answers with the class. Then students discuss in pairs whether the statements in 3 are true for them or their country. Finish with a class discussion and perhaps a show of hands on whether the statements are true or not.

a) to keep ahead of   b) the turn of   c) By far the most   d) have a good chance of   e) no limit to   f) has in store for   g) By the year   h) at the expense of   i) come up against   j) for economic reasons

Close up (p 70)

Will for predictions & assumptions

1 Pairwork. Students read the predictions and find examples of the verb patterns.

  a) 2 – won't colonise; 7 – will continue
  b) 3 – will be producing
  c) 1 – will have landed
  d) 4 – won't be contacted; 5 – won't be banned
  e) 6 – will have been developed

2 Ask students to think about what the difference in meaning is between the five forms. While they are working on this, draw the timelines below on the board. Check answers with the class and then ask them to work in pairs and match each of the verb patterns with a timeline.

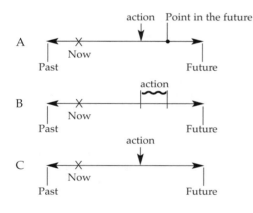

Timeline A *will* + perfect; perfect passive
Timeline B *will* + continuous
Timeline C *will* + infinitive; *will* + simple passive

3 Students work individually or in pairs to add *probably* to each of the predictions in 1 and study its position.

  1 By the end of this century we will probably have landed a spaceship on Mars.
  2 We probably won't colonise Mars as it is far less hospitable than Earth.
  3 In a hundred years' time we will probably be producing babies outside the womb.
  4 We probably won't be contacted by aliens.
  5 Genetic engineering on humans probably won't be banned this century.

  6 By the end of the millennium techniques will probably have been developed to redesign human DNA.
  7 The development of computers will probably continue until they are more intelligent than humans.

In positive sentences *probably* usually goes after *will*. In negative sentences it goes before *won't*.

4 Give students time to read the sentences and complete them. Allow them to compare their answers in pairs before checking with the class.

  a) will have taken
  b) probably won't go
  c) will be cooked / will have been cooked
  d) will probably be asked
  e) will be sitting
  f) will probably have had
  g) will probably have been cleaned

5 Students work individually to change the sentences so they are true for them. This could involve changing an affirmative to a negative or vice-versa, changing the time or place or any other aspect of the sentence. Do one or two about yourself as examples. Allow students to compare answers in pairs.

6 Pairwork. Students read the text and discuss whether it is true for them. You could then have a brief whole class discussion of the text.

7 Pairwork. Students look at the uses of *will* in the text in 6 and decide whether they refer to the past, present, future or a combination of times. Check answers with the class. Refer students to the Language reference section on page 72.

  you'll probably have been studying – combination of times – reference to past and present
  you'll feel – present / any time
  won't have – present / any time
  will sometimes give – combination of times / any time
  you'll have been using, you will have bought, will possibly also have read, you'll have made, you will have been invited – combination of times of past with present result

8 Go through the examples with the whole class and then put students into pairs. Students work individually to write their assumptions and predictions about their partner. Go round offering help and encouragement and make sure they are using a variety of the verb phrases and time expressions. Do not allow them to consult their partners.

9 Pairwork. Students compare their sentences with their partners and find out how accurate their assumptions and predictions are. You could get them to read their sentences to each other using the subject *you*. Ask them to report back to the class on how happy they were with the predictions made about them and on how accurate their predictions were.

Future worlds (p 72)

Books closed. Choose two or three of the questions from the discussion exercise and have a brief class discussion. Tell students they are going to have a more in-depth discussion about similar issues later.

1 Groupwork. Students get into their groups and choose one of the pairs of topics. Encourage the groups as much as you can to choose different topics.

2 Groupwork. Each group chooses a secretary to take notes. They then discuss the questions.

3 Groupwork. Each group chooses a spokesperson.

Whole class. Go through the box of presentation tips with the class and elicit any other useful tips they can think of. Remind them that the Language toolbox contains useful language for use in presentations.

Groupwork. The members of each group work together, using the secretary's notes, to prepare the presentation their spokesperson will give. Remind them to look at the list of points in c) which should be covered by their presentations. You could set a time limit for the presentation, for example, no more than three minutes.

4 Whole class. Groups take turns to make their presentations. You could have a class vote on which one is the most realistic, optimistic and pessimistic.

Video games: a new art form? (p 73)

1 Groupwork. Students discuss the questions. Ask them to describe in some detail their favourite game and why they like it. You could pair game-playing students with non-game-playing students to ensure everyone is involved.

2 **35 SB p 151**

Go through the instructions with the class and read the information in the card file about Steven Poole's book. Students then work in pairs to write their questions. Play the recording for students to listen and find out if their questions are answered.

35

(I = Interviewer; S = Steven Poole)

I: *How popular are video games, and why are they so popular?*

S: *Video games these days are extremely popular. One in four households in Britain has a Playstation and in 1999 the video game industry made nearly a billion pounds, which was 60*

percent more than cinema box office takings. So why are video games so popular? Well, they combine very fast moving, well-designed graphical images with very interesting sound design and music. But crucially they're interactive, so they change according to what you do from moment to moment, so the computer system concentrates on what you are saying to it, and poses you very interesting challenges and difficulties at very high speeds. So, in this sense, the video game is a much more challenging and involving art form than older things such as cinema or television.

I: *What was the first video game, and who played it?*

S: *The first commercial video game came along in 1971. It was called 'Computer Space'. Unfortunately it wasn't very successful because it was a very complicated game involving space ships and torpedoes and black holes and so forth. The same man who had invented that invented a game called 'Pong' in 1972 and that's when the video game explosion really took off. It was a very very simple tennis game. You had two white bats and a ball travelling across the screen making little blippy noises, and er, it was put in bars next to pinball machines and so on, and it became a very popular activity, more popular than the pinball.*

I: *So, how have games changed and developed since those early days?*

S: *The very early video games like 'Pong' just took place on one screen and the boundaries of the screen were the boundaries of the playing area. But then the space in video games started to get larger. The games started to scroll from side to side or up and down, so that the playing area became larger than the total size of one screen. The graphics in games slowly became more colourful and more detailed and then the big innovation took place in the 90s, which was the invention of full 3D. This meant that you started to control characters who explored fully realised, solid 3D environments. You could wander round landscapes and buildings and look at them from any angle.*

I: *There's a common criticism that video games are very violent. What's your view on that?*

S: *A lot of people think that playing violent video games might be bad for children; it might make them into violent people themselves. But I don't think that's true. After all, millions of people around the world play these games and the vast majority of them are very peaceful people and never pick up a gun in real life. The violence in video games after all is very crude, cartoon violence. It's very exaggerated. It bears no relation to real life and people who play video*

---

games know this. They aren't stupid. Now, it's certainly true that if a slightly disturbed child plays these video games too much, then he might become more violent, but then it's true that that sort of child would become more violent if he watched a film or listened to a heavy metal record, or did any one of a number of other things. Video games themselves can't be blamed for causing people to act violently in real life.

I: *What's the profile of a typical games player?*

S: *A lot of people still think the typical video game player is a teenage boy locked in his smelly bedroom, not having any kind of social life, just playing games all day. But that's not true. The average age of a Playstation owner nowadays is 26 and although video gamers in this country are still mostly male, because the games are largely designed by men and marketed to men, that's not the case in Japan or America where many more women have become interested in video games. Also, the idea that video gaming is an anti-social activity is no longer true at all. It's a very sociable one. Not only can you invite your friends round to your home to play a four-player game of 'Micro Machines', you can go to a bar and play games on networked PCs there. And these days of course, many many people over the world play video games on the Internet. Hundreds of thousands of people can be playing a game at the same time and they can be making friends on different continents through video games.*

I: *Do you think that video games could be considered an art form?*

S: *I think video games are close to becoming an art form in themselves. Certainly, when cinema was only around 30 years old, as video games are today, a lot of people thought films were mindless entertainment and rotted people's brains and were no good. But now we know that cinema is an art form and we have film critics who can analyse films and enhance our enjoyment of them, and I think in the future this will be true of video games as well.*

I: *What will the next developments be?*

S: *Well, the current research in video games is concentrating on artificial intelligence. People want to play video games that give a greater illusion of interacting with real characters. A game like 'Black And White' is brilliant at doing this, where you teach creatures who actually learn from you and then they go off and do their own thing and they seem to have their own brains and their own wills.*

3 Pairwork. Students discuss their questions and report back to the class.

b)

1 Video games now make more money than cinema box offices. In 1999 the video game industry made nearly a billion pounds, which was 60% more than cinema box office takings.

Steven says that video games are more challenging and involving as an art form than cinema or TV.

He compares cinema to video games in that when cinema was a new phenomenon, people thought films were mindless entertainment which rotted the brain. Now cinema is seen as an art form and critics analyse films and increase our enjoyment of them, and he predicts that this will happen to video games too in the future.

2 The first video game, 'Computer Space', was created in 1971 but wasn't successful. 'Pong' was invented in 1972. It was a simple tennis game but was very popular and it was the start of the video game industry.

Over time games started to scroll which meant that the playing area became larger than the size of the screen. Graphics became more colourful and detailed and in the 1990s full 3D in computer games was invented so players could control characters who explored landscapes and buildings from all angles.

3 Many people think that violent games are bad for children in that it might make them behave violently. However, millions of people play the games and are peaceful people. Steven does think that if a child who was slightly disturbed played violent games too much they might become violent, but he believes this would happen if they did other things too. Video games themselves can't be blamed for children's violence.

4 Most video gamers in Britain are male because of the way they are marketed and designed, but in Japan and America many more women are becoming interested in playing video games.

4 Students work individually to choose a topic. Play the recording again for students to write their notes. Be prepared to play it a third time if necessary.

5 Pairwork. Students compare notes with a partner who has chosen the same topic. Remind them to keep their notes safely as they will need them later.

Close up (p 74)

Using discourse markers

1 Whole class. Ask students if they know what discourse markers are (a variety of words and expressions used to link ideas and give coherent structure to both speech and writing and to help listeners and readers follow what you want to say).

Students then decide the correct position for each discourse marker. Do not check answers at this stage.

2 🔲 **36 SB p 151**

Pairwork. Students compare their answers. Then play the recording for them to listen and check.

> a) 1 But crucially 2 So, in this sense
> b) 3 But then 4 This meant that
> c) 5 After all 6 it's certainly true that
>   7 but then it's true that
> d) 8 Also 9 Not only
> e) 10 but now 11 as well

🔲 **36**

> a) *So why are video games so popular? Well, they combine very fast moving, well-designed graphical images with very interesting sound design and music. But crucially they're interactive so the computer system poses you very interesting challenges and difficulties at very high speeds. So, in this sense the video game is a much more challenging and involving art form ...*
>
> b) *The very early video games like 'Pong' just took place on one screen. But then the space in video games started to get larger. And then the big innovation took place in the 90s, which was the invention of full 3D. This meant that you started to control characters who explored fully realised, solid 3D environments.*
>
> c) *A lot of people think that playing violent video games might be bad for children but I don't think that's true. After all, millions of people around the world play these games and the vast majority of them are very peaceful people and never pick up a gun in real life. The violence in video games after all is very crude, cartoon violence. Now, it's certainly true that if a slightly disturbed child plays these video games too much, then he might become more violent, but then it's true that that sort of child would become more violent if he watched a film or listened to a heavy metal record ...*
>
> d) *... that's not the case in Japan or America where many more women have become interested in video games. Also, the idea that video gaming is an anti-social activity is no longer true at all. Not only can you invite your friends round to your home to play a four-player game of 'Micro Machines', you can go to a bar and play games on networked PCs there ...*

> e) *... a lot of people thought films were mindless entertainment but now we know that cinema is an art form and we have film critics who can analyse films and enhance our enjoyment of them, and I think in the future this will be true of video games as well.*

3 Pairwork. Allow students a few minutes to think about the questions individually and then ask them to compare their answers with a partner. Refer them to the Language reference section at the foot of this page and then check the answers with the whole class.

> a) but now, but then
> b) but crucially, but then it's true that, also, as well, not only
> c) so, in this sense, this meant that, it's certainly true that, after all
> Note: 'but then it's true that' could also go in c).

4 Students work individually to put the discourse markers in brackets in the correct positions in the sentences. Allow them to compare answers with a partner before checking with the class.

> a) Video games provide entertainment and also the opportunity to make new friends.
> b) Video games are the new films. After all, far more money is spent on games now than on going to the cinema.
> c) Most video gamers are men. But then it's true that most games have been marketed towards them.
> d) New technology allows games to have high quality sound and images. But crucially, it means that the player can interact with the characters and their surroundings.
> e) Video games can be violent and so, in this sense, could encourage children to act violently, but they are unlikely to be the only influence on their behaviour.

5 Whole class. Students complete the text individually and compare answers in pairs. To check, read the text aloud to the class, pausing at each gap for the students to add the missing discourse markers.

> 1 but now 2 Not only 3 as well
> 4 This means that 5 as well as

6 Whole class. Ask students to comment on the text and give their own opinions.

7 Remind students of the notes they made in 4 in the previous section (*Video games: a new art form?*) and ask them to write their articles. This can be set for homework.

Net work (p 76)

Closed books. Ask students when they last used the Internet. Get one or two students to tell the rest of the class when, what and why.

1 Pairwork. Students discuss the questions in pairs. Ask them to report back to the class how much they use e-mail and the Internet and what they use them for. Write their ideas on the board and elicit any further uses they can think of. Leave the notes on the board for the next exercise.

2 🔲 **37 SB p 152**

Play the recording. Students listen and see how many of their ideas are mentioned. Allow students to discuss the questions with a partner before checking with the whole class. Ask them if they identify with any of the speakers.

🔲 **37**

1

I'm terrible on the Net, I'm really, really bad at it, but I really enjoy it. I kind of start off surfing, looking for something specific. I might want some information on a particular, on a particular subject, but I get carried away, I get diverted, I end up looking at something completely unrelated, and inevitably, um, actually I have to confess I end up shopping, or window shopping anyway, which is, um, well, it's, it's, it's quite seductive on the Net because there's some really, really, really, funky shopping sites. You can pick up all sorts of different things and you can go through it and normally the graphics are like really good and, um, I've downloaded I think nearly all the, all the kind of sound software that you need, so I end up watching film bites on different products, and getting kind of, well, getting completely carried away. But I never get my credit card out, so that's quite good but on the other hand, I do tend to do it in the middle of the day which makes it a bit expensive, but, um, I really enjoy it.

2

I work as a doctor in a very busy medical practice, um, and I never thought I'd have time to use the Internet, but I discovered of course, how useful it is for e-mailing and sending messages, um, particularly work related messages, and I also I've, I've discovered that I can find information out much quicker than by looking up the telephone book for instance, or, or the newspaper to find out train times or maybe what's on at my local cinema, and if I have a problem, um, a professional problem, I can also get in touch with colleagues and find out their opinions. I don't use it socially though – I hardly ever use it to talk to friends. Frankly I still like the old-fashioned telephone.

3

Er, I'm fairly new to the whole kind of computer thing, but I have started to use the e-mail, um,

mainly for personal use and, um, I find it very handy if I forget someone's birthday, I can just sort of quickly send an e-mail, send a card which is quite nice, um, but I rarely use the Net, um, I have yet to work out how to do that, but I'm sure in the next couple of weeks I'm going to give it a go.

4

I use the Net for a couple of reasons, one because I have family that are scattered all over the world and I find that's a quite a good way to keep in touch with them and again it's quite cheap, but I primarily use it because I'm doing a degree part-time and I find it really helpful for various reasons and probably the best thing is that I can get in touch with the lecturers and the professors without actually having to speak to them in person which I find to be a plus. They are very hard to track down and they seem to be, it seems to be easier for them to communicate with me or with students in that way so, so that's one advantage and I suppose the other advantage is that on the Net you have access to various different libraries and so it is very easy to track down materials and books and reserve them or find out where they are anyway and, and find out if you have, you can gain access to them, so that's primarily why I use the Net.

Lexis (p 76)

1 Pairwork. Students look at the extracts and try to fill the gaps with appropriate words, either words they remember from the listening exercise or, failing that, anything that is appropriate. Do not check answers at this stage.

2 🔲 **38 SB p 152**

Play the recording for students to listen and check their answers. Ask students to check their answers with a partner before checking with the whole class. Acknowledge any suggestions from 1 that are also possible.

---

1 surfing   2 sites   3 downloaded   4 software
5 bites

🔲 **38**

a) *I kind of start off surfing, looking for something specific. I might want some information on a particular, on a particular subject, but I get carried away, I get diverted, I end up looking at something completely unrelated ...*

b) *... there's some really, really, really, funky shopping sites. You can pick up all sorts of different things ...*

c) *... I've downloaded I think nearly all the, all the kind of sound software that you need, so I end up watching film bites on different products, and getting kind of, well, getting completely carried away.*

3 Students match their answers to the definitions. Check answers with the class.

> a) software b) surfing c) sites d) bites
> e) downloaded

4 Whole class. Read the words and phrases in the box and ask students, individually, to put them into groups according to whether they associate them with e-mail, the Internet or both. Encourage students to mingle and to ask others for help with unknown words. Check answers with the class and write the terms in groups on the board. Elicit any other terms and add them to the groups.

> **e-mail:** attachment inbox
> **Internet:** search engine hyperlink home page
> bookmark graphics online chat room newsgroup
> **both:** server log on

5 Pairwork. Students choose three words or phrases from 4 and write definitions for them, using the definitions in 3 as a model. Students then close their books and exchange definitions with other pairs. They try to remember the words and phrases defined. This can be repeated with several pairs. To finish the activity, collect in the definitions and read some out to the class.

6 Pairwork. Students discuss the questions and then report back to the class.

Big brother is watching you! (p 77)

Closed books. If the TV programme *Big Brother* was shown in the students' country or countries, find out how many watched it and what they thought about it. If anyone is unaware of the programme, encourage students who watched it to explain the rules and what happened. If students are familiar with the same programme, ask them to share their thoughts on the candidates.

Pairwork. Students work individually to read the description and then discuss the questions in pairs.

Writing (p 77)

1 Pairwork. Students read the instructions and the advert. They then discuss what kind of people the producers are looking for and report back to the class.

Optional activity

Photocopy the letter on the right and give a copy to each pair of students in the class. Students read the letter and decide whether the writer has a good chance of being selected by the producers of *Big Brother* or not. Ask students to justify their decisions and have a class vote.

2 Whole class. Read the instructions with the class. Students then work individually (or at home) to write their application letters. Emphasise that these letters are from the ideal candidate; the students don't have to write about themselves, unless they want to. If this is done in class, allow the students plenty of time to think and write.

Big Brother
PO Box 258
London W1 5JZ

Via Piaggia 52
20065 Milan
Italy

Dear Big Brother
My name's Marco, I'm from Milan, I'm 29 years old and currently studying Psychology at university. I live at home with my five brothers, two sisters and my dog. The idea of sharing a house with another nine people doesn't bother me at all. I've done it all my life and survived (so far!). In our house, the person with the loudest voice wins, and it's usually me! Though I must admit I HATE anything to do with cooking or cleaning (my mother does all that for me). In my book, that is definitely a woman's job!

And why do I want to take part? Because it's a new experience, putting yourself on show 24 hours a day, and I think I can use it to help me in my studies. And of course, I want to win the prize. Isn't that why everyone's taking part?

And why are you going to pick me? Because I am exactly the person you're looking for: tall, dark, handsome and above all, photogenic. I love being with people, telling funny stories, playing practical jokes and generally fooling around. All my friends tell me I should be on TV!

I look forward to meeting you soon.

Yours
Marco Rossi
PS Viva Italia!

3 Groupwork. Divide the class into two groups. Groups exchange application letters. They have to select one candidate from the applications they receive and should discuss and decide on their selection criteria before they make their selection. The groups then take turns to report to the other group who have they chosen and why.

Test

Scoring: one point per correct answer unless otherwise indicated.

1 (2 points per answer)
  1 turn of 2 store for 3 chance of 4 come
  (up) against 5 limit to 6 by far 7 ahead of

2 1 'll be 2 'll be 3 won't start 4 'll still be doing
  5 'll get 6 'll arrive 7 will have landed
  8 'll be going 9 They'll probably be here soon.
  10 I probably won't be there until much later I'm afraid.
  11 We'll probably have got back by midnight at the latest.
  12 They'll probably be leaving in a little while.

3 1 but 2 After all 3 also 4 this means that
  5 not only 6 as well

4 1 attachment 2 online, chat room (2 points)
  3 home page 4 bookmarked 5 search engines
  6 hyperlink 7 inbox

Cyberspace Test

Name: _____   **Total:** _____ /40

---

1 Lexis – prepositional phrases *14 points*

Complete each sentence with a word from the box and an appropriate preposition. Use each word once.

> chance   turn   far   come   store   ahead   limit

1   It was made around the _____ _____ the century.

2   So, what have you got in _____ _____ me today?

3   We've got a good _____ _____ getting there on time if we leave now.

4   It'll be OK. We don't expect to _____ up _____ any problems.

5   There's no _____ _____ what computers might be able to do in the future.

6   She's _____ _____ the best person for the job.

7   We must continually make sure we keep _____ _____ all our competitors.

2 *Will* for predictions and assumptions *12 points*

Put the verbs in brackets into the correct form using *will*.

Nick: The phone's ringing . Do you want me to get it?

Ian: I'll get it, it (1) _____ (be) Pete. He said he'd ring about this time.

Carlos: You still here? You (2) _____ (be) late if you don't leave now.

Marco: I know – the car (3) _____ (not/start).

Freda: Can you come sometime after six? I imagine I (4) _____ (still/do) my homework 'til then.

Marta: Sure, I (5) _____ (get) the later bus, so I guess I (6) _____ (arrive) around six thirty if that's OK.

Amit: Do you think their plane (7) _____ (land) yet?

Ajay: Well, it should have arrived twenty minutes ago. I guess they (8) _____ (go) through Customs right now.

Put *probably* into the correct place in each sentence.

9   They'll be here soon.

10 I won't be there until much later I'm afraid.

11 We'll have got back by midnight at the latest.

12 They'll be leaving in a little while.

3 Discourse markers *6 points*

Complete the dialogue with the discourse markers from the box. Use each discourse marker once.

> but   as well   not only   also   after all
> this means that

A: Have you finally decided where to go then?

B: Hopefully to a couple of Greek Islands, (1) _____ I suppose I might change my mind yet again.
    (2) _____ , things haven't really gone to plan so far, have they?

A: And I hear that Gianni's (3) _____ going with you now. So, I guess (4) _____
    (5) _____ will you come back all tanned and relaxed, you'll be speaking fluent Italian
    (6) _____ !

4 Lexis – Internet and e-mail *8 points*

Rearrange the mixed-up words. The first letter is given.

1   Can you show me how to send an **amentchtat**?

2   We met **oienln** in a **caht romo**. We've been e-mailing each other ever since.

3   Do I need a password to view the **hmoe pega**?

4   Let's see which sites you've got **bomakkedor** then.

5   Which **sercah esgeinn** do you usually use?

6   Do you know what a **hrlipyenk** is?

7   Just let me check my **ionxb** for new mail.

9 *Law* Overview

The topic of this unit is the law. The grammar focus is on using modals to talk about the past and inversion after *neither/nor, so* and *such*.

Students start by looking at some silly questions asked in court. They then learn some courtroom vocabulary and use it to complete sentences. Practice in paraphrasing provides an introduction to the work on inversion which they will do later in the unit.

Students put various crimes in order of seriousness and discuss suitable punishments. They then listen to other people giving their opinions on appropriate punishments for different crimes. Next, they read some legal cases and give their judgements on them. A discussion on whether students have ever had anything stolen leads into a listening text about a woman whose car was stolen. Students then practise linking words that end in *t* and *d*.

The grammar focus is on using modals to talk about the past and students practise using modals to report speech or thought, speculate and make deductions, and comment or criticise. They then examine and use some collocations with *law* and go on to discuss some proposals for new laws.

Students read a legal anecdote and study the difference in style between broadsheet and tabloid newspapers. They practise writing a report for a tabloid paper. This leads into work on inversion. Finally students complete the lyrics of a Bananarama song and look at the use of metaphors and similes.

Section	Aims	What the students are doing
Introduction page 78	*Reading skills*: reading for detail	Reading extracts from court cases and determining which one does not contain a silly question.
In the courtroom pages 78–79	*Lexis*: vocabulary of the courtroom	Categorising words to do with law.
		Completing sentences with law words.
	Listening skills: listening for detail	Listening to conversations and deciding what crimes the speakers are talking about.
Test yourself pages 79–80	*Writing skills*: paraphrasing;	Paraphrasing sentences starting with given words.
	writing newspaper reports	Writing a newspaper report of a court case.
Crime & punishment pages 80–81	*Listening skills*: listening for detail	Ordering crimes by seriousness.
		Listening to people saying what punishments they would give criminals.
	Conversation skills: discussion	Discussing crime and appropriate punishments for crimes.
Legal wrangles pages 81–82	*Listening skills*: listening for detail	Listening to someone talking about a crime and identifying true and false statements.
	Pronunciation: word linking	Practising linking words with final *t* and *d* sounds.
Close up pages 82–83	*Grammar*: using modals to talk about the past	Matching modal verb phrases to functions.
		Practising using modals to report speech or thought, speculate about the past and comment or criticise.
Law pages 83–84	*Lexis*: law & its collocations	Using collocations with *law* to complete sentences.
	Conversation skills: discussion	Discussing your country's laws and proposals for new laws.
Legal anecdotes pages 84–86	*Reading skills*: reading for gist; reading for detail	Deciding on the best title for an anecdote.
	Lexis: formal words;	Matching formal vocabulary with less formal equivalents.
	newspaper styles	Differentiating between broadsheet and tabloid styles.
	Writing skills: writing a tabloid newspaper report	Transforming an article from broadsheet into tabloid style.
Close up page 86	*Grammar*: inversion after *neither / nor, so & such*	Studying newspaper extracts which use inversion.
		Rewriting sentences with and without inversion.
		Writing sentences with *so, such* and *neither / nor*.
Love in the first degree page 87	*Listening skills*: listening for detail	Completing the lyrics of a song.
		Listening to a song and discussing the use of metaphors.
		Writing your own similes.

Law Teacher's notes

Ask students to open their books at the first page of the unit and, in pairs, to describe the photograph. They should discuss who the person is, where he is and what he is wearing. Ask students how they would they feel if they were about to face this man in court and if they know why he wears a wig and a gown (it's a tradition: to give him an air of authority; to show the importance of what is taking place and to contrast it with everyday life). Ask if judges in students' own countries wear similar clothes. If not, how do they dress?

1 Explain that the extracts are all things said in court cases and all but one contain a silly question. Give students plenty of time to read them and decide which one does not contain a silly question.

> e) The final question was asked to help to confirm that the defendant was actually watching the TV.

2 Whole class. Students give their opinions on which extract they found the most amusing.

In the courtroom (p 78)

Closed books. Ask students if they have ever been in a courtroom. If anyone has, and is willing to talk about their experiences, encourage them to tell the class about it.

Lexis

1 Pairwork. Read the headings with the class and make sure everyone understands them. Students then work in pairs to put the words and phrases in the box under the correct headings.

> **crimes:** libel, contempt of court, arson, manslaughter, fraud, speeding
>
> **punishments:** suspended sentence, community service, solitary confinement
>
> **people:** jury, the accused, judge, counsel, witness
>
> **legal processes:** sue, award damages, weigh up the evidence, return a verdict, cross examine

2 Pairwork. Students add another word or phrase to each category and report back to the class. Check all the answers with the class.

Optional activity

You might like to have a vocabulary competition with points awarded for each word or expression that pairs can add to the headings. If other pairs have the same words, they each get 1 point. A pair that comes up with a word that no-one else has got gets 2 points.

3 Working in pairs or individually, students complete the gaps with words and phrases from 1. Check answers with the class.

> a) Libel
> b) the accused
> c) manslaughter
> d) sue
> e) weigh up the evidence, return a verdict
> f) suspended sentence
> g) Counsel
> h) Community service

4 Students work individually to write their gapped sentences. They then exchange them with a partner and try to complete the ones they receive.

5 🔊 **39 SB p 152**

Play the recording. Students listen and identify the crimes described. Be prepared to play the recording again if necessary.

> Conversation 1: libel
> Conversation 2: speeding
> Conversation 3: fraud

🔊 **39**

1
(D = David; M = Margaret)
D: *So, have you spoken to Mike?*
M: *Yes.*
D: *And does he reckon you have a case?*
M: *Well, he says I certainly have a case but it'll probably cost me more than it's worth to take them to court. So I'm not sure what to do.*
D: *Well, I think you should sue them, even if you only get minimal compensation. It's the principle that counts. People can't just go round spreading lies and rumours like that. What I mean is you have to stand up for yourself, you know, show that it's important to you.*
M: *Yes, I agree. The only reason I'm hesitating is because I don't want any more bad publicity.*
D: *Well it might not all be bad, and you know what they say, there's no such thing as bad*

publicity. But if you want a second opinion, the best person to ask is Fred MacIntyre.

M: *But surely it's too late now anyway? I mean it's been almost three weeks since they published the article ...*

2

(R = Rani; D = Daniel)

R: *... And then?*

D: *Well, I suppose what I should have said is 'Yes, officer. I'm sorry, but I was in a terrible hurry'.*

R: *But you didn't.*

D: *No, I tried to deny it, you know, make out that I couldn't possibly have been doing 100 miles per hour.*

R: *And?*

D: *And, he gave me an on-the-spot fine and said that if it happened again I'd lose my licence.*

R: *Ooh, how much?*

D: *Fifty pounds.*

R: *Oooh!*

D: *That's a lesson I won't forget in a hurry!*

R: *What, don't lie to a policeman?*

D: *No, it's better to be late than fifty pounds worse off!*

3

(F = Fiona; D = Doug)

F: *Yeah, being on the jury was a really weird experience.*

D: *How long did it last?*

F: *Umm, a couple of weeks. It was fascinating, seeing how a court works, you know, how formal it all is and everything. We had to stay in a hotel overnight because we couldn't come to a verdict in one day. That was quite exciting.*

D: *Really? What was it for then? Murder?*

F: *No, nothing that drastic! It was your usual story of a guy setting up a company, borrowing money from banks, getting things on credit and then using the company money to buy himself and his girlfriend some nice treats, you know, a Ferrari, a Rolex ...*

D: *A couple of diamond rings!*

F: *Exactly. But the main issue was that the accused used to be a local politician! Didn't you read about it in the papers? It was quite big news at the time.*

D: *Yeah, now you come to mention it, I do remember something ... John Limes or something like that?*

F: *Yes, John Limey.*

D: *And what did you decide?*

F: *Well, in the end the verdict we returned was unanimous – guilty!*

Paraphrasing

The caption for the cartoon is in Welsh. Students will see the translation for it when they do 4 on page 80.

Make sure students understand that to paraphrase is to say the same thing using different words.

1 Pairwork. Students read the sentences in pairs and decide which conversation they come from. Check answers with the class.

> a) Conversation 3
>
> b) Conversation 2
>
> c) Conversation 1
>
> d) Conversation 3
>
> e) Conversation 1

2 Students work individually to paraphrase the sentences in 1 starting with the words given. It is probably a good idea to do the first one with the class or demonstrate with another example of your own. Do not check answers at this stage.

3 Pairwork. Students compare their paraphrases and see if there are any differences between them. Then check answers with the class.

> a) We returned a unanimous verdict – guilty.
>
> b) I won't forget that lesson in a hurry.
>
> c) Fred MacIntyre is the best person to ask.
>
> d) Seeing how a court works was fascinating.
>
> e) They published the article almost three weeks ago.

4 Give students plenty of time to paraphrase these sentences and to think about their answers. Allow them to compare answers in pairs before checking with the class. Alternatively, give students the answers on a handout and allow them time to check their own answers and notice any differences. They can then make any necessary corrections to their own sentences.

> a) 1 It was in Wales where a recent court case was held.
>
>   2 Wales was where a recent court case was held.
>
> b) 1 A Welshman who was accused of shoplifting stood in the witness box.
>
>   2 Accused of shoplifting was a Welshman who stood in the witness box.
>
> c) 1 Defending him was a Welsh lawyer.
>
>   2 The lawyer defending him was Welsh.
>
> d) 1 'May I speak to the jury in Welsh', the lawyer asked the judge towards the end of the trial.

2 The lawyer asked the judge towards the end of the trial if he could speak to the jury in Welsh.

e) **1** Not wishing to appear biased towards English, the judge agreed.

2 In order not to appear biased towards English, the judge agreed.

f) **1** A verdict of not guilty was returned (by the jury).

2 Not guilty was the verdict that was returned (by the jury).

g) **1** What puzzled the judge was that the defendant was obviously guilty.

2 The defendant was obviously guilty, which puzzled the judge.

h) **1** Not being able to speak Welsh, the judge hadn't understood what the lawyer had said.

2 As the judge didn't speak Welsh, he hadn't understood what the lawyer had said.

5 Ask students to say what changes or additions they think will be necessary to turn their sentences into a newspaper report (avoid repeating the subject in consecutive sentences, add discourse markers, etc.). You could show students one or two real newspaper reports as examples (if you have access to the Internet it is very easy to download example newspaper reports). Then give them time to write their reports. Discourage them from looking at page 135 until they have finished.

6 Students compare their reports with the one on page 135 and notice similarities and differences. You could display the finished reports on the classroom wall for other students to read and enjoy.

Crime & punishment (p 80)

Closed books. Brainstorm as many different crimes as you can – serious or petty. One way of doing this is for each student to write a crime on a piece of paper and then pass the paper to another student who adds another crime. Repeat this until the students can think of no more crimes. Each paper should now have several crimes written on it. With the whole class, check the meaning of any unfamiliar vocabulary. Now open books and see how many of the crimes mentioned by the class are in the box.

1 Check students understand the vocabulary and then ask them to work individually to put the crimes in order of seriousness and decide on a punishment for each one.

2 Pairwork. Students compare results and report back to the class. Ask them to justify their decisions and encourage any discussion.

3 🔲 **40 SB p 152**

Read the questions with the class before you play the recording and make sure students understand the task. Then play the recording. Ask students to work in pairs and compare answers. Do not check answers at this stage.

🔲 **40**

1

Well, I think if you do something like go into somebody's garden without asking them first, then, then I think that it's not too bad so you shouldn't, you shouldn't be punished for it, but I really think that you should go and say sorry.

2

Well, I suppose it's not really an offence, is it, not, not a serious offence? I just think people do it without thinking. Um, they see other people do it so they do it themselves and then you end up with a really filthy street. People should think more about the environment, about their surroundings and perhaps rather than punishing them they should, they should have a deterrent fine or, or, you know, enough of a fine to make them think twice about doing it again, frankly.

3

Well, let's be honest, it's the most serious thing you can ever do, isn't it? I mean it's the most brutal thing you can ever do and I personally think it should be an eye for an eye, a tooth for a tooth, a life for a life. If you're going to do this kind of thing, you know, you deserve what you get.

4

Well, my mother always said that when she was a little girl, she had her mouth washed out with soap and water and I think that is still the best way. I really do.

5

Um, I'm not really sure to be honest. Er, I think, ban, a ban I think. Er, six months, a year, depending on how much you've had I suppose, but I don't really have a strong opinion about it.

6

I think give the person a bucket and a cloth and make them scrape the stuff off the walls themselves. I think it's really important. You have to see the consequences of your actions and be made to fix up your own mess. Other than that, maybe give them art classes, so they do it properly.

7

Well, I think this is, you know, a really violent theft. You know, it's a dreadful crime and I think you should be quite heavily punished for it really. Um, I think you should get at least fifteen years. I mean, this might act as a deterrent, especially for younger people thinking that it's just a bit of fun and, um, it's maybe an easy way of getting money.

8

Well, first of all I think the damage these things do should not be underestimated. This is in no way a nuisance crime. It is extremely, extremely serious. It can have worldwide effects. It can lose businesses and individuals millions of pounds and I think the punishment should reflect this. It's a difficult one because I think perhaps prison is too harsh but perhaps we should consider community service. I mean, a lot of these people that commit this kind of crime are obviously extremely talented and have a lot of knowledge and maybe that could be put to better use. Or perhaps a large fine. Er, gosh, how much I don't know, but that would be decided by the courts, but I think that would certainly make these criminals, because that's what they are, think twice about doing it again.

9

Well, I think it should be imprisonment for quite a long time because this is a crime that can also involve torture and can also involve murder as well, so it is a very serious crime and it can do an enormous amount of damage to the victim if they survive and to the victim's family, so I think it's quite a serious offence.

4 Play the recording again. Students note down the punishments suggested by the speakers. At this stage check answers to 3 and 4 with the class before asking students to do the discussion exercise. They then discuss whether they agree or disagree with the suggested punishments.

3

a) 1 trespassing 2 dropping litter 3 murder
   4 swearing in public 5 drink driving
   6 graffiti 7 mugging 8 creating and
   releasing computer viruses 9 kidnapping

b) Speaker 3 refers to murder, which is not one of the crimes listed.

4

a) 1 you should go and say sorry

   2 a fine to make them think twice about doing it again

   3 an eye for an eye, a tooth for a tooth, a life for a life (capital punishment)

   4 wash mouth out with soap and water

   5 a ban depending on how much you've had

   6 give the person a bucket and cloth and make them clean the walls, or give them art classes

   7 at least fifteen years in prison

   8 community service or a large fine

   9 imprisonment for quite a long time

b) Students' own answers.

Discussion (p 80)

1 Groupwork. Students discuss the questions. Encourage them to take notes of their discussion (they can appoint a secretary) and report back to the class.

2 Group or pairwork. Students read the cases and discuss the questions. They then report back to the class to find out if there is general agreement.

Legal wrangles (p 81)

1 Pairwork. Students discuss the questions. Ensure they understand the meaning of *insured*. Ask one or two students to report to the class anything interesting from their discussions.

2 ▭▭ **41 SB p 153**

Read the statements with the class. Then play the recording for them to listen and mark the statements true or false. Be prepared to play the recording again if necessary. Ask students to compare their answers with a partner before checking with the class.

a) false b) true c) true d) false e) true
f) true g) false h) false

▭▭ **41**

(T = Tim; A = Anne)

T: *Have you ever had anything stolen?*

A: *Er, yes I have, a brand new car! I'd had it for just under a month.*

T: *You're kidding!*

A: *No!*

T: *You were insured of course?*

A: *Of course, but the insurance company wouldn't pay up.*

T: *What do you mean wouldn't pay up? I mean, a brand new car and you didn't insure it against theft?*

A: *Of course I did, and I was insured against theft ... but they just didn't want to pay up. It was a bit of a complicated case ... Fortunately my boyfriend at the time was a lawyer so in the end we managed to sort it out.*

T: *So, what happened then?*

A: *Well, you see, these three teenagers stole my car ... they'd broken out of this special school for young offenders and well, it seems they wanted to run away, so they decided to pinch a car – my car! Anyway, while they were driving away they started arguing and drove the car straight into a tree.*

T: *Oh no!*

A: *The car was a write-off, a total write-off. I couldn't believe it when I saw it!*

T: *What about the kids?*

A: *Well, they weren't seriously hurt or anything, miraculous really, considering ... but they got arrested of course and sent back to the school. I was just relieved I'd taken out insurance and I was already thinking I'd get another car with the insurance money ... maybe buy a second hand one this time and make a bit of money on the deal!*

T: *Sounds like a good idea ... but they wouldn't pay up you said?*

A: *Yeah, when I explained to the insurance company what had happened, they told me they would need to see my insurance documents. So, I went down to the garage where my car had been towed, only to find that all my documents had mysteriously disappeared from the glove compartment.*

T: *So what did you do?*

A: *Well, I went back to the insurance people and explained the situation and they said it didn't matter because they had their own copy of the original contract and that anyway, I wasn't covered.*

T: *But didn't you say ...*

A: *Well, I thought I was covered but they said I was insured against theft, but that the car had been found, so technically it was no longer stolen. The problem was that I wasn't covered for any damage incurred in the event of theft.*

T: *Surely they can't include such a ridiculous clause?*

A: *Well, apparently they can and they did. The box with this condition had been ticked. I hadn't read all the small print in the contract.*

T: *But why not? You really should have read it before signing it you know. You were almost asking for trouble.*

A: *Thanks! Yeah, I suppose with hindsight I ought to have done, but I couldn't be bothered at the time.*

T: *But couldn't you have asked your boyfriend to check it over for you? He was a lawyer, wasn't he? Or you could have asked a friend.*

A: *Well, I suppose I could have done, but you know how these things are, they're standard forms so I thought I'd be all right. Anyway, I have no idea if I had actually ticked the box or not. I might have done but I didn't have my copy and so they might have simply ticked the box themselves to save them having to pay out the equivalent of £8,000.*

T: *They wouldn't have done that surely? That's quite a serious accusation ...*

A: *I don't know. They certainly could have done it if they'd wanted to.*

T: *It would have been far too risky, I mean, you might have found your copy of the contract.*

A: *Not if they had it.*

T: *What do you mean?*

A: *Well, the man who ran the insurance company office was the brother of the man who owned the garage where my car was towed. I reckon they must have taken it from the car, along with all the other documents.*

T: *That sounds too far-fetched, they wouldn't have dared do something like that, surely? I mean, I know you must have been upset at the time, and of course, you may be right ... but they can't have just stolen the documents like that!*

A: *I know it all sounds very improbable, but it all looked terribly suspicious at the time.*

T: *So what happened in the end then?*

A: *Well, my boyfriend decided the best way to get the money back would be to sue the boys' school, which he did, and four years later we got the money back. Not that I saw much of it.*

T: *What, all swallowed up by the lawyers?*

A: *Yeah, my husband.*

T: *Oh, you married your boyfriend!*

A: *Yeah, to avoid the legal fees!*

Word linking (p 81)

1 Pairwork. Students look at the phrases and decide when the underlined consonants are pronounced and when they are silent. Do the first one with the whole class as an example to ensure that they understand the task. Encourage students to do the exercise by saying the words aloud, listening carefully to each other, and deciding what sounds right or what they think a native speaker would say.

2 〰 **42 SB p 153**

Play the recording for students to listen and check their answers. Be prepared to give them help and clarification.

Final *t* and *d* are generally dropped when followed by a sounded consonant. They are generally pronounced when followed by a vowel sound. In *could have asked* the *d* of *could* is sounded because the unstressed *have* starts with a schwa (ə).

〰 **42**

a) a brand new car

b) they just didn't want to pay up

c) second hand

d) What did you do?

e) I went back

f) they said it didn't matter

g) I was insured against theft

h) I ought to have done

i) I couldn't be bothered

j) you could have asked a friend

3 Pairwork. Students decide which final *t* and *d* sounds are silent. Again encourage them to read the questions aloud to see what sounds right.

Silent letters are underlined

a) Wha<u>t</u> do you think abou<u>t</u> the woman in the story?

b) Wha<u>t</u> would you have done if you'<u>d</u> been her?

c) Do you read everything you sign?

d) Wha<u>t</u> was the las<u>t</u> thing you signed?

e) Have you ever ha<u>d</u> to go to a police station? Wha<u>t</u> for?

4 Pairwork. Students discuss their answers to the questions in 3. Monitor and remind students to link the words as they ask each other the questions.

Close up (p 82)

Using modals to talk about the past

1 Pairwork. Students read the modal verb phrases and match them to the functions. Do the first one with the whole class as an example.

a) 1 b) 1 c) 3 d) 3 e) 3 f) 1
g) 2 h) 2 i) 2 j) 2 k) 2 l) 2

2 Pairwork. Students discuss the questions in pairs and then check their answers with the whole class.

a) all the sentences refer to the past

b) reporting speech or thought: would, could
speculating / making deductions: might, must, would, can't, could
commenting / criticising: should, ought to, could

c) Reporting speech or thought uses modal + infinitive (although a perfect could be used as well).

When referring to the past, speculating / making deductions and commenting / criticising use modal + perfect (in these cases the modal + infinitive can't be used).

3 Pairwork. Students work in pairs to decide which two sentences are wrong and then correct the modal verbs. Check answers with the class. If students have trouble with past modals, go through the Language reference section on page 83.

a) Anne can't have been very happy when she found her car had been stolen.

b) Correct

c) Correct

d) Anne must have made a mistake about the insurance company.

4 Go through the example with the class. Students then work individually or in pairs to rewrite the sentences. Check answers with the class.

Suggested answers

a) They might / could have changed the original contract.

b) You shouldn't have signed a contract without reading it first.

c) You might / could be wrong.

d) The garage owner might / could have taken the documents.

e) The boys' parents wouldn't take any responsibility for their actions.

5 Give students one or two example sentences about yourself and then ask them to work individually to write their three sentences. Students then compare their sentences with a partner and find out more information about the ideas in them. They can report back to the class about anything interesting in their discussion.

Law (p 83)

Collocations

1 Read the expressions in the box and ask students in pairs to match them with a–i. Check answers with the class.

a) in trouble with the law

b) a law unto herself

c) no-one is above the law

d) take the law into my own hands

e) laying down the law

f) my word is law

g) against the law

h) law-abiding

i) by law

2 Students work individually to complete the sentences. Allow them to compare answers in pairs and then check with the class.

a) law-abiding

b) no-one is above the law

c) in trouble with the law

d) take the law into my own hands

e) laying down the law

f) a law unto herself

g) my word is law

h) by law

i) against the law

Note: chewing gum is against the law in Singapore.

Discussion (p 84)

1 Groupwork. Students discuss the questions and report back to the class.

2 Groupwork. Working in the same groups, students read the proposals and discuss the questions.

3 Groupwork. Groups compare together the outcomes of their discussions. You may want to form new groups with one member from each of the original groups.

4 Whole class or in small groups. Ask students for their responses to the question. Encourage them to give reasons for their opinions.

Legal anecdotes (p 84)

1 Explain to the students that they are going to read a short text describing a court case. Students then read the anecdote and decide on the best title. Give them plenty of time to do this. Allow students to compare their answer with a partner before checking with the class.

It pays to do your homework

2 Pairwork. Students discuss the questions. Check answers with the class.

a) He was trying to win compensation for an injury he claimed he had received at work.

b) He was photographed to provide evidence for the trial that he wasn't injured.

c) The lawyer for the insurance company didn't know that he had a twin brother.

d) The lawyer would have felt humiliated and embarrassed.

Lexis (p 85)

1 Give students a few minutes to look back and find the formal words in the anecdote. Do the first one as an example. Allow students to check their answers with a partner before checking with the whole class.

a) prominent   b) seeking   c) prior to
d) engaged   e) severe   f) further   g) depicted
h) commenced   i) in due course   j) to deceive

2 Students read the information about tabloid and broadsheet newspapers. Find out if the information is true for their country or countries as well, particularly as regards writing style. Students then read the newspaper extracts and decide if they are from tabloids or broadsheets. Tell them to ignore the gaps at this stage.

a) story A, story C   b) story B, story D

3 Working individually, students complete the extracts with words and phrases from 1, deciding whether formal or informal words are more appropriate. Allow them to compare answers in pairs before checking with the class.

1 well-known   2 started   3 severe   4 engaged
5 depicting   6 tricked   7 before   8 Further
9 seeking / to seek   10 in due course

Writing (p 86)

1 Pairwork. Students choose one of the stories and finish it in the appropriate style. Make sure all the stories are used. Go round offering help and encouragement. You might like to ask students to do this on a piece of paper which can be displayed on the classroom wall for other students to read. Alternatively, put students into groups of four and get each student to complete one of the stories. They then combine their stories to make a page of a newspaper. These pages can be displayed in the classroom.

2 Students rewrite the anecdote on page 84 for a tabloid newspaper. They could do this for homework. Again, the results could be displayed for other students to read.

Optional activity

Students could make a class newspaper as a mini-project:

1 Divide the class so that each pair or small group is responsible for one page of the newspaper. These pages could be, for example, front page, sports page, TV and entertainments page, showbiz and music page, foreign news page, home news page, local news, etc.

2 Decide with students whether the style of your newspaper will be tabloid or broadsheet.

3 If you are not in an English-speaking country, students could choose some interesting stories and articles from recent newspapers and translate them into English to produce their page of the newspaper. Perhaps they could also invent some stories of their own.

4 If you are in an English-speaking country, then students could choose some stories and articles and rewrite them – if the class has decided to produce a tabloid style newspaper, you could choose stories from broadsheets and rewrite them in the style of a tabloid and vice-versa.

5 An alternative is to make a newspaper about your school or local community. If so, ask students to find some stories from local newspapers, write about things they know or invent some stories!

6   Decide how long you want the mini-project to last and whether it will be just in class time or also for homework. Perhaps you could devote a part, say 30 minutes, of the next few lessons to this.

7   Once all the pages have been completed, put them together to produce the newspaper.

Close up (p 86)

Inversion after *neither/nor*, *so* & *such*

1   Pairwork. Students read the sentences and discuss the question. Check answers with the class.

> After *nor*, *so* (+ adj) and *such*, the verb and the subject are inverted.

2   Point out that inversion of subject and verb is characteristic of a more formal style. Students rewrite the sentences as they would appear in a tabloid, ie with no inversion, and with any other necessary changes to vocabulary and style. Allow them to compare their answers in pairs before checking with the class. Refer students to the Language reference section at the foot of the page.

> *Suggested answers*
> A   The attack was so horrific that reports say that police who found the body couldn't immediately identify it as the body of Martine Moon.
> B   She got such a lot of attention from men around the world that it is likely that the reason for the murder was jealousy.
> C   Reports say that the Agency have not been able to finish building the craft which will go to the planet, and they haven't been able to find the right people to be sent up in it either.

3   Students work individually to match the the two halves of the sentences. Ask them to check their answers with a partner and then check with the whole class.

> A 4   B 5   C 1   D 3   E 6   F 2

4   Students rewrite the sentences using inversions and making any other necessary changes. Remind them to look at the Language reference section on this page if they still have problems. Allow students to compare their sentences with a partner. In the meantime, write the correct sentences on the board. Ask the students to work with their partners to compare the sentences to the answers and notice any differences and correct any mistakes.

> a)   The north of the country doesn't have theatres, nor does it have opera houses.

> b)   So determined is the government to stop young people smoking that it has banned tobacco advertising.
> c)   He is neither young, nor is he good looking, but he's very popular.
> d)   So happy were they with the results that they have recommended the company to all their colleagues.
> e)   Such was the outcry over the new proposals that the government is having to reconsider its plans.
> f)   Such was the confusion over who was telling the truth that the jury failed to reach a verdict.

5   Students work individually to write sentences about current news stories. Prepare one or two examples of your own. You could find and bring to the class some articles that contain sentences that can be transformed, give them to the students and ask them to identify the sentences and then make the transformations.

6   Groupwork. Students compare and discuss their sentences.

Love in the first degree (p 87)

Closed books. Write the title on the board. Explain that it is the title of the song. Ask students to guess what the song is about. (It is the title of a song comparing being in love to being in prison. *First degree* is a term used in the United States to describe the most serious kind of murder – that where the murderer deliberately planned the murder in advance.) Students listen to the song with their books closed and see if their suggestions were right. Then they open their books.

1   Students read the information about Bananarama and complete the song with the words and phrases from the box. Do not check answers at this stage.

2   ▭▭ **43 SB p 153**

Play the recording for students to check their answers. Play it again for them to sing along if they wish.

> ▭▭ **43**
> *Love in the first degree* by Bananarama
> *Last night I was dreaming I was locked in a prison cell*
> *When I woke up I was screaming, calling out your name*
> *Whoa, and the judge and the jury*
> *They all put the blame on me*
> *They wouldn't go for my story*
> *They wouldn't hear my plea*
>
> *Only you can set me free*
> *'Cos I'm guilty*
> *Guilty as a girl can be*
> *Come on baby can't you see*
> *I stand accused of love in the first degree*
> *Guilty*
> *Of love in the first degree*

Someday I believe it, you will come to my rescue
Unchain my heart you're keeping and let me start
anew
The hours pass so slowly
Since they've thrown away the key
Can't you see that I'm lonely
Won't you help me please

Only you can set me free
'Cos I'm guilty
Guilty as a girl can be
Come on baby can't you see
I stand accused of love in the first degree
Guilty
Of love in the first degree

Guilty of love, guilty of love in
Guilty of love, guilty of love in
Guilty, of love in the first degree
And the judge and the jury
They all put the blame on me
They wouldn't go for my story
They wouldn't hear my plea

3 Ask students if they think the prison metaphor is a good one. In what way is being in love like being in prison? Note that a metaphor is the application of a descriptive term or phrase to an object or action. This is used imaginatively but not literally. This is different from a simile which is an overt comparison using the preposition 'like' or 'as' to compare two things. Students then complete the sentences which are all similies.

Possible answers

a) Love is like a battlefield in the war between men and women.

b) Life is like the sea; sometimes it's calm and at other times it's rough and difficult to deal with.

c) Money is like grains of sand as it slips through your fingers.

4 Students write a comparison of their own.

Test

Scoring: one point per correct answer unless otherwise indicated.

1   1 damages   2 confinement   3 weigh
  4 examined   5 sentence   6 verdict
  7 manslaughter   8 arson   9 speeding
  10 fraud   11 kidnapping   12 trespassing
  13 libel   14 mugging

2   1   I didn't like it and neither did they.

  2   Such was the weather that we didn't leave the house for days.

  3   So gorgeous was he that I couldn't take my eyes off him.

  4   We left early and so did my friends.

3   1 couldn't   2 would   3 can't   4 would
  5 must   6 shouldn't   7 might   8 could
  9 must   10 could

4   Hi Sue,

  Just a short note to say thank you for the wonderful time I had at your school. I have now got a new job working for a very *well-known* company in my country. They were *looking for* someone to translate reports into English. The job *starts* next week.

  Before leaving the UK, I was feeling quite nervous about returning to my country and I have to say that I still haven't got used to being back here.

  Hope you like the postcard. It *shows* my home city. I'll write again *later*.

  Best wishes, Mamiko

5   1 c)   2 b)   3 e)   4 a)   5 f)   6 d)

Law Test

Name: _____   **Total:** _____ /40

1 Lexis – crime and punishment *14 points*

Complete the missing words.

1   He was awarded d_____ of $100,000.

2   He spent three months in solitary c_____ .

3   We need to w_____ up the evidence very carefully.

4   The defendant was cross e_____ for forty minutes.

5   She was given a suspended s_____ .

6   The jury returned a v_____ of not guilty.

Add the missing vowels.

7 m_nsl_ _ ght_r   8 _rs_n   9 sp_ _ d_ng   10 fr_ _d

Write the crime for these definitions.

11   Taking someone against their will and demanding money for their release.

_____

12   Unlawfully entering land or a property.

_____

13   Publishing a false statement which can damage someone's reputation.

_____

14   Robbing someone with violence, in a public place.

_____

2 Inversion after *neither*, *nor*, *so* and *such* *4 points*

Correct the mistakes in these sentences.

1   I didn't like it and neither they did.

2   Such the weather was that we didn't leave the house for days.

Complete b) so it has the same meaning as a).

3   a)   He was so gorgeous that I couldn't take my eyes off him.

    b)   So _____ .

4   a)   We left early and my friends did too.

    b)   We left early and so _____ .

3 Using modals to talk about the past *10 points*

Choose the correct alternative.

1   I'm afraid I **couldn't** / **shouldn't** find it. Sorry.

2   What **would** / **ought** you have done in my position?

3   He **can't** / **mustn't** have seen us.

4   Surely he **would** / **must** have come over and talked to us if he had.

5   They **must** / **could** have been so worried about her.

6   You really **mustn't** / **shouldn't** have done that.

7   It **can** / **might** have been him, but I can't say for sure.

8   You **could** / **would** have told me! Why didn't you?

9   It simply **must** / **should** have been him.

10   Those guys in the pub **could** / **should** have stolen my purse. They looked very suspicious.

4 Formal and informal language *6 points*

Read the postcard and find six examples of where the writer has inappropriately used formal language. Replace it with the correct form of the more neutral language in the box.

> before   look for   show   later   start   well-known

Hi Sue,

Just a short note to say thank you for the wonderful time I had at your school. I have now got a new job working for a very prominent company in my country. They were seeking someone to translate reports into English. The job commences next week.

Prior to leaving the UK, I was feeling quite nervous about returning to my country and I have to say that I still haven't got used to being back here.

Hope you like the postcard. It depicts my home city. I'll write again in due course.

Best wishes, Mamiko

5 Lexis – law collocations *6 points*

Join the two halves to make complete sentences.

1   She's a law   a)   down the law.

2   He's often   b)   in trouble with the law.

3   She took the law   c)   unto herself.

4   She's always laying   d)   above the law.

5   Don't do that. It's   e)   into her own hands.

6   He sometimes thinks he's   f)   against the law.

10 *Firsts* Overview

The topic of this unit is firsts, both in the sense of winning and being the first to do something. The grammar focus is on contrast and patterns with *get*.

Students start by looking at some quotations which are about winning and succeeding. They discuss which offer the best advice. They then read about the first of a new type of car rally which ordinary people can take part in. They practise using some of the vocabulary from the text and then look at extracts from the text which show ways of expressing contrast. They practise using *but*, *whereas* and *however* to make contrasts.

Students look at collocations with *first* before reading a text about an extreme physical challenge: being the first to climb Mount Everest without oxygen. They discuss why people undertake such challenges and listen to two people talking about a psychological study on what drives people to do such things. Students then discuss other great human achievements and challenges they themselves have faced.

A section on practising word stress is followed by listening to three people talking about coming first and doing things for the first time. Students match the conversations to pictures before examining some of the lexis in more detail. They then practise using patterns with *get* and finding alternatives to such expressions.

The anecdote in this unit is about coming first or doing something for the first time and is followed by an opportunity for students to test their knowledge of the passive. Finally, students read a description of different personality types and do a short quiz about them. They then write their own questions for the same quiz.

Section	Aims	What the students are doing
Introduction page 88	*Conversation skills:* fluency work	Matching first and second halves of quotations.
		Discussing which quotation offers the best advice.
It's not the winning ... pages 88–89	*Reading skills:* reading for gist	Reading an article about the World Cup Rally and checking comprehension.
	Lexis: phrases from the reading text	Matching phrases from the reading text and completing sentences with them.
Close up pages 90–91	*Grammar:* contrast	Contrasting things using *but*, *whereas* and *however*.
Firsts page 91	*Lexis:* collocations with *first*	Matching expressions with *first* and completing sentences with them.
Great firsts pages 92–93	*Reading skills:* reading for detail	Reading about the first person to climb Mount Everest without oxygen.
	Lexis: vocabulary of physical challenges	Completing an extract with vocabulary of physical challenges.
		Discussing why people take on extreme physical challenges.
	Listening skills: listening for detail	Listening to two people discussing a psychological study on why people take on physical challenges.
	Pronunciation: word stress	Identifying and practising word stress.
First prize page 94	*Listening skills:* listening for gist	Listening to three conversations and matching them to pictures.
	Lexis: idioms and phrasal verbs	Choosing the correct word to complete idioms in sentences.
Close up pages 94–96	*Grammar:* patterns with *get*	Examining the use of expressions with *get*.
		Replacing *get* in sentences with alternative words.
		Rewriting sentences using *get*.
	Conversation skills: fluency work	Anecdote: talking about coming first or doing something for the first time.
Test yourself pages 96–97	*Grammar:* passives	Completing a text with verbs in the passive.
		Rewriting sentences using the passive.
Making the first move page 97	*Reading skills:* reading for gist	Reading a quiz about personality types.
	Writing skills: writing questions	Writing more questions for the quiz.
	Conversation skills: discussion	Discussing the outcome of the quiz.

10 *Firsts* Teacher's notes

Ask students to look at the photographs on the first page of this unit and say what they have in common and what the connection is with the unit title (they both show someone winning – coming first at something). Ask them to identify the circumstances and to say how they think the people feel.

1 Students work in pairs to match the two halves of the quotations. Check answers with the class.

> a) 4   b) 5   c) 2/6   d) 6/2   e) 1   f) 3

2 Whole class. Ask students to discuss the questions.

It's not the winning ... (p 88)

1 Pairwork. Students discuss the questions and report back to the class. Encourage students to find out as much information as possible.

2 Ask the students to read the article and note down the four differences. Allow them to check their answers with a partner before checking with the class.

> ordinary drivers
>
> paying for themselves / no sponsorship deals allowed
>
> ordinary showroom cars
>
> no technical support allowed

3 Pairwork. Students discuss the questions and report back to the class.

> a)   two: a navigator and a driver
> b)   to give normal drivers a chance to take part in a big rally and to boost the sales of normal family cars
> c)   to promote the rally
> d)   it hasn't been possible because of the high cost
> e)   Students' own answers.

Lexis (p 89)

1 Tell the students that they should try to match the two halves of the phrases without looking back at the text. Students then check their answers against the text.

> a) 6   b) 4   c) 8   d) 1   e) 2   f) 5   g) 3   h) 7

2 Students complete the sentences using the phrases in 1. Allow them to check answers with a partner before checking with the class.

> a)   Ardent fans
> b)   armchair rally driver
> c)   High profile
> d)   once in a lifetime
> e)   mass production
> f)   multi-million
> g)   against the clock
> h)   precise details

3 Pairwork. Students discuss the questions and report back to the class.

Close up (p 90)

Contrast

1 Go through the instructions with the class and do the first one as an example. Students then work individually to find what is being contrasted and to identify the discourse markers. Remind them of the work they did on discourse markers in Unit 8 and refer them to the Language reference section on page 91 if they have difficulty. Allow them to compare answers in pairs before checking with the class.

> **a)**
>
> | | |
> |---|---|
> | Sentence A: | the name / the concept |
> | Sentence B: | multi-million pound sponsorship deals / paying their own way |
> | Sentence C: | high-tech or vintage cars / ordinary, everyday cars |
> | Sentence D: | drivers in the old rally / drivers in the new rally |
> | Sentence E: | professional rally drivers / ordinary car drivers |
> | Sentence F: | all other aspects of the old rally / all other aspects of the new rally |
>
> **b)**
>
> | | |
> |---|---|
> | Sentence A: | but |
> | Sentence B: | but |
> | Sentence C: | whereas |
> | Sentence D: | However |
> | Sentence E: | Whereas |
> | Sentence F: | however |

2 Students work in pairs to complete the sentences by putting *but*, *whereas* or *however* in the gaps.

> a) However / But   b) but / whereas
> c) Whereas   d) however   e) however / but

3 Still working in pairs, students look back at the sentences in 2 and see how *but*, *whereas* and *however* are used. They then complete the sentences. Ask students to check their answers in the Language reference section on page 91 and then check answers with the class.

> a) However (unless it's at the end of the sentence)
> b) Whereas
> c) However, but
> d) However, But, whereas

4 Give the students a few minutes to complete the sentences and compare them with a partner. Check answers with the class.

> a) however   b) but   c) However
> d) Whereas   e) but   f) but

5 Pairwork. Students work individually to rewrite the sentences in 4 so that they are true for themselves. They then discuss them in pairs.

Closed books. Ask the students to work in pairs and to find six 'contrasts' between them. The following can be given as suggested topics: likes / dislikes, places they want to visit, what they are doing next weekend, how they feel about studying, habits, etc. The students each write sentences stating these contrasts, but each student must use a different discourse marker for each fact. For example, Silvia: *Whereas I really like watching football, Juan really hates it.* Juan: *I hate football, but Silvia really likes it.* Ask the students to read out some of their sentences.

Optional activity

Students each write a paragraph about their favourite sport or pastime, explaining why they prefer it to other sports / pastimes. They should include all three discourse markers at least once. Go round offering help and encouragement and making sure they use the three discourse markers correctly. They then compare paragraphs in pairs and discuss differences and similarities.

Firsts (p 91)

Collocations

1 Students match the expressions and meanings. Check answers in pairs and then with the class.

> a) 6   b) 7   c) 8   d) 9   e) 3   f) 1   g) 10
> h) 5   i) 4   j) 2

2 Students work in pairs to complete the sentences. Check the answers with the whole class by asking students to say which expression from 1 they used for each sentence.

> a) first aid   b) first night   c) first language
> d) first class   e) first-hand   f) first lady

3 Pairwork. Students choose questions to answer and take turns asking and answering.

4 Students work in pairs or small groups to discuss the questions. Check answers with the whole class, making sure that the students are clear about how the meaning changes when *first* is replaced by *second*.

> second language: means a new language the speaker has learnt
> second class: means inferior
> second-hand: means not new

5 Elicit other expressions students know with *first* or *second*.

> Other expressions with first and second include:
> first come, first served; first things first; 'I don't know the first thing about it'; first born; second to none; second best; second nature; second rate; on second thoughts

Great firsts (p 92)

Closed books. Divide the class into groups and give the groups a few minutes to think of, say, 4–6 *Who was the first ...?* questions, for example *Who was the first person on the moon?* Pair the groups. They then ask each other their questions with the team that answers the most correctly being the winner.

1 Whole class. Read the information about Reinhold Messner and the questions. Students then read the text and find the answers. Allow them to check answers in pairs before checking with the whole class.

> a) He was hoping to be the first to climb Everest without bottled oxygen.
> b) He faced opposition because others thought he was putting himself at risk of severe brain damage and other extreme physiological demands.
> c) Getting dressed took them two hours, they had to use hand signals to communicate, progress was slow, trekking through snow was exhausting so they had to climb more difficult rock ridges, they felt extreme exhaustion, they had to gasp for breath, Messner felt apathetic, breathing was so difficult they hardly had the strength to go on, Messner felt like his mind was dead.

2 Groupwork. Students discuss the questions and report back to the class.

3 ▭ **44 SB p 154**

Go through the questions with the class before you play the recording. Students make a note of their answers. Do not check answers at this stage.

▭ **44**

(D = David; S = Sue)

D: *Have you seen this article about why men want to climb Everest?*

S: *Well, because it's there, surely?*

D: *That's not what the article reckons. It reckons that they do it for the attention.*

S: *What? Well, I suppose that could be true but I can think of a lot of easier ways of getting attention!*

D: *Yeah, but this article says that psychologists reckon their desire to climb high mountains can be traced back to the fact that they just weren't shown enough love by their mothers.*

S: *Oh, give over!*

D: *No really, there's an article here on the Internet. It says they're making up for this lack of motherly love and attention by doing daring, dangerous feats.*

S: *Whatever next!*

D: *And it has some pretty harsh things to say about the kind of people who are attracted to mountaineering.*

S: *Yeah?*

D: *Yeah. Listen to this, 'Mountain men are "overdependent on external admiration ... intensely envious, exploitative in relations with others".'*

S: *Wow! That's a bit harsh, they have after all been neglected by their mothers. Did they canvass any mountaineers on this finding?*

D: *Yeah, there are a couple of good quotes actually. What about this one: 'Maybe mountaineers should do a study of narcissism, competition and the desire for fame among academics', Alan Hinkes.*

S: *Who?*

D: *Alan Hinkes, you know, that English climber ...*

S: *Oh yeah, he's trying to be the first Englishman to climb all the highest peaks isn't he?*

D: *Yeah, that's the one.*

S: *So, does he have anything to say in his defence?*

D: *Well, his answer's pretty straightforward really, he just says he does it for fun; 'You are out exercising in the middle of fantastic scenery with some good mates. It is a very simple pleasure ... that's all.'*

S: *Mmm, a nice leisurely hike in the summer I can understand. Hiking up an enormous mountain, no.*

D: *Mmm, and then there's the danger element too. I can kind of understand the challenge of seeing how far you can push your body, you know, test yourself to the limits and all that, but not to the point of putting your life in danger.*

S: *Yeah, I reckon they must be really driven by something, a need to prove themselves, a need to achieve something really special. I don't think that's necessarily negative, I mean we wouldn't make any progress at all, would we, if we didn't try to do the impossible ... that's how progress happens.*

D: *Yeah, good point, but at what cost? I mean it's one thing to put your own life in danger, but what about the effects on other people? I mean, some of these people have families, and what about the sherpas and the local guides?*

4 Pairwork. Students compare their answers and decide if the speakers mentioned any of the points raised in their discussion in 2. Be prepared to play the recording twice if necessary. Check answers with the class. Ask students to comment on the opinions expressed by the speakers.

---

a) That climbers do it for attention because they weren't given enough love by their mothers and need external admiration.

b) For fun, for the danger element, to test yourself, a need to prove oneself, a need to achieve something special.

Lexis (p 93)

1 Students complete the extract. Do not check answers at this stage.

2 ▭ **45 SB p 154**

Play the recording for students to listen and check their answers. Then check answers with the whole class.

---

1 challenge   2 push your body   3 test yourself to the limits   4 putting your life in danger
5 driven   6 prove   7 achieve   8 progress

▭ **45**

D: *Mmm, and then there's the danger element too. I can kind of understand the challenge of seeing how far you can push your body, you know, test yourself to the limits and all that, but not to the point of putting your life in danger.*

S: *Yeah, I reckon they must be really driven by something, a need to prove themselves, a need to achieve something really special. I don't think that's necessarily negative, I mean we wouldn't make any progress at all, would we, if we didn't try to do the impossible ...*

3 Students complete the sentences. Make sure they realise they may have to modify the words and phrases. Allow them to compare answers in pairs before checking with the class.

> a) driven
> b) test themselves to the limits
> c) progress
> d) challenges

4 Pairwork. Students discuss whether or not they agree with the sentences in 3. Finish the exercise by asking for a show of hands for each statement and asking students to report on their discussion.

5 Pairwork. Students read the list of achievements and discuss the questions. Finish the activity with class discussion of this. Note: *apnoea* is pronounced /ɑpˈniːə/.

Word stress (p 93)

1 Students work individually. Encourage them to find the word stress by saying the words aloud and deciding what sounds right.

2 🔲 **46 SB p 154**

Play the recording for students to listen and check their answers.

> 🔲 **46**
> The main stress is underlined.
> a) <u>al</u>titude b) coordi<u>na</u>tion c) ex<u>ci</u>ting
> d) <u>chal</u>lenge e) e<u>mer</u>gency f) a<u>chieve</u>ment
> g) appa<u>ra</u>tus h) mountai<u>neers</u>
> i) circum<u>na</u>vigate j) as<u>cent</u>

3 Pairwork. Students turn to their respective pages and follow the instructions. They take turns to read words to their partner and mark the stress.

> The main stress is underlined.
> **Student A**
> a) <u>con</u>quer b) <u>ma</u>rathon c) im<u>pos</u>sible
> d) inter<u>na</u>tional e) at<u>ten</u>tion
> **Student B**
> a) <u>sum</u>mit b) pio<u>neer</u> c) ex<u>pe</u>dition
> d) <u>dan</u>gerous e) communi<u>ca</u>tion

Closed books. Ask the students, working in the same pairs as in the A/B exercise they have just completed, to add words with the same stress pattern to each of the words in the exercise. They could be given a time limit, with the winners being the pair with the most words. Alternatively, they continue until they have, say, at least four words for each stress pattern.

First prize (p 94)

Closed books. Ask students if they have ever won first prize for anything. If they have, ask them what they won.

1 🔲 **47 SB p 154**

Play the recording. Students match the conversations to the pictures.

> Conversation 1 = picture C
> Conversation 2 = picture A
> Conversation 3 = picture B

> 🔲 **47**
> **1**
> (M = Martin; K = Kate)
> M: *Well, I never win anything. Did you ever win anything?*
> K: *Well, yes I did, actually. Yes, I came in first in this little competition in the local newspaper, and it was this competition where you had to, um, finish the phrase 'School is ...'.*
> M: *Right.*
> K: *And design a poster and so I said, because I was quite a good student at the time, I said 'School is the key to a new and better world.' And I had a little rocket ship blasting off and everything ...*
> M: *So you were how old then?*
> K: *I was eleven.*
> M: *Oh, eleven, right, right. So what did you win then?*
> K: *Well, I won a twenty dollar gift certificate to Hathaway House Bookshop, and I spent the whole summer kind of eking it out because twenty dollars was quite a lot back then, so I still have the books that I bought and I still have the 'Wuthering Heights' and ... yes, so ...*
> M: *So how do you feel when you look at those books?*
> K: *It was a proud moment for me and my mother.*
> M: *Lucky you.*
> **2**
> (J = Jenny; H = Howard)
> J: *... I got my fifty pence back. Have you ever won anything?*
> H: *Oh, do you know I've won a couple of things actually. The first thing that springs to mind is, um, I was quite young and away on holiday*

with my family and extended family, um, at a holiday camp.

J: *Oh, right.*

H: *Lots of organised games and things like that and I think my sister and the older kids were off doing something else and, er, my mother entered me into the Tarzan Call competition.*

J: *I'm sorry, the what?*

H: *The Tarzan Call competition. Don't you remember? Ooooooh, oooooh, ooooh. I used to be much better at it than that. So, anyway, there I was in this big draughty hall with loads of other kids who were all up on stage. I remember we were extremely late for this thing and, er, I was fully clothed and my mother undressed me. I was quite young, about five, down to my pants.*

J: *Why?*

H: *My underpants. Well, because Tarzan always ran around in a loincloth.*

J: *Oh, I see. All the other kids were ...*

H: *They were all there in their trunks or something like that, so there I was, on stage doing the Tarzan Call competition and extremely nervous – first time in front of an audience, but I won. I can't quite remember what I did win, I just remember the feeling of coming first. It was great.*

J: *Exciting.*

H: *Yeah.*

3

(E = Emma; R = Rob)

E: *Well, I suppose you've had lots of girlfriends, but I mean, can you even remember the first one?*

R: *The first one? Oh, oh yes I can. OK. Thirteen years old, a girl called Lucy Dunkerly who I fancied for ages. I was thirteen.*

E: *Oh, how old was she?*

R: *Twelve. I had fancied her for ages. I eventually plucked up the courage to ask her out and she said yes and I was so shocked it was ridiculous. And, I sort of, I used to live in this village really far away from sort of the town where we sort of used to live near and I had to get my dad to drive me out so that we could pick her up and I took her to see this terrible film, I can't even remember the title of it, but it had Michael J. Fox in it and it was really bad. I remember always sort of people giving advice to you saying, 'Oh, don't sit on the back row,' and all this kind of thing because it will make ... and everyone will poke fun and everything and it was so embarrassing and eventually we sort of sat in the middle of the cinema and watched this film and it was really nice. And at the end of the night got picked up and sort of taken*

home, and that's when I sort of got my first kiss as well, which was very, very frightening. I probably did really badly as well, but, um, ...

E: *Well, it's not a competition. How did you feel, sort of, did you see her again?*

R: *Yeah, we did. We continued going out for about three weeks.*

E: *That long!*

R: *Which is nothing, really, is it? But ...*

E: *It's a lot when you're eleven or thirteen.*

2 Whole class. Ask students to identify which conversations were about coming first and which about doing something for the first time.

> a) Conversations 1 and 2
>
> b) Conversation 3

Lexis (p 94)

1 Allow students a few minutes to complete the expressions individually and then ask them to compare their answers with a partner. Then check with the whole class.

> a) out   b) up   c) to   d) out   e) around
> f) up   g) off

2 Pairwork. Allow students to discuss the meanings of the expressions in pairs before checking with the whole class.

> a) eke out = to make something last as long as possible
>
> b) pluck up the courage = to feel brave enough to do something
>
> c) springs to mind = to think of something suddenly
>
> d) ask someone out = to invite someone to go on a date with you
>
> e) run around = to move about quickly and freely from one place to another (of a child)
>
> f) pick up = collect
>
> g) to be off (somewhere) = to be away from your usual place (home, work, etc.)

3 Pairwork. Students discuss whether the sentences are true for them. Ask some students to report back on their discussion to the class.

Close up (p 94)

Patterns with *get*

1 Students look at the three sentences and decide where *get* can be replaced by *received*, *ask* and *were*.

a) 3 b) 1 c) 2

2 Students work individually to replace *get* with one of the words in the box. Check answers in pairs and then with the class. Ask them to notice what patterns follow *get* for each different meaning. Refer students to the Language reference section on page 95 to clarify any problems they may have.

a) manage b) ask c) became d) received
e) have f) was

3 Go through the example with the class so they can see how sentences can be rephrased to avoid using *get*. Students then work individually to rephrase the sentences. Allow them to check answers in pairs before checking with the whole class.

Suggested answers
a) He's a great instructor, so patient. He's the one who encouraged / convinced me to start skiing again after the accident.
b) I don't know if I'm going to have the opportunity to finish this report before we go out.
c) Come on! It's about time we started on this new design, isn't it?
d) Let's start painting, otherwise we won't finish before dark.
e) I persuaded / convinced everyone to listen to the band's new album and now they've all bought it!

4 Pairwork. Students rewrite the sentences using *get*. Do the first one or two as examples and make sure they understand this may involve changes to the sentence structure. Check answers with the class.

a) I got the chance to go abroad for the first time when I was ten.
b) I was hopeless at sports when I was at primary school; I never got chosen for any of the teams.
c) I got my brother to do my homework for me when I was younger.
d) At this time of year we get busloads of tourists visiting our town.
e) We're having a few problems with our car; it's really difficult to get it started it in the mornings.
f) I saw a great film last week – it really got me thinking.
g) I always get really nervous the night before an exam.
h) I usually get my hair cut once a month.

i) It's so hot at the moment, I'm finding it really difficult to get to sleep at night.
j) I'm quite shy when I first meet someone but once we get talking, I'm fine.

5 Pairwork. Students discuss whether any of the sentences they wrote are true for them. You might like to ask them to rewrite the ones that are not true in order to make them true.

Anecdote (p 96)

See Introduction, page 4, for more ideas on how to set up, monitor and repeat Anecdotes.

1 Give students plenty of time to think about what they are going to say, to read the prompt questions and to prepare their stories.

2 Pairwork. Students take turns to describe their experiences of coming first or doing something for the first time.

3 Pairwork. Students find three similarities or differences (or both) between their stories and report these to the class.

Test yourself (p 96)

Passives

1 Ask students to skim the story quickly, ignoring the gaps, and to answer the questions. Allow students to check their answers in pairs before checking with the whole class.

a) more developed
b) we don't know – it's still to be confirmed
c) Students' own answers

2 Students work in pairs to complete the story by putting the verbs in brackets in the appropriate passive form. You might like to do the first one as an example. Check answers with the class.

1 were still being finalised
2 was first established
3 was only made
4 are issued
5 has been reported / is reported
6 is believed
7 are still to be confirmed
8 has previously been stated / was previously stated
9 is expected / will be expected / could be expected
10 has been released

3 Students work in pairs to rewrite the sentences using the words given and a passive. Check answers with the class.

a) Brazil is / are expected to win the next World Cup.

b) Unemployment is reported to have risen steeply.

c) 1,000 people are estimated to have lost their homes due to the recent floods.

d) It is assumed that only ten people were injured following last night's rail accident.

e) It is reported that the actress has been offered a role in Cedric Scheybeler's new film.

4 Whole class or small groups. Students discuss whether they have read or heard any similar stories in the news recently.

Making the first move (p 97)

1 Go through the instructions with the class. Students then read the three descriptions and discuss with a partner which they think best describes themselves. If the students know each other well, they can choose which best describes their partner.

2 Students read the first two questions in the quiz and answer them first for themselves. They then decide what a typical initiator, follower or ditherer's answer would be. Do not check answers at this stage.

3 Pairwork. Students compare their answers. Check with the class.

a) Students' own answers

b) **Question 1**

Initiator: answer a

Follower: answer b

Ditherer: answer c

Question 2

Initiator: answer b

Follower: answer a

Ditherer: answer c

4 Groupwork. Students write four more quiz questions using new situations and giving an answer for each personality type. Make sure all the students have a copy of the questions they are writing for the next stage.

5 Groupwork. Students work with partners from a different group and discuss their answers to both their own and their partner's questions.

6 Ask students to say whether they have changed their minds about their personality types. If so, ask them to say why.

Test

Scoring: one point per correct answer unless otherwise indicated.

1 1 Whereas   2 however   3 but / whereas
   4 However   5 But   6 whereas / but

2 1 emergency   2 coordination   3 summit
   4 pioneer   5 apparatus   6 international
   7 impossible   8 conquer   9 mountaineers
   10 communication   11 marathon   12 dangerous

3 1 to go   2 to agree   3 packed   4 going
   5 to wait   6 stolen   7 running   8 invited
   9 developed   10 to give

4 1 lifetime   2 foremost   3 clock   4 class
   5 high   6 light   7 aid   8 plucked   9 mind
   10 hand   11 limit(s)   12 first

10 *Firsts* Test

Name: _____   **Total:** _____ /40

---

1 Discourse markers *6 points*

Complete the sentences by adding *but*, *however* or *whereas*.

1 _____ most people prefer the band's second CD, I much prefer their first one.

2 I loved living in the city as a child. My sister, _____ , hated every minute of it.

3 I love cooking, _____ I hate the washing up.

4 They don't take reservations. _____ , we could go anyway and take our chances.

5 If the weather's bad, jogging isn't much fun. _____ if it's a nice warm day, it's a great way to exercise.

6 A lot of people like office life, _____ I prefer working from home.

2 Word stress *12 points*

<u>Underline</u> the main stress in these words.

1 emergency

2 coordination

3 summit

4 pioneer

5 apparatus

6 international

7 impossible

8 conquer

9 mountaineers

10 communication

11 marathon

12 dangerous

3 Patterns with *get* *10 points*

Put the verbs in brackets into the correct form.

A: I hear you got (1) _____ (go) to Paris at long last.

B: Yeah, I finally got James (2) _____ (agree) to come with me. First, we nearly missed the plane. I've never known anyone take so long to get their bags (3) _____ (pack). We didn't get (4) _____ (go) until about an hour before the plane was due to leave and we just made it. They had

to get the plane (5) _____ (wait) for us. And would you believe it, as soon as we arrived, James got his bag (6) _____ (steal).

A: Oh, dear. So it wasn't the romantic weekend you'd hoped for?

B: Well, James then got me (7) _____ (run) all over Paris buying stuff to replace the things he'd had stolen. As I was doing this I met some really nice French people and I got (8) _____ (invite) to a party they were having. James was in a bad mood and he refused to go with me.

A: And ...?

B: Well, you'll see when I get the photos (9) _____ (develop). Oh, and I'm getting your friend Pierre (10) _____ (give) me some French lessons!

4 Lexis – general *12 points*

Complete the missing words.

1 It's a once in a l_____ opportunity. You'd be mad not to go.

2 First and f_____ , I'd like to thank you all for the help you gave me.

3 It was a bit of a race against the c_____ , but we finished it just in time.

4 Her work is always first c_____ . You can't fault it.

5 He's very h_____ profile. Always in the papers.

6 It's a long journey. We'd better set off at first l_____ .

7 He's away on a first a_____ course at the moment.

8 I finally p_____ up the courage and asked him out.

9 Nothing springs to m_____ at the moment, I'm afraid.

10 I heard it first-h_____ . It's true, believe me.

11 He's always testing himself to the l_____ . If he's not skiing, he's hang-gliding or skydiving!

12 At f_____ , we were really nervous, but we loved it in the end.

Photocopiable

11 Stories *Overview*

The topic of this unit is stories and storytelling. The grammar focus is on the future seen from the past.

Students start by looking at and discussing some pictures from traditional stories. They then examine the qualities needed by a good storyteller and listen to an interview with Helen East, a professional storyteller. They take notes on what she says and write an article on storytelling.

Students look at the structure of a good story and put the story of Androcles and the lion in the most logical order. They listen to Helen telling a story and identify the structural features they have already discussed and the way she uses her voice to add to the atmosphere. They then read some examples of urban myths and practise telling them to each other. They then write an e-mail version of them for a website.

Students read the short story *Hearts and Hands* by O. Henry and discuss the actions of the characters in the story. They then do some work on compound adjectives. Next, students read an article and listen to a radio programme about the millennium celebrations in London. They discuss what went wrong and look at vocabulary to describe things that don't go according to plan.

A section on the future as seen from the past is followed by listening to three people talking about plans which had to be changed. Students then tell each other about a time when they had to change their plans, when things didn't live up to their expectations or when things worked out better than they had expected. Finally, they work in groups to write a short story, using a picture and a description as inspiration.

Section	Aims	What the students are doing
Introduction page 98	*Conversation skills:* fluency work	Discussing questions related to illustrations of stories.
Story telling page 98	*Listening skills:* listening for detail;	Discussing the qualities of a good storyteller.
	taking notes	Listening to an interview with a professional storyteller and taking notes.
	Writing skills: article	Writing an article on storytelling.
Close up pages 99–100	*Grammar:* telling stories	Analysing the different sections of a story.
		Putting a story in the correct order.
	Listening skills: listening for detail	Listening to a story and identifying the sections and the features of storytelling.
	Pronunciation skills: intonation	Matching extracts from the story to features used by storytellers in their voices to add atmosphere.
		Practising features of intonation in storytelling.
Urban myths page 101	*Reading skills:* reading for detail	Reading an urban myth and retelling it to a partner.
	Speaking skills: storytelling	Talking about and telling urban myths.
	Writing skills: narrative	Writing an urban myth for use on a website.
Telling tales pages 101–103	*Reading skills:* reading for gist & detail	Reading *Hearts and Hands*, a short story by O. Henry and deciding whether statements are true or false.
	Lexis: compound adjectives	Identifying compound adjectives used in the story and using them to replace clauses in sentences.
	Conversation skills: fluency work	Discussing lies.
The best laid plans ... pages 103–104	*Reading skills:* reading for detail	Reading an article about London's millennium celebrations and identifying events and times.
	Listening skills: listening for detail	Listening to a radio programme about the millennium celebrations and matching phrases to people and events.
	Lexis: vocabulary of things going wrong	Matching words and phrases with definitions. Completing a TV review with words and phrases.
Close up pages 104–105	*Grammar:* the future seen from the past	Examining ways of expressing the future seen from the past.
		Completing extracts from a radio programme.
		Reordering sentences to make them logical.
A change of plan page 106	*Listening skills:* listening for detail	Listening to stories of plans that had to be changed.
	Conversation skills: fluency work	Anecdote: talking about a change in plans, a time when things didn't live up to expectations or a time when things went better than expected.
The glass elevator page 107	*Writing skills:* narrative	Preparing for writing a story by looking at a photograph and listening to a description.
		Writing a story collaboratively in groups.

11 Stories Teacher's notes

Closed books. Ask students to close their eyes and think back to their childhood and think about the stories that their parents, grandparents or teachers told them or read to them. Which ones do they remember most clearly? Which ones did they enjoy most? Who were the main characters? Were there any which frightened them? Working in pairs, the students discuss this, telling each other any stories their partner is unfamiliar with. Ask a few students to report their discussions back to the whole class. You could get one or two students to tell unfamiliar stories briefly to the whole class.

1 Pairwork. Students look at the pictures and discuss the questions.

a) Picture 1: Pinocchio
   Picture 2: Robin Hood
   Picture 3: Aladdin

b) Robin Hood: an English legend, loosely based on fact, that dates back to the time of the Crusades. Robin was a famous robber who 'stole from the rich to give to the poor'.

   Pinocchio: originally written as a political allegory about the unification of Italy, with the wooden puppet standing for the new nation in search of an identity, Pinocchio is nowadays more famous for having a nose that grows when he tells a lie.

   Aladdin and the lamp: One of the best-known stories of *The Thousand and One Nights*, a collection of ancient oriental tales in which Aladdin, a poor Chinese boy, finds a magic lamp. When he rubs it he summons up a genie who can grant his every wish. He becomes rich, marries well and lives a long and happy life.

c) Students' own answers. Students will probably be familiar with Disney style characters.

d) Robin Hood: England
   Pinocchio: Italy
   Aladdin: the Middle/Far East

e) Students' own answers.

Story telling (p 98)

1 Groupwork. Students discuss the questions and report back to the class.

2 Whole class. Read the information about Helen East with the class. Then ask students to read the list and say which areas they would be most interested in hearing about.

3 📼 **48 SB p 155**

Play the recording. Students listen and tick the topics in 2 which the speaker talks about. Ask them if she mentioned the points they were interested in.

Topics talked about: a, b, e, f, i, j

📼 **48**

(I = Interviewer; H = Helen)

I: *Helen, let me first ask you a bit about your background. We're here in London but you weren't born here, were you?*

H: *No, I was born in Sri Lanka and after that I lived for a while in Norway and in Nigeria and my father moved on to Iceland – I've spent a lot of time there and I've also lived for some time in India so, I've spent a lot of time in many different cultures that have a very strong oral tradition, but I decided to come to England and settle in England when I was about twenty-one, twenty-two and I moved to London.*

I: *What exactly does a professional storyteller do?*

H: *Everything. A professional storyteller has to work with all ages, and in all situations and they have to be able to tell all different kinds of stories. I think traditionally professional storytellers were the people who were genealogists and historians and everything else was domestic storytelling – whether it be the passing of news and information by people travelling from village to village or whether it be the stories that mothers, fathers and grandparents told to their children, or the stories that friends told each other, they were all happening domestically, but what has happened now is that domestic storytelling has all but died out and so the job of a professional storyteller is to cover everything. So you must work with history and information about the past. You also have to work with the whole area of belief – myth, which goes into religion. You have to work in education, so you have to use teaching stories that are teaching all ages about simple behaviour and about complex moral and social issues and you also have to tell as a mother does to a child to create that intimacy, that close connection between teller and listener. Stories are told inside, outside, in bizarre as well as very* normal situations, so really a professional storyteller has to be able to do all different kinds of storytelling.

I: *And how did you first get into storytelling?*

H: *Well, I've always been into storytelling as long as I can remember – I was listening to stories, reading stories, and telling anybody who'd listen and luckily I had a younger sister who would listen and in fact wouldn't go to bed unless I told her stories, and then my friends, they like stories, but actually professionally it was accidental. When I arrived in London I saw an advert for a storyteller wanted to work in Brixton, to work in the streets and the adventure playgrounds and on the housing estates and the idea, it was for the libraries, the idea was to encourage people by hearing stories to come into the library and read them.*

I: *And what do you think is the universal appeal of stories?*

H: *I think primarily it's human contact. What stories do is they connect people to each other, to the listener, put all the listeners together, listener to teller, listeners to each other, they connect you with your inner world, your private dreams. They connect you with the natural world, with the environment all around you, and at the same time they entertain you, they amuse you, and they are put in a form that are memorable, so you can carry them away with you. So I think that's the universal appeal of stories and of course they're free! Now stories, when I say stories, I mean everything – could be a joke, could be an anecdote, could be a family story, a little bit of family history, could be a personal event that did happen, could be a wildly exaggerated tall tale that might have a grain of truth. It could be a folk tale, a wonder tale, it could be a ghost story, a myth, something to do with that great scale of human belief or it could be what we call an urban myth. An urban myth is set in an urban rather than a rural situation and it deals with primarily urban considerations and one of the most important urban considerations is living all together – it's people, it's society, so an urban myth is a rumour often with an element of humour and it's a rumour that's rooted in possibility and it has a contemporary ring but yet these stories that people think happened here and now, they are very, very often hundreds and hundreds and hundreds of years old. One of the most common urban myths is the story of the vanishing hitch-hiker. Everybody knows somebody who knows somebody who knows somebody that this happened to and yet this story actually has its antecedents in ancient Rome and perhaps even before that, only naturally the girl wasn't picked up in a car, she*

was picked up in a coach or a chariot or lifted onto the back of a horse, but the story remains the same.

4 Go through the instructions with the class. Then play the recording again for them to make notes.

a) Her background: Born in Sri Lanka, then lived in Norway, Nigeria, Iceland and India. Came to England at 21 or 22 and moved to London.

b) Her first job as a storyteller: Saw an advert for a storyteller in Brixton to work in the streets, adventure playgrounds and housing estates to encourage people to go into libraries and read stories.

e) The job of a professional storyteller: Has to work with all ages, in all situations and be able to tell all different kinds of stories. Must work with history and information about the past. Has to work with beliefs and in education, using stories to teach. Has to create intimacy between listener and teller. Has to be able to do all different kinds of storytelling.

f) The traditional role of storytellers: Professional storytellers were historians and genealogists. Domestic storytellers passed news by travelling and within families or to friends.

i) The universal appeal of stories: Their appeal is in human contact, connecting people with each other and with their inner worlds and private dreams. Stories connect you with the natural world and the environment and they entertain, amuse and are memorable. And they're free.

j) Different types of stories: Stories can be jokes, anecdotes, family stories, family history, personal events that really happened, exaggerated tales which might have a grain of truth, folk tales, wonder tales, ghost stories, myths or urban myths.

5 Pairwork. Students compare notes and add anything they missed.

6 Pairwork. Students work together to write their articles. Make sure they keep to the 200 word limit. If you have photocopying facilities available, they could write one copy of the article between them and make one copy for their partner.

Close up (p 99)

Telling stories

1 Pairwork. Students match the sections and definitions. Check answers with the class.

a) 3 b) 4 c) 1 d) 5 e) 2

2 Elicit the correct order for the sections from the students. There is some information about the different parts of a story in the Language reference section on page 100.

> introduction, background, problem, resolution, comment

3 Students read the story of *Androcles and the lion* and put the paragraphs in order.

> Correct order: paragraph C, A, E, D, B.

4 Ask students if they have heard the story before and if they know any others like it. Encourage them to tell their stories to the class, reminding them again of the stages of storytelling outlined in the Language reference section on page 100.

5 🔲 49 SB p 155

Read the questions with the class and play the recording. Elicit answers to the questions.

> a) yes   b) It is unlikely to be true.

🔲 **49**

(I = Interviewer; H = Helen)

I: *Do you have an urban myth you can tell us?*

H: *Well, I know lots of urban myths but this one actually happened to me, so it wasn't so much an urban myth as a really disturbing experience. You see, what happened was, it was when I first moved to London and I was driving up from the North and I was rather nervous because I had only just passed my driving test and I had a very old car and it was also very bad weather. So I was driving along and rather anxiously leaning over the wheel and peering out and then all of a sudden somebody stepped out right in front of me and I only just managed to jam the brakes on and I zipped into the slip road and I thought I'd hit whoever it was, so I jumped out of the car, shaking all over, and there was a girl. She was about fourteen, she was dressed in a very short mini-skirt and a tank top. She was soaking wet and she was still standing in the middle of the motorway. So I yelled and screamed at her because I had been so scared and then I noticed that she was crying, so of course I calmed down and I got her out of the road and I asked her if she needed some help and she said, 'I want a lift'. So I let her get into the car and we started driving along and it turned out that she was going to London as well, she was going to Streatham. She had been out at a party and she lived actually at 29*

Gleneldon Road. I remember it was really impressed in my mind. So we were driving along and then I noticed that she was shivering and this being an old car I didn't have any heating or anything so I told her that I had a coat in the back that she could borrow. This was a while back, you know, when those big fur coats were in fashion.

So, she wrapped herself up in that and we drove, and I must say I forgot about her because she stopped talking. I suppose she must have fallen asleep, and I just concentrated on the road. It must have been quite late when we got to London, and as we drove in off the ring road, there was a little bit of a problem, and I had to brake very suddenly and automatic reflex, I just flung my arm out in front of my passenger, forgetting that you know, she had a seat belt, and when I looked round to make sure she was all right, she wasn't there.

So then I had to stop and pinch myself and I was sure I hadn't been dreaming but she definitely wasn't there and I got out the car and I looked at the car and I got back in the car, and then I looked in the back, and my coat wasn't there either. I couldn't believe that it was just a dream, I couldn't explain the disappearance of the coat, so in the end I drove all the way to Streatham, and I found this road – Gleneldon Road – and I found number 29 and I stopped outside it and of course it was about one o'clock in the morning by then, but there was a light on, so I went and I knocked and the door was opened by a woman who was probably late 30s, 40s perhaps, but she looked just like this girl. So I just stared at her, and after a while she said, 'Yes? Yes?' and she made as if to shut the door. Well, I suppose it was late at night, and I said, 'Excuse me, it's just that I've just, I just gave a lift to your daughter,' and she looked at me and her face crumpled up and she said, 'How could you, how could you?' I didn't know what was going on, and I said, 'I'm sorry, what is it?' and she said 'My daughter is dead'. I said, 'I'm so sorry, I'm so sorry, it must have been somebody else. It's just such a coincidence. She said this was her address and I picked her up, oh, it must have been about seven or eight hours ago, I picked her up just outside York on the M1.'

She stared at me then, and she said, 'My daughter died on the M1, outside York exactly a year ago.' My legs started to give way underneath me. I couldn't believe it, and then I thought to myself, 'But what about the coat?', and I said, 'But how can it be, because she got in the car and I talked to her and she was there, and she even put my coat on, and a ghost wouldn't put on a coat.' And the woman said, 'Well, if you don't believe me, go and look at

*her grave.' And there and then she came out,
and she was still in her slippers but she took me
up the road and left and right and there was a
big church. She stopped at the gate of the
churchyard and she said, 'My daughter, she's in
there, the third grave to the right of the church.
You'll excuse me if I don't go any further.'*

*So of course I understood and I went in and it
was very dark, but there was a light outside the
church and I could just make out the third
grave. Sure enough, it was fairly new, grass just
growing, flowers on it, and I looked – date, the
girl had died exactly that day a year before.
Fourteen years old. But folded up on the grave
was my fur coat.*

*It's hard to believe, isn't it? If it hadn't happened
to me, well I wouldn't be telling you now.*

6 Whole class. Look at the list of features. Students match them to the extracts from the story. Allow students some time to think about it individually first, then to compare their answers with a partner before checking answers with the class.

> a) 4   b) 5   c) 6   d) 2   e) 1   f) 3

7 Students work with a partner and look at the tapescript on page 155 and find examples of the features listed in 6. Check answers with the class

> a) reporting thoughts directly – no further examples.
>
> b) reporting speech directly – Many examples, including: *and she said, 'I want a lift'; after a while she said, 'Yes? Yes?'; I said 'Excuse me, it's just that I've just, I just gave a lift to your daughter,'*
>
> c) making the story personal – *If it hadn't happened to me, well, I wouldn't be telling you now.*
>
> d) asides to the listener – *It's hard to believe, isn't it?*
>
> e) adding detail – *this being an old car I didn't have any heating or anything; she was soaking wet; she was going to Streatham; who was probably late 30s, 40s perhaps*
>
> f) repetition – *I got out of the car and I looked at the car and I got back in the car; I couldn't believe that it was just a dream; I couldn't explain the disappearance of the coat.*

8 ⊙ **50 SB p 156**

Read the instructions and the list with the class. Then play the recording. Students match the extracts to the techniques.

> a) extract 1   b) extract 3   c) extract 2

> ⊙ **50**
>
> **1**
>
> *So I yelled and screamed at her because I had been
> so scared and then I noticed that she was crying, so
> of course I calmed down and I got her out of the
> road and I asked her if she needed some help and
> she said, 'I want a lift'.*
>
> **2**
>
> *... and she even put my coat on, and a ghost
> wouldn't put on a coat.*
>
> **3**
>
> *Sure enough, it was fairly new, grass just growing,
> flowers on it, and I looked – date, the girl had died
> exactly that day a year before. Fourteen years old.
> But folded up on the grave was my fur coat.*

9 Students look again at the tapescript on page 156 and prepare to shadow read. See Unit 4 page 51 in this book for the procedure for shadow reading. Play the recording again. Students read aloud at the same time as Helen.

Urban myths (p 101)

1 Students read the file card on urban myths. They find any differences between the story told by Helen and those described here.

> The only difference is that Helen told the story as
> though it had happened to her, not to someone
> she knows.

2 Whole class. Read the titles and ask students if they think they know any of them.

3 Groupwork. Students turn to their respective pages and follow the instructions. Each group has an urban myth to read and a series of questions to discuss. Monitor and check answers with the groups as they are discussing.

> **Group A**
> 1   a) Students' own answer.
>   b) The suspense that's built up makes it a good story.
>   c) The fact that spiders crawled out of the cyst.
>
> **Group B**
> 1   a) Students' own answer.
>   b) The suspense that's built up makes it a good story, and the twist at the end.
>   c) The fact that the man in the car behind was trying to save her, not kill her.
>
> **Group C**
> 1   a) Students' own answer.

> b) The twist at the end makes it a good story.
>
> c) The trick question.
>
> d) The moral is: don't lie to teachers.

4 Groupwork. Students form groups of three with students who have all read different stories. They take turns to tell their stories and afterwards discuss the questions. Ask members of the groups to feed back on their discussion and encourage students to share similar stories.

5 This writing exercise could be done for homework. Encourage students to finish their writing before they compare their stories with the ones at the back of the book.

Optional activity

There are several websites dedicated to urban myths. They can be found by typing in 'urban myths' or 'urban legends' into any search engine. The students could, if the school or they themselves have the facilities, visit one or more of these sites and bring an urban myth to the next lesson to share with the other students.

Telling tales (p 101)

Closed books. Write *telling stories* and *telling tales* on the board. Ask students what the difference is between them. (One meaning of *telling tales* implies some form of deception. It can also mean telling someone in authority about something that someone else has done and is particularly used for children telling parents or teachers about their friends' bad behaviour. *Telling stories* is generally a more positive thing, implying telling stories for entertainment, though it can be used to imply that someone is exaggerating.)

1 Whole class. Students look at the pictures and, in open class, suggest answers to the questions. Do not confirm or deny any answers at this stage.

2 Students read the story. Elicit the correct answers to the questions in 1.

Note: 'pen' as used in the story is short for 'penitentiary'.

> The young man is a prisoner, being taken to jail by the older man, who is a prison officer. The woman is an old friend of the young man.

3 Encourage students to decide whether the statements are true or false without looking back at the text. Do not check answers at this stage.

4 Pairwork. Students discuss their answers and look back at the story if necessary.

> a) false (They sat there because it was the only empty seat in the carriage.)
>
> b) true, though only momentarily.
>
> c) false
>
> d) true

> e) true
>
> f) false
>
> g) false (It was the marshal who said that he was thirsty, though it was probably only an excuse to get the young man out of the embarrassing situation.)
>
> h) false (The older man was the marshal; he was only pretending to be a prisoner.)
>
> i) false (He was the prisoner.)
>
> j) true (He was ready to pretend that he was the prisoner in order to help the young man save himself from an embarrassing situation.)

Optional activity

Ask students to read back through the story and identify / make a note of any occasions where the speakers aren't telling the truth. They should then check with a partner, or in small groups. This encourages them to read the story very carefully and promotes noticing by motivating them to discuss the language being used. Most of the 'lies' told are, in fact, omissions or assumptions made by the listener.

> 'I see you know the marshal here.'
>
> 'He's taking me to Leavenworth Prison.'
>
> 'Say, Mr Marshal.'

This could lead into a brief class discussion of what a lie is, which in turn leads nicely into the discussion questions.

5 Pairwork. Students discuss the questions and report back to the class.

Compound adjectives (p 103)

1 Pairwork. Students look at the compound adjectives in the box and answer the questions. Check answers with the class.

> a) good-looking: the young man
> sad-faced: the older man
> roughly-dressed: the older man
> grey-gloved: the woman's hands
>
> b) *Suggested answers*
>
> the young man: newly-arrested, quick-thinking
> the woman: wealthy-looking, softly-spoken, fair-skinned, smartly-dressed
> the older man: grey-haired, quick-thinking
>
> c) *Suggested answers*
>
> slow-moving: train, traffic
> well-informed: person (politician, speaker, etc.)
> record-breaking: speed, length, height
> stress-induced: headache, tiredness, heart attack
> well-behaved: children, pet
> time-consuming: homework, task
> comfort-loving: person, pet

2 Students work individually or in pairs to think of an answer for each one. Then elicit suggestions from the class.

> a) carefully-made   b) time-saving
> c) tasty-looking   d) quick-drying

3 Again, allow students to do this individually or in pairs before checking with the class.

> a) well-mannered   b) quick-tempered
> c) fun-loving   d) hard-working

4 Go through the instructions and the example with the class. Students then work individually to replace the *italicised* clauses with compound adjectives. Allow them to compare answers in pairs before checking with the class.

> *Suggested answers*
> a) The building was a real eyesore. It was very cheaply-built.
> b) She was wearing a new sweet-smelling perfume that didn't really suit her.
> c) He was well-educated and could speak knowledgeably on a range of topics.
> d) He's quick-thinking and always makes intelligent contributions.
> e) She's smooth-skinned and she has a beautifully clear complexion.
> f) We bought some gorgeous handmade plates.
> g) Peter's parents are very broad-minded – they let him do whatever he wants.

5 Students use each of the compound adjectives in 4 to describe people or things they know. Ask them to compare answers with a partner.

The best laid plans ... (p 103)

Pairwork. Students discuss how they celebrated the new millennium. Encourage them to report back to the class on any interesting information.

1 Read the questions with the class. Students then read the text and find the answers. Check answers with the class.

> a) River of fire, firework display, opening of the London Eye
> b) River of fire: midnight
>   Firework display: midnight–12.15am
>   Opening of the London Eye: 8.30pm

2 ▱ **51 SB p 156**

Read the questions with the class before you play the recording. Students make notes of their answers as they listen. Do not check answers at this stage.

▱ **51**

(B = Becky; J = John)

B: *Good evening and welcome to the first show of the year 2000! Today we have John Ruskin in the studio with us. John's been following the events of the Millennium, and I must say John, you're looking remarkably wide awake.*

J: *If only! You don't look so bad yourself! Were you one of the hordes lining the river last night, waiting to see the river of fire?*

B: *No, I took up a last minute invitation from some friends to whizz down to the coast for a house party!*

J: *You did well. Most Londoners were not impressed by the party laid on by the capital. The river of fire didn't really live up to expectations. It was supposed to be one of the most spectacular pyrotechnic shows ever seen, measuring 60 metres in height and travelling down the Thames at the incredible speed of 1,240 kph ... but a slight technical hitch meant that 99% of the population didn't actually see it.*

B: *So there was a river of fire then?*

J: *Yes, but it was only visible by helicopter!*

B: *Fantastic! So the crowds lining the banks of the Thames must have been pretty disappointed.*

J: *Yes, I think we all were really. The organisers are blaming the weather conditions but I think they miscalculated how much, or should I say, how little, people would have been able to see from the ground. The helicopter crews flying over the city to cover the events claim to have had superb views. I must admit I thought the fireworks display in Paris was much better.*

B: *Yes, it was spectacular wasn't it? The whole of the Eiffel Tower lit up like that. Amazing!*

J: *Yes, especially considering the terrible weather and the flooding that France has been suffering over the last week. There was talk at one point of having to call the whole thing off: it didn't sound like it was going to happen.*

B: *Really?*

J: *Yes, but they pulled it off – and in superb fashion, really put us to shame in fact what with the, well, you know, the mix up with the tickets for the Dome, the fiasco with the trains, the London Eye ...*

B: *Oh yes!*

J: *I mean, it was going to be one of the centrepieces of the whole evening. Tony Blair was to have opened it with a Star Wars type laser show but it all fell through. Thanks to bad organisation and bad time management it just didn't happen ... they just didn't get their act together in time. The Ferris wheel failed some fairly routine safety check at the last minute. I mean, that's pretty bad, isn't it? France had to contend with a major hurricane and they managed to pull everything off without a hitch!*

B: *Typical!*

J: *And then of course there was the Millennium Experience party at the Dome. Up to a third of the tickets hadn't been distributed by yesterday so the guests had to pick them up at the train stations on the way, and that was a fiasco. The train service was slow and irregular and some of the guests actually never made it to the Dome. In fact the whole thing was almost called off because of a bomb scare ...*

B: *A bomb scare?*

J: *Yes, apparently a hoax caller phoned to say that a bomb would go off in the Dome at midnight. The organisers were on the verge of evacuating the Dome at 10.45, minutes before the main show was due to begin – but the Queen stood her ground – and, as we know, the show went on.*

B: *Sounds like a bit of a disaster all round really ...*

J: *Well, it wasn't all bad news. On a happy note, there were no rushes at the hospitals and everything seemed to pass off very peacefully. Most medical staff had had their leave cancelled to cover what they had imagined would be a flood of party victims, but it seems that in fact it turned out to be a very quiet night. And of course the Millennium Bug was a bit of a no-show. To date, the only failures reported here in the UK were a weather vane in Portsmouth and a set of traffic lights in Inverness.*

B: *Could it all have been an elaborate hoax on the part of the IT technicians to get a bit of extra cash over the holiday?*

J: *Well, yes it might well have been ...*

3 Pairwork. Students compare their answers and decide whether the evening was a success or not. Check answers with the class.

a) river of fire, opening of the London Eye

b) No – the river of fire had a problem with it which meant that 99% of the population didn't see it and the London Eye opening didn't happen because it failed a safety check.

c) fireworks display in Paris, the ticket mix up for the Dome party, slow and irregular train service, bomb scare at the Dome

d) rushes at hospital, the Millennium Bug

The night wasn't the success it was supposed to have been.

4 Pairwork. Students match the phrases to the people and events. You could split the pairs and get the students to

check their answers with another partner. Do not check answers with the class at this stage.

5 Students turn to the tapescript on page 156 to check their answers.

a) 5   b) 5   c) 3   d) 8   e) 7   f) 1   g) 2
h) 4   i) 4   j) 6

6 Students work individually to read the definitions and identify the matching *italicised* words and phrases in 4. Allow them to compare answers in pairs or small groups before checking with the class.

1 g   2 h   3 j   4 c   5 d   6 b   7 a   8 e
9 f   10 i

7 Students use the expressions from 4 to complete the text. Check answers with the class.

1 fiasco   2 called off   3 hitch
4 get their act together   5 mix up   6 fell through
7 live up to expectations

Students can then go on to discuss what their favourite soap opera is and what happened in the last episode.

Close up (p 104)

The future seen from the past

1 Students use the phrases in the box to complete the extracts. Do not check answers at this stage.

2 **52 SB p 156**

Play the recording for students to listen and check their answers.

a) was supposed to be one of the most spectacular

b) didn't sound like it was going to

c) was going to be one of the centrepieces, was to have opened it

d) would go off, were on the verge of evacuating, was due to begin

e) would be a flood

52

a) *It was supposed to be one of the most spectacular pyrotechnic shows ever seen, measuring 60 metres in height and travelling down the Thames at the incredible speed of 1,240 kph.*

b) *There was talk at one point of having to call the whole thing off: it didn't sound like it was going to happen.*

c) *... it was going to be one of the centrepieces of the whole evening. Tony Blair was to have opened it with a Star Wars type laser show but it all fell through.*

d) *... apparently a hoax caller phoned to say that a bomb would go off in the Dome at midnight. The organisers were on the verge of evacuating the Dome at 10.45, minutes before the main show was due to begin – but the Queen stood her ground ...*

e) *Most medical staff had had their leave cancelled to cover what they had imagined would be a flood of party victims, but it seems that in fact it turned out to be a very quiet night.*

3 Pairwork. Students look at the box in 1 and find the verb phrases in *italics*. They discuss the questions. Check answers with the class. Go through the Language reference section on this page if they have trouble with these structures.

a) on the verge of (+ -*ing*)

b) no

c) were on the verge of

4 Students reorder the words and phrases to form sentences. Allow them to compare answers with a partner before checking with the class.

a) We were supposed to be going to the seaside but the car broke down so we didn't go.

b) I was going to do my homework last night but I didn't feel very well so I went to bed early.

c) The plane was due to leave at 8.30 but there was heavy fog and we were delayed by six hours. OR We were due to leave at 8.30 but there was heavy fog and the plane was delayed by six hours.

d) I was to have met the minister at the opening but he was delayed at the last minute.

e) We had imagined that the exam would be really difficult, but actually it was pretty easy.

f) We were on the verge of giving up hope when the rescue party arrived.

5 Pairwork. Give an example or two about yourself and then ask students to discuss very briefly any similar situations that they have been in.

A change of plan (p 106)

Closed books. Ask students to think about a time when they decided to do something but unfortunately had to change their

plans at the last minute. Ask them, in pairs, to describe the details briefly to each other. Get one or two students to report their discussions to the whole class. Be careful to keep this brief so that they do not pre-empt the Anecdote activity on page 106.

Alternatively, ask students to look at the cartoon and establish a link between it and the section title 'A change of plan'.

1 **53 SB p 156**

Read the questions with the class before playing the recording. Students make notes of their answers. Do not check answers at this stage.

 53

1

I had planned to go on holiday to South America. I was supposed to go visit friends and travel around for six weeks. It was my dream to visit Machu Picchu in Peru. I'd been thinking about it for years and so I had booked time off of work and I had my itinerary all worked out and I had bought all my hiking gear and everything, but luckily I hadn't paid for the ticket yet because you see, what happened was this big problem came up at work. A client had moved the deadline forward and so I actually had to cancel the whole trip and I ... I couldn't believe it actually, I really could not believe it. I was so disappointed because I had been hoping and thinking and dreaming about this for years and, um, so this friend of mine suggested that we should just go to Egypt, after the project deadline, um, just sort of a last minute thing, and I, you know, I was very stressed by that point and I definitely was in need of a holiday so, so we went and in fact I ended up doing a scuba diving course in the Red Sea and now I am a convert to diving. I can't, you know, get enough of it, so I am really glad that things turned out the way they did in the end.

2

Ah, well, there's a, there's a funny story there actually. You see, this job wasn't actually the job that I'd applied for. I, um, I had been offered the post of a lecturer in a university in Kuala Lumpur, and you know I quite fancied, I was up for the travel and everything, I was very excited, and er, so I'd made all sorts of plans. You know and I'd, I'd done all the boring medical stuff. I had the jabs, bought the guide books and, er, and of course I had completely axed the winter wardrobe, which was a little foolish as it turned out, but as I was going to be there for two years, you know, what did one need you know, the winter woollies for? And I was really looking forward to living in a tropical climate. I thought, 'Well this will be a nice change', and er, there I was, my bags practically packed and their economy crashed and they cut back on their budgets and there was no job and, er, that was a month before I was due to leave. So there I was, I practically didn't have a home to live in because, of course, I'd given up the tenancy on my flat and, er, so I mean I was frantic. I was looking in the journals, you know, 'Oooh, where do I find another job?' and it was a terrible time of year to job hunt believe me, and then I couldn't believe it. I mean, suddenly here was this job in Madrid. Well, I mean, it was a total change of plan because actually it does get very cold in Madrid in the winter. I don't know whether people have been there, but believe me it does, so of course it was a complete new winter wardrobe and, er, there I was. But, erm, ah, no, I'm glad it worked out like that really because I mean I, I love Madrid and I've been there for three years now, and I may stay for longer, you know.

3

Well, I'd organised a surprise party for my friend's 30th birthday and it was at my home and oh, it was great. We, a couple of friends and myself, we'd decorated the house out with streamers and balloons and it looked fantastic and this big banner saying 'Happy Birthday' and we'd prepared loads of food and the, the house was going to be just bursting because we'd invited close to fifty people. And the guests were supposed to arrive half an hour before my friend was due to turn up, so it could all be a surprise. And we, I told her to come and meet me at my house because she thought we were going to go out for dinner. Um, I sort of, all this pretext had been made up and everything, so all of our friends arrived and then all of a sudden, twenty minutes before she was supposed to turn up, I get this phone call from my friend saying that her dad was ill and she had to go and see him, and she wouldn't turn up until much later. So, there was nothing I could do. I had all these people at the house so we just decided to start the party. Um, and she did, you know, my friend turned up and she was still surprised and it was lovely, um, I was a bit upset that the surprise got ruined because we had gone to so much trouble but the party was brilliant. It all went you know, really well, but, um, it taught me never to plan a surprise again because you never know what is going to happen.

2 Pairwork. Students compare their answers. Check with the class.

> a) Story 1: holiday to South America
> Story 2: job in Kuala Lumpur
> Story 3: surprise birthday party
> b) Story 1: deadline at work moved – had to cancel holiday
> Story 2: economy crashed – job fell through
> Story 3: ill father – friend whose party it was couldn't come to the party until later

> c) Story 1: disappointed
> Story 2: frantic
> Story 3: upset
> d) Story 1: went on a scuba diving holiday
> Story 2: got a job in Madrid
> Story 3: started the party without the guest of honour

Anecdote (p 106)

See Introduction, page 4, for more ideas on how to set up, monitor and repeat Anecdotes.

1 Give students plenty of time to choose a situation, read the prompt questions and decide what they are going to talk about. Remind them that the Language toolbox is there to help them with useful language. If it is practical, try to make sure all three situations are chosen equally throughout the class.

2 Pairwork. Students take turns to tell their stories. Encourage the listening partner to listen attentively and ask follow-up questions to elicit more details.

3 Pairwork. Students discuss whether their stories had anything in common.

The glass elevator (p 107)

Whole class. Focus attention on the photograph. Ask students what they can see and where they think it is. Ask them to say briefly what kind of a story they think could be inspired by this photograph.

1 📼 **54 SB p 157**

Go through the instructions with the class. Students look at the photograph and listen as you play the recording. They imagine the scene that is described.

> 📼 **54**
>
> *It's twilight on a cold winter's evening. You are in a tall building in the middle of a large city. You are on one of the top floors. You are getting ready to leave. You walk towards the lift. It's a glass elevator on the outside of the building. The lift arrives. You get in. The view is beautiful with all the lights of the city coming on against the backdrop of the turquoise twilight sky. The lift starts to go down. You look out at the view. Suddenly the lift stops and the lights go out. You realise that the lights have gone out throughout the city.*

2 Groupwork. In groups of four, students discuss and decide on the characters in their story.

3 Each student chooses one of the characters. They then work individually to think about answers to the questions for their character.

4 Students work individually to write the first part of the story from their character's point of view. Make sure they write in the first person.

5 Groupwork. Each member of the group reads their story to the others. They discuss the questions and come to an agreement about what is going to happen.

6 Students work individually to continue the story from their character's point of view, using the information agreed on by the group.

7 Groupwork. Members of the group swap stories and read each other's. They see how far their stories coincide and decide if they have a favourite version.

The stories could be displayed in the classroom for other students to read and enjoy.

Test

Scoring: one point per correct answer unless otherwise indicated.

1 1 f) 2 d) 3 g) 4 e) 5 a) 6 c) 7 h)
   8 b)
   9 fun-loving   10 quick-tempered
   11 hard-working   12 well-mannered
   13 broad-minded   14 hand-made

2 (2 points each for 5–8)

   1 She was on the verge of telling me something when he came into the room. I wonder what it was she wanted to say.

   2 We had been worried that there would be rain later.

   3 We were going to go to Greece, but we changed our minds at the last minute and came here instead.

   4 Originally the President was to have opened the new gallery, but he won't be able to make it I'm afraid.

   5 I was going to go out tonight, but I'm a bit tired so I'll stay in I think.

   6 We were supposed to be meeting Tom and Sue later, but they've just phoned to say they can't make it.

   7 She was on the verge of leaving, when they rang to tell her not to come.

   8 We had expected that they would be here by now.

3 (2 points for 7–10)

   1 up   2 through   3 off   4 on / ahead
   5 off   6 together

   7 confusion

   8 a (small) problem

   9 something that fails, often resulting in disorganisation and embarrassment

   10 something that failed to happen

Stories Test

Name: _____   **Total:** _____ /40

1 Lexis – compound adjectives *14 points*

Join the two halves to make compound adjectives.

1	record-	a)	consuming
2	stress-	b)	haired
3	good-	c)	spoken
4	quick-	d)	induced
5	time-	e)	thinking
6	softly-	f)	breaking
7	smartly-	g)	looking
8	grey-	h)	dressed

Complete the compound adjectives.

9   She's a f_____- loving sort of person. She always enjoys life to the full.

10 He's quite q_____- tempered so don't take it personally if he suddenly gets angry with you.

11 They're really h_____- working. You can always rely on them to get the job done.

12 He's extremely w_____- mannered at all times. My parents love him!

13 I'm sure he'll understand. He's pretty b_____ -minded about most things.

14 The vase was h_____-made and very fragile.

2 The future seen from the past *12 points*

Correct the mistakes in these sentences.

1   She was on the verge to tell me something when he came into the room. I wonder what it was she wanted to say.

2   We had been worried that there would to be rain later.

3   We were going go to Greece, but we changed our minds at the last minute and came here instead.

4   Originally the President was have opened the new gallery, but he won't be able to make it I'm afraid.

Put the words in *italics* into the correct order to complete the sentences.

5   I *go out / was / to / going* tonight, but I'm a bit tired so I'll stay in I think.

_____

6   We *supposed / be / to / were / meeting* Tom and Sue later, but they've just phoned to say they can't make it.

_____

7   She *on / of / was / the / leaving / verge*, when they rang to tell her not to come.

_____

8   We *expected / that / had / be / would / they* here by now.

_____

3 Lexis – general *14 points*

Complete the sentences by adding the missing words.

1   It didn't really live _____ to our expectations.

2   Our plans fell _____ at the last minute.

3   The party's been called _____ . Their parents aren't going away after all.

4   Despite the rain, the football match went _____ .

5   They managed to pull everything _____ without the slightest problem.

6   They need to get their act _____ if they're going to be successful.

What do the following words mean?

7   a mix-up _____

8   a hitch _____

9   a fiasco _____

10 a no-show _____

12 *Words Overview*

The topic of this unit is words. The grammar focus is on *whatever, however, wherever*, etc. and patterns with *have*.

Students start by looking at words with unusual features. They then look at some words which are new to the English language and speculate about what they might mean. They match definitions with words and then write their own definitions. They then listen to some people talking about current issues using new words and then discuss their own opinions on these issues.

Next, students look at the use of words which end with *-ever*: *whoever, whichever, however*, etc. They use them to complete and correct sentences and discuss their answers to some questions which use these words. They then look at collocations with *word*, match them to their meanings and write a dialogue containing some of them. The focus then moves to the written word and letter writing styles. Students identify types of correspondence and read some advice on correct letter writing. They encounter some of the vocabulary used to talk about letter writing and practise writing an invitation, apology or thank you letter.

A section on patterns with *have* is followed by listening to people playing word games. Students identify the rules of the games and then play them themselves. They then read some extracts from the autobiographies of three famous people and match them to the people. They then prepare and write a short account of an event or moment of significance in their own lives.

Finally, students read a short text by Mark Twain advocating the simplification of English spelling. They practise identifying silent letters in ordinary words and in English place names. They also read a limerick highlighting the difference between spelling and pronunciation in several English words.

Section	Aims	What the students are doing
Introduction page 108	*Lexis*: fun with words	Matching words with their special features.
New words pages 108–109	*Lexis*: new words in English	Answering questions about words.
		Looking at some words which are new to English and speculating on their meanings.
		Writing definitions for words.
	Listening skills: listening for gist and specific information	Listening to people using new words and giving your own opinion about the issues they discuss.
Close up pages 110–111	*Grammar*: *whatever, however, wherever*, etc	Matching beginnings and endings of sentences.
		Completing sentences with *-ever* words.
		Discussing questions with *-ever* words.
Words page 111	*Lexis*: *word* & its collocations	Matching expressions with *word* to their meanings.
The written word pages 112–113	*Reading skills*: types of correspondence	Identifying types of correspondence.
		Reading advice about letter writing and identifying mistakes made by letter writers.
	Lexis: vocabulary of letter writing	Identifying words associated with letter writing.
		Completing a paragraph about writing invitations.
	Writing skills: letter writing	Writing an apology, an invitation or a thank you letter.
Close up pages 114–115	*Grammar*: patterns with *have*	Studying the structure and use of expressions with *have*.
World languages page 115	*Conversation skills*: discussion	Discussing languages around the world.
Word games page 115	*Listening skills*: listening for gist	Listening to people playing word games and determining what the rules are.
	Conversation skills: fluency work	Playing word games.
In their own words page 116	*Reading skills*: reading for detail	Reading extracts from autobiographies and matching them with famous people.
		Identifying events described in the texts and how the writers felt.
	Writing skills: autobiography	Writing about an important event or moment in your life.
Spelling simplified page 117	*Reading skills*: reading for detail	Reading a text on spelling by Mark Twain.
	Pronunciation: silent letters	Identifying the silent letters in words.
		Practising the pronunciation of some English place names which contain silent letters.

12 *Words* *Teacher's notes*

Whole class. Ask students to look at the quotes and discuss which they prefer and why.

Students find the words in the box that answer the questions. Allow them to compare answers with a partner and then check answers with the class.

> a) madam (a palindrome)
>
> b) smoke and fog, breakfast and lunch (portmanteau words, supposedly created by Lewis Carrol)
>
> c) suggested rhymes: choice / voice, brunch / crunch, smoke / joke, fog / log / jog, lunch / bunch / munch, smog / bog, madam / Adam
>
> d) choice
>
> e) facetious
>
> f) feedback

Optional activity

Just for fun, ask the students if they can think of any other palindromes or portmanteau words in English, or, if they exist, in their own languages. You could tell them some English ones:

Palindromes: mum, dad, radar, civic, rotator, level, refer, noon, peep, sees, did, eve, nun, pop or the phrases – 'sums are not set as a test on erasmus', 'a man a plan a canal: Panama'.

Portmanteau words: motel – motor and hotel, camcorder – camera and recorder, Oxbridge – Oxford and Cambridge, infomercial – information and commercial, Franglais – French and *anglais*, Spanglish – Spanish and English.

New words (p 108)

Lexis

1 Groupwork. Students discuss the questions. (They may be interested in a couple of very long words used by schoolchildren in Britain to test their friends: *antidisestablishmentarianism* and *floccipaucinihilipilification*.)

2 Groupwork. Groups get together (or put together members from different groups in new groups) to compare their answers and see how many were the same. Check answers with the class and write any interesting vocabulary on the board.

3 Pairwork. Students look at the list of new words and phrases and answer the questions. The words are all ones which have come into use fairly recently. Do not give answers at this stage.

4 Students, working in the same pairs, read the sentences and see if they guessed the meanings correctly in 3. Check with the whole class.

5 Students match the definitions with three of the words in 3. Check answers with the class.

> a) road rage   b) spin doctor   c) retail therapy

6 Students work individually to write three more definitions. Make sure they don't write the word itself in the definition. They then show them to a partner who has to identify each word being defined. Ask some students to read their definitions out to the class. Try to include all the words.

> **to clamp:** to immobilise a car which has been illegally parked by putting a lock on the wheel so it cannot be moved. A clamp is the lock which is put on the car
>
> **decaf:** abbreviation for decaffeinated, which refers to coffee or tea which has had the caffeine removed from it
>
> **gap year:** a year off between school and university when you can travel or work to gain experience
>
> **hacker:** a person who uses computers to break into systems without permission
>
> **quality time:** time spent giving your full attention to something, usually family
>
> **road rage:** a driver's uncontrolled, aggressive behaviour, apparently caused by the stress of modern driving
>
> **scratch card:** a card that you buy with an area you scratch off to see if you have won a prize
>
> **semi-skimmed:** milk which contains less fat than normal milk
>
> **spin doctor:** a person who is employed by a political party to ensure that information is presented to the public in a positive light
>
> **retail therapy:** going shopping in order to cheer yourself up
>
> **GM food:** genetically modified food – food which has had the information in its genes changed
>
> **bad hair day:** originally a day when your hair wouldn't look right, putting you in a bad mood for the day. Now a day when nothing goes right.

7 Whole class. Elicit students' opinions on the questions.

Listening (p 109)

1 📼 **55 SB p 157**

Go through the instructions with the class before playing the recording. Students listen and tick the words they hear from the box in 3 on page 108. They then decide what the relationship between the speakers is. Don't check answers at this stage.

📼 **55**

1

(C = Claire; K = Karen)

C: *Do you want tea or coffee?*

K: *Whichever you're having.*

C: *Coffee. Decaf or normal?*

K: *Normal. I need some caffeine.*

C: *Milk?*

K: *Yeah. Full fat.*

C: *I've only got semi-skimmed.*

K: *That's fine.*

C: *There you are.*

K: *Thanks.*

C: *So what are you going to do this afternoon?*

K: *I thought I might go off and get some retail therapy in.*

C: *Good idea ... but whatever you buy, make sure you put it on his credit card!*

K: *Yes, I will. When are you picking Mum up from the station?*

C: *Twenty past five.*

K: *OK, so let's meet up at about eight then?*

C: *Yeah, fine.*

2

(D = DJ; R = Robin Jones)

D: *This afternoon we've got Robin Jones in the studio, talking about GM food. Robin, where do you stand on the GM food argument then?*

R: *Whenever I hear people getting het up about GM foods it really makes me angry. I mean, we've been genetically modifying things for centuries and nobody says a word, but the idea of doing it with a bit more sophistication and everyone starts flapping and fussing.*

D: *But that's only right. I mean, we don't know what the effects of altering a plant's DNA are going to be.*

R: *Effects, effects! What are you worried about? Is eating too many genetically modified peas or whatever going to turn you into a monster?*

D: *Ah, but what happens if eating too many genetically modified peas gives you cancer?*

R: *How can peas give you cancer?*

D: *Well you never know. It depends what they put into the pea's DNA.*

R: *Well, it's not going to be something carcinogenic is it? More likely something to make them frost resistant to keep the farmers happy and greener and bigger to keep the customers happy.*

3

(M = minister; S = secretary)

M: *... 705*

S: *0338 1945705.*

M: *That's it. So now wherever I am you can contact me, but only in real emergencies.*

S: *OK.*

M: *And on no account whatsoever must you give my number out. Whoever calls, just say you'll make sure I get their message.*

S: *But what about other ministers?*

M: *Especially the other ministers. However much they pester you, don't give them the number.*

S: *OK. Where are you off to now?*

M: *To get some quality time in with my kids.*

S: *OK. And when will you be back in?*

M: *Not until tomorrow morning.*

S: *Don't forget you have an appointment with Reginald Clarke at ten.*

M: *Who?*

S: *The spin doctor.*

M: *Oh yes, Reg. Fine Thanks for reminding me. I think I'd like the meeting in the Blue Room.*

S: *No problem, Sir.*

2 Pairwork. Students compare their answers. Check answers with the class.

a) Conversation 1: sisters
Conversation 2: DJ and interviewee
Conversation 3: minister and secretary

b) decaf, semi-skimmed, retail therapy, GM food, quality time, spin doctor

3 Groupwork. Students work in groups of three or four. Allow them time to read through the questions and decide which ones they want to answer. Encourage them not to work through the list from top to bottom. They discuss two or three of the questions. They can appoint a secretary to take notes and report back to the class on what they have discussed.

Close up (p 110)

-ever

1 Quickly brainstorm as many words as possible which end with *-ever*. Write them on the board. Working individually or in pairs, students match the two halves of the sentences. Check answers with the class.

> a) 2   b) 3   c) 6   d) 5   e) 1   f) 4

2 Students complete the sentences and check their answers with a partner. Go round monitoring progress. If they are having trouble refer them to the Language reference section on page 111 and then check answers with the class.

> a) Whatever, wherever   b) Whichever
> c) However   d) whatever   e) However
> f) whenever   g) Whoever   h) Whenever
> i) wherever

3 Students work individually to decide which of the sentences are correct and which are wrong. They change the incorrect sentences. Ask them to compare answers in pairs and go round offering help, if necessary. Then check with the class.

> a) I'm going to find her, wherever she is.
> b) correct
> c) Whichever dress you choose, make sure it's not too revealing.
> d) It doesn't matter who takes the letters to the post, as long as they go today.
> e) correct
> f) However much chocolate she eats, she never puts on weight!
> g) Whoever's on the phone, I'll ring them back later.

4 Students work individually or in pairs to rewrite the sentences using the words in the box in 2. Do the first one as an example. Check answers with the class.

> a) However long it takes, I'm going to speak English like a native.
> b) Whatever you do, I'll always love you.
> c) Wherever I go, I'll never forget you.
> d) Whenever I go to London I take the train.

5 Pairwork. Students discuss whether the statements are true for them and give more information on the things that are true. Finish the activity with a quick show of hands on whether each sentence is true or not.

Words (p 111)

Collocations

1 Students read the dialogues and match the expressions with *word* to the meanings. Ask them to check with a partner and then check answers with the class.

> a) 7   Word of mouth
> b) 5   to put into words
> c) 3   words fail me
> d) 6   In a word
> e) 4   a man of few words
> f) 8   in other words
> g) 9   I'll take your word for it
> h) 1   you have my word
> i) 2   You're putting words in my mouth

2 Whole class. Brainstorm other expressions students know with *word*. If you prefer, they could do a dictionary search and each find one or two new expressions.

> *Students may know some of these expressions*:
> A word of warning
> Without a word
> To keep your word
> Have a word in someone's ear
> Word for word

3 Pairwork. Students write a short dialogue containing at least three of the expressions in 1. Go round offering help where needed. Ask several pairs to perform their dialogues for the class.

The written word (p 112)

1 Students work individually to read the notes and identify the correspondence type. Check answers with the class.

> a) thank you letter   b) e-mail   c) letter of apology

2 Pairwork. Students discuss the questions and report back to the class.

> a) and b)   Students' own answers.
> c)   Other types of correspondence include: postcard, job application, letter requesting information, 'letter to the editor', memo, note.

3 Students read the extracts and match the titles to them. Allow them to discuss this with a partner. Check answers with the class.

> a) 5   b) 6   c) 2   d) 1   e) 3   f) 4

4 Establish that a correspondence convention is a style of writing or form of words typical of a particular type of writing. Students read the extracts carefully and note down any that are new to them.

5 Pairwork. Students compare and discuss their notes. They then report back to the class.

6 Working in pairs, students look back at the notes in 1 and decide what mistakes the writer of each one has made, according to the extracts. Check answers with the class.

> a) The writer should have signed off with a full name and perhaps used something other than simply 'Yours'.
>
> b) The writer didn't need to include 'Dear Chris' as it's an e-mail, and he should have signed off with a name instead of just an initial.
>
> c) The writer should have offered to replace the vase.

Lexis (p 113)

1 Students scan the extracts to find words and phrases to match the meanings. Allow them to check with a partner and then check answers with the class.

> a) address   b) recipient   c) dictates
> d) sign off   e) hospitality   f) to duplicate
> g) get straight to the point   h) snail mail

2 Pairwork. Students use their answers from 1 to complete the text.

> 1 get straight to the point   2 dictates
> 3 address   4 recipient   5 hospitality

Writing (p 113)

1 Students choose one of the options to write. Make sure all the options are chosen by at least two students where feasible.

2 Give students time to write and to consult the reading extracts for help. This could be done for homework.

3 Pairwork. Students exchange work with someone who has chosen the same option where possible. They read each other's work and make suggestions for improvements. They can then rewrite their own work, taking into account their partner's suggestions. Again, this could be done for homework.

Optional activity

Students could write one of the letters to a classmate. Either put students into pairs and they write to each other or Student A writes to Student B, B writes to C, C writes to D, etc. They give the letter to the classmate, who writes an appropriate reply and returns it. These could be homework activities.

Close up (p 114)

Patterns with *have*

1 Pairwork. Students look at the *italicised* verb phrases and answer the questions. Check answers with the class.

> a) you'll have people flaming you
> b) to have someone read over the letter

2 Whole class. Ask students to look at the sentences and discuss with a partner whether they mention results or arrangements. Then read the sentences aloud or get individual students to read them. For each one, ask students to say whether they mention results or arrangements.

> a) result   b) result   c) arrangement   d) result
> e) arrangement   f) result   g) result

3 Whole class. Elicit answers. If students have difficulty, remind them that the Language reference section on page 115 gives more information on these points.

> a) *have* + someone/something + *-ing*
> b) *have* + someone/something + infinitive

4 Give one or two examples to the class. Then give students a few minutes to think of some examples of their own.

> *Possible answers*
> a) talking about someone who's ill in hospital
> b) talking to mechanics fixing a car
> c) talking about house repairs
> d) talking about a late night party
> e) talking about a newly-decorated flat
> f) talking to a friend who's got a TV acting job
> g) talking to someone who hasn't seen their friend for a few days

5 Students choose the correct forms to complete the sentences. Check answers first in pairs and then with the class.

> a) It's been a long time since I've had a visitor from abroad come to stay at my house.
>
> b) I always have my brother check my homework for me before I hand it in.
>
> c) My father's great at telling jokes; he sometimes has us crying with laughter.
>
> d) I saw a really exciting film last night; it had me sitting on the edge of my seat.
>
> e) My mother works such long hours that she has someone do the cleaning and cooking for her.

6 Students match the sentence halves. Check answers with the class.

> a) 3   b) 5   c) 4   d) 2   e) 6   f) 1

7 Pairwork. Ask students to discuss their answers to 6. Encourage them to give details for situations they have experienced personally.

World languages (p 115)

Discussion

1 Groupwork. Students discuss the questions.

2 Groupwork. Groups join together (or put together members from different groups to form new groups) to compare their findings and see how similar their ideas and opinions are. Finish the activity with a class discussion.

Word games (p 115)

Closed books. Ask students to say what popular word games they know which are played in their country or countries. Ask them to explain briefly the rules of some of them.

1 📼 **56 SB p 157**

Make sure students understand the task and then play the recording. Students listen and make notes about the rules of each game. Check answers with the class.

> **Game 1:** One player chooses a topic (for example, film titles) and gives an example starting with the letter 'A' and then each player in turn has to think of another example beginning with the next letter of the alphabet.
>
> **Game 2:** One player says a word and the next player has to say a word beginning with the last letter of the previous word.
>
> **Game 3:** One player chooses a topic for another to speak about for a minute. If the player says 'er' or 'um' they are out.

> 📼 **56**
>
> **1**
>
> (A = Andy; B = Beryl; E = Emma; C = Chris; D = Donna)
>
> A: *OK, Emma, you choose the topic ...*
>
> E: *Er, films.*
>
> B: *That's too difficult!*
>
> C: *No it's not!*
>
> B: *OK.*
>
> D: *I'll start! 'American Beauty'.*
>
> A: *OK. It goes clockwise, so Chris, you're next!*
>
> C: *'Black Beauty'.*

> E: *'Charlie's Angels'.*
>
> A: *'Dracula'.*
>
> B: *'Elephant Man'.*
>
> D: *Err, 'Forrest Gump' ...*
>
> **2**
>
> (A = Ann; K = Katy; P = Pete; M = Mike; S = Sue)
>
> A: *I'll start and Katy and Pete can go next as they know the game. Let's start with 'umbrella'. Your turn Katy.*
>
> K: *Avocado.*
>
> P: *OK, operation.*
>
> A: *Your turn Mike. Have you got it?*
>
> M: *Yes, I think so. November?*
>
> A: *Yes! Your turn, Sue.*
>
> S: *Er – banana?*
>
> All: *No! Try again.*
>
> S: *Garlic.*
>
> All: *No!*
>
> S: *I give up.*
>
> A: *OK. My go again. What was the last word? November? Um, rubbish.*
>
> K: *Helicopter.*
>
> P: *Radio.*
>
> M: *Orange.*
>
> S: *I think I've got it – elephant!*
>
> A: *Well done! Let's play something else ...*
>
> **3**
>
> (H = Helen; K = Kiki; J = John)
>
> H: *Right Kiki, your topic is libraries. I'm timing you. Your minute starts ... now!*
>
> K: *Oh no! Right, libraries are really interesting places. They're full of books and they're somewhere you can go when you want to find out all sorts of information, especially if you haven't got access to a computer. Um, ...*
>
> J: *Ha! You said 'um'. My turn ...*

2 Groupwork. To illustrate, play one of the games with a few students in front of the whole class. Students then play a round of each game.

In their own words (p 116)

1 Whole class. Before students work in pairs to discuss what they know about the people in the photographs, establish some basic information about all three people.

Pairwork. Students discuss what else they know about the people in the photographs.

> **Nelson Mandela:** President of South Africa from 1994 to 1999. He was jailed for life in 1964 by the

government of South Africa for his anti-apartheid activities. He then spent 27 years in prison, despite international efforts to secure his release. On his release at the age of 71, he was elected president of the African National Congress and worked for the unification of South Africa, securing the abolition of the apartheid system and the establishment of multi-racial government. He is widely praised for the non-violent way the country passed to majority rule. In 1993 he won the Nobel Peace Prize jointly with F W de Klerk. After South Africa's first free elections in 1994, he became the country's first black president. He retired in 1999.

Muhammad Ali: Born Cassius Clay (he took the name Muhammad Ali after his conversion to Islam), he is widely regarded as the best heavyweight boxer of all time. He first came to public attention when he won the light heavyweight gold medal at the Rome Olympics in 1960. He became Heavyweight Champion of the World when he beat Sonny Liston in February 1964. It was after this fight that he changed his name. He was stripped of his title when he refused to join the United States army on religious grounds and did not fight for three and a half years. The US Supreme Court eventually upheld his right to refuse to join the army and in 1971 he challenged Joe Frazier for the heavyweight title and lost. However, he regained it in 1974 by beating George Foreman in Zaire. He then succesfully defended the title ten times before losing to Leon Spinks in 1978. When he beat Spinks later the same year, he became the first boxer ever to regain a championship twice. Now he is suffering from Parkinson's disease, probably brought on by a career of blows to the head. At the Atlanta Olympics in 1996, he was given the honour of lighting the Olympic flame.

Geri Halliwell: Formerly a member of the Spice Girls pop group and then known as 'Ginger Spice', Geri Halliwell now has a solo singing career. She also works as a goodwill ambassador for the United Nations.

2   Students read the extracts and work individually to decide who is writing in each one. Do not check answers at this stage.

3   Pairwork. Students compare their answers to 2. Do not check answers with the class yet.

4   Students read the longer extracts from the autobiographies and identify the authors. Check answers with the class before asking them to discuss the two questions in pairs and report back to the class.

1   Muhammed Ali (talking about his boxing match against Sonny Liston; at first he was scared, then he became more confident)

2   Geri Halliwell (talking about when the Spice Girls record *Wannabe* went to the top of the charts; happy and proud, but also a little sad and homesick)

3   Nelson Mandela (talking about his release from prison; surprised and a little alarmed, happy and confused, joyful)

5   Pairwork. Students check their answers to 2 with the texts. Then check with the whole class.

a) Geri Halliwell   b) Muhammed Ali
c) Muhammed Ali   d) Geri Halliwell
e) Muhammed Ali   f) Nelson Mandela
g) Geri Halliwell   h) Nelson Mandela

6   Go through the instructions with the class. Tell them that the event or moment they choose could be the first time they did something, their first day at school or their first job, a time when they won a competition or met their partner. It could be the last time they did something, perhaps their last day in the house they lived in as a child.

If you wish, after they have made notes in preparation for writing, put students in pairs. Students tell each other about what they're going to write about before they start writing. Their partners interview them about the experience, asking as many interesting questions as possible about their partner's feelings and reactions. Students then review their notes before writing their piece.

They should also decide on the order in which they are going to put the information and the language they will need before they start to write. Alternatively this could be done as a peer feedback stage after the students have written their piece, with the partners conducting a follow-up interview asking for additional information.

Students write their autobiographical pieces. This could be done for homework. If you choose to do it in class, go round monitoring and offering assistance where needed.

Optional activity

Another possible activity would be for students to interview each other in the roles of the three celebrities whose autobiographical extracts they've just read.

Spelling simplified (p 117)

Books closed. Ask students to say whether they think spelling in their own language is easier or more difficult than spelling in English. If so, why? Ask students if there are any words that are commonly misspelt in their language and what the root of the problem is.

1   Pairwork. Students discuss the questions and report back to the class. Write the words they say they misspell on the board to clarify the spelling.

2   Pairwork. Students look at the information about Mark Twain and then, in pairs, read the text aloud with each partner reading a paragraph.

3 Whole class. Ask if students approve of any of his suggestions.

Silent letters (p 117)

1 Students read the sentences and cross out the silent letters. Do the first one as an example, or write your own example on the board. Tell them there may be more than one silent letter in each sentence. Allow students to check answers with a partner and then check with the class.

> The silent letters are underlined.
>
> a) Knowing how to pronounce English words correctly is important but there's no doubt that it is one of the hardest things to learn.
>
> b) Keep your receipt if you want to return a purchase otherwise there's no guarantee you'll get your money back.
>
> c) I had a really bad case of pneumonia earlier this year. Even watching the TV was tiring so I spent most days just listening to the radio.
>
> d) Psychiatrists can be very vague. They'll rarely give you a direct answer to a question.
>
> e) During the flight the plane will climb to 10,000 metres above sea level.

2 Ask students if there are any place names in their country that foreign visitors find difficult to pronounce. They read the English place names and cross out the silent letters. Encourage them to read the names aloud and to try to decide what sounds correct. Do not check answers at this stage, but allow students to compare notes with each other.

3 ▭ **57 SB p 157**

Play the recording for students to listen and check their answers.

> The silent letters are underlined.
>
> a) Gloucester   b) Leicester   c) Grosvenor Square
> d) Brighton   e) Greenwich   f) Guildford

> ▭ **57**
>
> a) Doctor Foster went to Gloucester in a shower of rain.
>
> b) Have you been to Leicester Square? You see people from every country under the sun there.
>
> c) I'd love to live in Grosvenor Square – it's a very desirable part of London.

> d) My cousins live in Brighton.
>
> e) Greenwich has a fantastic market on Sundays.
>
> f) Guildford's about an hour's drive out of London.

Ask students to read the limerick out in pairs and then check with the class. Ask students to rewrite the misspelt words in the limerick and notice the relationship between sound and spelling. There is further work on this in the workbook.

4 Whole class. Elicit further examples of English words the students know which have silent letters. You could put students into pairs or small groups, set a time limit, say five minutes, and ask the teams to write down as many words as they can with silent letters. The winning team is the one with the most correct words.

> Other words with silent letters include: comb, lamb, knee, knife, sign, psychology, write

Test

> Scoring: one point per correct answer unless otherwise indicated.
>
> **1** 1 complaining   2 check   3 working   4 repair
>
> **2** 1 whichever   2 Whatever   3 Wherever
> 4 whatever   5 However   6 however
> 7 whoever   8 whenever
>
> **3** The silent letters are underlined.
>
> 1 The flight lasts just over three hours.
>
> 2 You need a receipt for the guarantee to be valid.
>
> 3 She lives in Brighton, about half a mile from the sea.
>
> 4 I don't know for sure, but I doubt he'll be there.
>
> 5 Her answer was quite vague, don't you think?
>
> **4** 1 e)   2 f)   3 a)   4 c)   5 b)   6 d)
>
> 7 Illegally breaks into computer systems and programs.
>
> 8 Decaffeinated coffee
>
> 9 A light meal eaten mid-morning. The word is a combination of breakfast and lunch.
>
> 10 Milk
>
> **5** 1 my   2 in   3 of   4 for   5 into   6 of
> 7 me   8 a

12 Words Test

Name: _____ **Total:** _____ /40

---

1 Patterns with *have* *4 points*

Put the verb in brackets into the correct form – infinitive or present participle.

1   We'd better turn the music down or we'll have the neighbours _____ (complain).

2   I'm having someone _____ (check) the car this afternoon. There's something wrong with the brakes.

3   You should get Tom to look at it. He'll have it _____ (work) in no time.

4   He had the builders _____ (repair) the damage to the wall.

2 *-ever* *8 points*

Complete the sentences with the words from the box. Some of the words can be used more than once.

> whichever   whenever   wherever   whatever
> whoever   however

1   It's up to you. You can have _____ of them you like.

2   _____ you decide to do, let me know straightaway.

3/4 _____ she is in the world and _____ she's doing, she always phones home once a week.

5   _____ many times you explain it to him, he never seems to understand.

6/7 You can invite _____ many people and _____ you like. It's your birthday.

8   The best thing about Internet shopping is that you can do it _____ you like, day or night.

3 Silent letters *10 points*

Cross out the silent letters. There are two words with silent letters in each sentence.

1   The flight lasts just over three hours.

2   You need a receipt for the guarantee to be valid.

3   She lives in Brighton, about half a mile from the sea.

4   I don't know for sure, but I doubt he'll be there.

5   Her answer was quite vague, don't you think?

4 Lexis – new words *10 points*

Join the two halves of these words and phrases.

1   scratch   a)   doctor

2   retail   b)   rage

3   spin   c)   food

4   GM   d)   year

5   road   e)   card

6   gap   f)   therapy

Answer the questions.

7   What does a hacker do? _____

8   What is decaf? _____

9   What is brunch? _____

10 What can you buy which is semi-skimmed? _____

5 Lexis – collocations with *word* *8 points*

Complete the sentences by adding the missing words.

1   I won't tell anyone at all. You have _____ word.

2   Stop putting words _____ my mouth. You know that's not what I mean.

3   We get most of our customers by word _____ mouth.

4   OK, I'll take your word _____ it. I just hope you're correct that's all.

5   I often find it difficult to put my feelings _____ words.

6   He really is a man _____ few words.

7   Aaaarrgh! Words fail _____ sometimes. I just don't know what to say.

8   In _____ word, the answer is no!

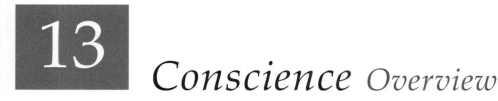

13 Conscience *Overview*

The topic of this unit is conscience and it covers a range of things from attitudes and giving money to charity to feeling guilty about things we have done. The grammar focus is on special uses of the past simple.

Students start by looking at some photographs of people collecting money. They identify the odd one out and discuss the issues surrounding giving money. They then focus on giving money to people in the street, particularly beggars, and discuss their attitudes to this. They practise special uses of the past simple for giving opinions and then go on to look at the various uses of the word *rather*.

Next, students listen to people talking about raising money for charity. They discuss what is said and examine the conversational techniques used by the speakers to express their arguments. Students then practise using sentence stress to match answers to questions. In the next section, students work together in groups to plan a fund-raising event and give a presentation to the class of their group's plans.

Students then talk about holidays and read an article on the effects of mass tourism on tourist destinations. They discuss the issues raised by this and learn some vocabulary of global situations. Finally, they look at some collocations with *conscience* and discuss things which make them feel guilty.

Section	Aims	What the students are doing
Introduction page 118	*Conversation skills*: fluency work	Identifying the odd one out from four pictures and discussing issues around giving money to people in the street.
Spare change page 118	*Listening skills*: listening for detail	Listening to people talking about giving money to people in the street.
	Conversation skills: discussion	Discussing attitudes to giving money to beggars.
Close up page 119	*Grammar*: special uses of the past simple	Studying the use of the past simple after expressions such as *It's high time* and *I'd rather*.
		Completing sentences and comparing opinions.
Rather you than me page 120	*Lexis*: rather	Identifying the different uses of the word *rather*.
		Rewriting sentences using *rather*.
Charity begins at home pages 121–122	*Listening skills*: listening for detail	Listening to people talking about raising money for charity and taking notes.
		Identifying ways of expressing your point of view in an argument.
	Pronunciation: sentence stress	Practising using sentence stress to change meaning and match appropriate responses to questions.
	Lexis: vocabulary of collecting money for charity	Completing extracts from the listening with words associated with fund raising.
All in a good cause page 123	*Speaking skills*: presentations	Preparing and giving a group presentation on plans for a charity fund-raising event.
Travelling with an easy conscience pages 123–125	*Reading skills*: reading for gist	Talking about holidays.
		Reading an article about the effects of tourism on tourist destinations and matching headings to paragraphs in the text.
	Conversation skills: discussion	Discussing the issues raised by the text.
	Lexis: vocabulary of global situations	Completing a text on ethical consumerism.
Conscience page 126	*Lexis*: collocations with *conscience*	Completing sentences with collocations with *conscience*.
	Conversation skills: discussion	Ranking actions that make you feel guilty.
		Discussing having a guilty conscience.

Conscience *Teacher's notes*

Books closed. Brainstorm the type of people who ask for money on the street. Ask students to do this in groups first. Give them a time limit of two or three minutes and then put their answers on the board.

Whole class. Students open their books and see if the photos show people that they included in their list. Elicit the answer to question a). Then, working in pairs, the students discuss the other questions.

> a) The person collecting for charity is the odd one out – they're not collecting for themselves.
>
> b) and c)   Students' own answers.

Spare change (p 118)

1   ▭ **58 SB p 158**

Read the questions with the class, then play the recording. Do not check answers at this stage.

> ▭ **58**
>
> **1**
>
> *Well, I don't think it's such a good idea to give money because, er, well, I'd be really worried that somebody would spend it on alcohol rather than something nourishing or, you know, because they always say, like, 'penny for a cup of tea' or whatever. Um, so what I think I might do is, um, buy a sandwich or hot drink or something in winter or … and give it to them there, or maybe find some old clothes.*
>
> **2**
>
> *Yes, I usually put a couple of coins in a donation box, um, I mean, obviously if it's, if I'm not in a hurry and it's easy to get at the change. Um, the thing I don't do is I don't believe in giving money to beggars.*
>
> **3**
>
> *Well, I never give any money to anybody. As far as I'm concerned it just encourages them. You know, I pay my taxes so the state will look after these people. I mean that's what we're paying all these high taxes for and you know what, quite frankly, I just think it's sheer laziness. I mean, I think they could get up off their bums and get a job if they really wanted to. It's just that they don't want to work.*

> **4**
>
> *Well, I don't mind giving money to people who are doing something to earn it, I mean, you know I'd rather they actually did something to earn the money, you know like, like street artists or, or buskers. I mean, I think someone who is actually playing music, it puts people in a good mood on the way to work, so you know, I usually give those people something. A few pennies.*
>
> **5**
>
> *Yeah, I never give money on the street any more. Um, I, um, I do give money through my bank, um, to charities that, um, I'm particularly concerned about. Once a month they get money from my bank. And that way I find I know where it's going and it also means that you're giving extra money because of tax relief.*
>
> **6**
>
> *It really annoys me. These people with their squeegies. I don't see why I should give money for cleaning my windscreen. I haven't, I haven't asked them. I think it's high time that the government did something about it because it really is annoying. No, I never give them anything.*

2   Pairwork. Students compare their answers to the questions in 1 and say whether or not they agree with the speakers. Check answers with the class. Be prepared to play the recording again if necessary.

> a)   Speaker 1: no   Speaker 2: yes   Speaker 3: no
>   Speaker 4: yes   Speaker 5: no   Speaker 6: no
>
> b)
>
> Speaker 1 doesn't give money because it might be spent on alcohol. She might buy a sandwich or hot drink for someone in need instead or give some old clothes.
>
> Speaker 2 gives to people collecting with boxes but not to beggars.
>
> Speaker 3 doesn't give money because she pays enough in taxes and thinks beggars are lazy.
>
> Speaker 4 gives money to people doing something to earn it like buskers.
>
> Speaker 5 doesn't give money to people in the street but pays through the bank.
>
> Speaker 6 doesn't give money to windscreen cleaners as they haven't been asked to do it. She finds it annoying.

3 Groupwork. Students discuss the questions and report back to the class.

Optional activity

Students could produce a questionnaire on people's attitudes to giving money in the street. Brainstorm six to eight questions based on the previous activities. Here are some example questions:

When did you last give to a charity? (a) in the last month; (b) in the last year; (c) longer than a year ago; (d) never

When did you last give to a homeless person? (a) in the last month; (b) in the last year; (c) longer than a year ago; (d) never

Which kinds of charities do you prefer to give to? (a) children's; (b) environmental; (c) animal; (d) political; (e) other

The questionnaire could be used within the class to produce a class survey or used to survey students from other classes or the students' friends and families. The results could be displayed as a poster.

Close up (p 119)

Special uses of the past simple

1 Pairwork. Students discuss the questions. Monitor them as they work. Check answers with the class.

> a) past simple
> b) a desired situation
> c) If only, for example, *If only I was better paid*; I wish, for example, *I wish I had a bigger car*; conditional, for example, *If I was a pop star, I'd ...*

2 Whole class. Allow students a few minutes to do this exercise on their own and then ask individual students to read the sentences aloud. Ask other students to say if they think the sentences are correct and to change them if they think they are wrong. If they are having problems, refer them to the Language reference section on this page.

> a) I'd rather Jack paid for dinner.
> b) I'd rather Jack didn't work at the weekends.
> c) I'd rather Jack cleaned the house.
> The verb changes to the past simple when the subject of the verb following 'I'd rather' changes.

3 Students work individually to complete the sentences. Allow them to compare answers with a partner before checking with the class.

> *Suggested answers*
> a) stopped   b) got / found   c) started
> d) took   e) did   f) spent

4 Students work individually to complete the sentences.

5 Pairwork. Students compare their sentences in pairs or small groups.

Optional activity

You could repeat 4 and 5 several times with students commenting on a different topic each time. Either choose the topics yourself or ask students to suggest them. After sharing their ideas orally, students could report back to the class on the most common opinions, most extreme opinions, etc.

Rather you than me (p 120)

Lexis: *rather*

1 Pairwork. Students look at the picture and answer the questions. Check answers with the class.

> a) 9, 3   b) 10 (3)   c) 1   d) 2, 8   e) 4, 5, 6, 7

2 Whole class. Elicit suggestions from the students as to what the expression means. You could ask them to use it in a sentence which demonstrates its meaning. Make sure they are aware that this expression is used as a stand alone sentence and most frequently as a response. For example, A: I've got to spend the whole weekend at a conference with the boss. B: Rather you than me.

> I'm glad it's you that's having to do (whatever), and not me!

3 Working individually, students add *rather* to the sentences. Ask students to read out their sentences to a partner then invite individual students to read out their sentences to the class. Ask other students to say if they agree or not.

> a) It was rather late when we got home so I didn't return your call.
> b) The new art gallery looks rather like a spaceship.
> c) Well, actually, I rather like the idea of getting some pizzas and just watching TV.
> d) I didn't really enjoy it; we walked rather too far for my liking and I was pretty stiff the next day.

4 Give students plenty of time to rewrite the sentences and allow them to compare their answers in pairs before checking with the class. You could do this by writing the sentences on the board and asking students to compare theirs. This encourages and develops their self-correcting and noticing skills.

> a) You mean you had to do five three hour exams! Rather you than me!

b) I'd rather watch a film than read a book for relaxation.

c) They asked us, or rather, forced us to work overtime at weekends.

d) I'd rather have gone to bed early last night instead of having visitors. / I wish I had gone to bed early last night, rather than having visitors.

e) I'd rather have stayed at home, but I had no choice in the matter.

f) I'd rather do something cultural on holiday instead of just lying on a beach.

5 Students work individually to complete the sentences.

6 Pairwork. Students compare their sentences. You could get them to walk around the class sharing their sentences with each other and trying to find other students with the same sentence or idea.

Charity begins at home (p 121)

Closed books. Write the title of this section on the board and ask students to speculate on the meaning. (The saying is often quoted by people who believe that one should take care of the interests of one's family and friends before looking after strangers.) Ask them if they have the same or a similar expression in their language.

1 Groupwork. Students look at the photos and discuss the questions. Ask a spokesperson from each group to report back to the class.

2 59 SB p 158

Go through the questions with the class so they know what information they are listening for. Then play the recording. Students make notes in answer to the questions. Do not check answers at this stage. Be prepared to play the recording again if necessary. It will be quite difficult for students to do this after hearing it only once.

Note: 'quid' is slang for pound and 'bob' is slang for shilling, an old form of currency in Britain. 'A few bob' is a small amount of money.

59

(D = Daniel; S = Sue; J = Jake)

D: *So, you did a parachute jump for charity?*

S: *Uh, huh, I must have been mad because it was the most frightening thing I ever did, but as far as I know, it seemed to, you know, do the trick ... it seemed to raise quite a lot of money.*

D: *I've always wanted to do a parachute jump but I, I've never really had the kind of guts to do it.*

J: *I can see the fun of a parachute jump but what does the charity get out of it?*

S: *Well, they get the money that you, you know, you get sponsored by people or they ...*

J: *What? You ring people up and say, give me so much money and I'll jump out of an aeroplane?*

S: *Yeah, yeah, because I think people are more willing to do that because the, you know because it's something that kind of is right at the edge of the sort of comfort zone, so people are going, 'Oh I wouldn't do that, I'll, I'll give ... '*

D: *Did you raise a lot?*

S: *I don't really know, you know, that's one thing that does bother me that you know, you never really know how much these charities ...*

J: *That bothers me too, I mean, what does it cost to take an aeroplane up? You know, and presumably they have to insure you, um ...*

S: *Yeah, I suppose so, but then, you know, people wouldn't do it, would they? I mean they wouldn't be organised if you didn't, if they didn't raise money, if the ...*

D: *Well, that's right. I mean you, you, you have to have some sort of ... I mean, before we had any kind of a welfare system, um, charities were the only, the only way that we could possibly er, er, support people who were less fortunate than we were.*

J: *But wouldn't it be more sensible to do something you know with a, with a purpose, like collect money for food or ...*

D: *Well, there is something to an event. OK, if you have a big event it focuses people's attention on things and you can generate more money with a, with a larger event than you can with just going door to door ...*

S: *Yeah, you can have celebrities along and you know they can all ...*

J: *Yeah, well, they're doing it for publicity. What are they getting out of it?*

S: *I think they want to give as well, you know, they want to give something. It's like these sort of champagne receptions, you know, you've got to get, the charity's got to get a profile, haven't they, so they won't get photos in the paper unless you've got some celebrities.*

J: *Yes, but what worries me is how much they spend setting up the event. You know, it's really expensive now and you, you know, I get letters from people saying, come to this black tie ball to raise money for a particular charity, tickets are 150 quid each.*

D: *But on the other hand what's the alternative? The alternative is that maybe a lot of homeless people go hungry if somebody doesn't do something, and it takes an awful lot to get people off their butts to go and do stuff.*

J: *But it's such a contradiction that, you know, people will revel in something luxurious in order to help people who have got nothing. I mean ...*

S: Yeah, but, you know, the thing is that it must, it absolutely must make money for the charities because they wouldn't bother doing it ...

J: I reckon if you saw the figures at the end of that. I mean I know that these big fund-raising things ... I know for instance that whoever organised it, is on a percentage of what money is raised ...

S: Oh, you're just being cynical.

J: I'm being realistic. I'm being realistic because I think that by the time you've paid for the event, you know, probably that champagne's cost a lot of money, the food's cost a lot of money, hiring a hotel ...

S: Maybe people donate it though, you never know, do you?

D: And also, it's, there's got to be a bottom line level of help for people and at least if something is going through it's got to be better than nothing ...

S: I tell you what does bother me though ...

J: It's just to make you feel good though, isn't it. I mean, this is just to make you feel good about yourself.

S: No, I think ...

D: I think that's a bit simplistic ...

S: Yeah.

D: And not necessarily accurate at all. I think we are moving from a time of extreme selfishness to a time of a bit more benevolence. I think people have got to a point now where we, we do feel a bit guilty about things and so we should. And so we should. There's a huge inequality in the world now and it's about time we did start doing things and ...

S: There's one thing that does bother me though, and like these big organisations. You sometimes hear in the newspapers or whatever that the money you actually give doesn't actually get through to places like Africa or ...

J: Quite, because of the administration is absolutely enormous.

D: That's why I like ...

J: People jetting around the world, you know, um, staying in smart hotels, um, distributing money. I mean how much of your, of your money to a, to a famine charity actually buys food?

D: Well, that's what makes ... there's a lot of great things now ... of course if you go out and look on the web and things like there's all these great erm, sites where people ...

S: Oh yeah, you can press a button and erm ...

D: ... where you can actually press a button and donate, and donate a cup of rice, er, there's, they have a row of sponsors and by pressing the button ... oh, the World Hunger site is a really good example of that ...

S: Mmm, yeah, I do that.

D: ... where you, where you press a button and, er, they donate a cup of rice to ...

J: I can see the sense of that. That seems much more sensible to me than jumping out of an aeroplane, frankly, for a few bob.

S: Well, thanks very much!

3 Pairwork. Students compare their answers to 2. Check answers with the class. Students then discuss the questions in this exercise.

> **2** a) Students' own answers.
>
> b) Sue did a parachute jump for charity.
>
> c) Other ways of raising money mentioned: collecting money for food, collecting door to door, big celebrity events (eg: champagne reception, black tie ball), donating through web sites
>
> d) No. Jake thinks that big events and those which celebrities are involved in cost too much to organise. He'd rather collect food or do something practical. They do all agree that donating through a website is more likely to cost less to administer and is more likely to actually get through to the people who need it.
>
> e) Problems and doubts: you don't know how much money actually gets through to the people who need it; events cost a lot of money to organise; celebrities only take part in these events to raise their own profiles; people take part in charity events to make themselves feel good
>
> **3** a) Daniel b) Jake c) Jake d) Daniel
>   e) Sue f) Daniel g) Sue h) Jake

4 Play the recording again. Students listen and read the tapescript on page 158 at the same time. They find and underline phrases which support their answers to 3.

> *Suggested answers*
>
> a) 'The alternative is that maybe a lot of homeless people go hungry if somebody doesn't do something, and it takes an awful lot to get people off their butts to go and do stuff.' 'There's a huge inequality in the world now and it's about time we did start doing things and ...'
>
> b) ... well, they're doing it for publicity. What are they getting out of it?' '... people will revel in something luxurious in order to help people who have got nothing.'

c) 'What? You ring people up and say, give me so much money and I'll jump out of an aeroplane?' 'That bothers me too, I mean, what does it cost to take an aeroplane up? You know, and presumably they have to insure you, um ...'

d) 'Well, that's right.'

e) 'I tell you what does bother me though ...' 'No, I think ...'

f) '... if you go out and look on the web and things like there's all these great erm, sites where people ... where you can actually press a button and donate, and donate a cup of rice, er, there's, they have a row of sponsors and by pressing the button ... oh, the World Hunger site is a really good example of that ...'

g) 'but then, you know, people wouldn't do it, would they? I mean they wouldn't be organised if you didn't, if they didn't raise money, if the ...'

h) 'People jetting around the world, you know, um, staying in smart hotels, um, distributing money. I mean how much of your, of your money to a, to a famine charity actually buys food?'

5 Pairwork. Students compare their phrases. Then check with the whole class.

Sentence stress (p 122)

1 Pairwork. Students decide where the main stress falls in the question. Encourage them to read it aloud to see what sounds right.

> The main stress is likely to fall on the 'pa' of parachute and the 'cha' of charity, though this depends on the context.

2 Pairwork. Students practise saying the question aloud, altering the stress each time to match the replies. Do not check answers at this stage.

3 Again, encourage students to read the sentences aloud to find what sounds right. Do not check answers yet.

4 🔊 **60 SB p 158**

Play the recording. Students listen and check their answers.

> See stress underlined in tapescript.

> 🔊 **60**
>
> a) A: *So, you did a parachute jump for charity?*
>   B: *No, I did a bungee jump.*
>
> b) A: *So, you did a parachute jump for charity?*
>   B: *No, it was my sister.*

c) A: *So, you did a parachute jump for charity?*
   B: *No, I did it for fun.*

d) A: *So, you did a parachute jump for charity?*
   B: *No, but I'm thinking about doing one.*

5 Pairwork. Students decide who is A and who is B. As read out the question, varying the position of the stress each time and Bs listen to the stress and respond appropriately.

6 Pairwork. Students reverse roles and do the same with a different question.

> Stress underlined
>
> a) So, were you collecting money for Oxfam?
>   No, for the Save the Children fund.
>
> b) So, were you collecting money for Oxfam?
>   No, actually, we were collecting old clothes.
>
> c) So, were you collecting money for Oxfam?
>   No, I was ill that day.
>
> d) So, were you collecting money for Oxfam?
>   Erm, no, for our school actually.

Lexis (p 122)

1 Students work individually to complete the extracts. Allow them to compare answers with a partner if you wish but do not check answers at this stage.

2 🔊 **61 SB p 159**

Play the recording for students to listen and check their answers.

> a) raise b) sponsored c) collect d) event, door to door e) profile, celebrities
> f) go hungry g) feel good about h) donate

> 🔊 **61**
>
> a) *... as far as I know, it seemed to, you know, do the trick ... it seemed to raise quite a lot of money.*
>
> b) *... they get the money that you, you know, you get sponsored by people ...*
>
> c) *But wouldn't it be more sensible to do something you know with a, with a purpose, like collect money for food or ...*
>
> d) *... you can generate more money with a, with a larger event than you can with just going door to door ...*
>
> e) *... the charity's got to get a profile, haven't they, so they won't get photos in the paper unless you've got some celebrities.*
>
> f) *The alternative is that maybe a lot of homeless people go hungry if somebody doesn't do something ...*

g) *I mean, this is just to make you feel good about yourself.*

h) *... you can actually press a button and donate a cup of rice ...*

3 Allow students time to complete the questions. Then ask them to check their answers with a partner before asking individual students to supply the missing words.

a) raise   b) sponsored   c) celebrities, event
d) collecting, door to door   e) feel good about

4 Pairwork. Students discuss the questions in 3 and report back to the class.

All in a good cause (p 123)

1 Groupwork. Students read and consider the points in the box, reaching a decision on each point. Go round offering help with vocabulary, if necessary. Allow plenty of time for discussion at this stage. Ask the groups to appoint a secretary who will keep a note of the decisions they make. They will need these notes when preparing their presentation.

2 Groupwork. Students nominate a spokesperson and follow the instructions for preparing their presentations. Remind them of the tips on giving presentations on page 73 and the useful language in the Language toolbox.

3 Whole class. Allow plenty of time for each group to make its presentation. Go through the questions with the class first to ensure that the audience realises that they have to make a judgement. This will encourage them to listen attentively each time. Encourage them to ask questions at the end of each presentation.

The class can then vote on the most original idea and the most practical idea. Allow time for the groups to reform and discuss their opinions before they are asked to vote. Obviously they must vote for another group, and can't vote for themselves!

Travelling with an easy conscience (p 123)

Closed books. Remind students that the unit title is *Conscience*. Ask them to say what aspects of conscience have been covered so far. Then ask what they think the expression *an easy conscience* means (someone who has an easy conscience has no feelings of guilt about their behaviour). Elicit that the opposite is a *guilty conscience*.

1 Groupwork. Students discuss the questions and report back to the class.

2 Students work individually to read the article and decide if the author would have approved of their last holiday. Ask students to discuss this first in pairs and then to report back to the class on why or why not.

3 Pairwork. Students match the headings to the numbered sections of the text. Check answers with the class.

a) 6 b) 5 c) 1 d) 4 e) 3 f) 2

4 Pairwork. Ask students to discuss the questions. Check answers with the whole class.

a) where you decide to go, who you travel with, how you behave when you get there, how you can benefit poor communities, staying away from areas with poor human rights records, travelling outside tourist compounds and luxury hotels, visiting villages, learning about the country's culture, purchasing local products, dressing appropriately

b) Students' own answers.

5 Groupwork. Students discuss the questions and report back to the class.

Optional activity

If students are from the same country or city, they could produce a poster advising tourists on how to make the most of their visit while at the same time suggesting how they can benefit the local community and not have any negative impact. The poster could have the headings 'Please do ...' and 'Please don't ...'. If students are from different places, they could make the poster about the city they are currently in.

Lexis (p 125)

1 Students work individually to match the words and phrases from the text to the definitions. Allow them to check their answers with a partner and then check answers with the class.

a) habitats
b) issues
c) livelihoods
d) human rights abuses
e) poverty stricken areas
f) boycotts
g) impact
h) campaigns

2 Students complete the text with words and phrases from 1. Allow them to compare with a partner before checking answers with the class.

1 issues
2 boycotts
3 campaigns
4 impact
5 habitats
6 human rights abuses
7 poverty stricken areas
8 livelihoods

3 Pairwork. Students discuss the questions. Finish the activity with a brief whole-class discussion.

Conscience (p 126)

Collocations

Whole class. Give students a few minutes to complete the sentences, choosing words and phrases from the box, and then ask individual students to read the completed sentences aloud. The rest of the class can say if they think each sentence is correct or not.

> a) on his conscience
> b) a clear conscience / an easy conscience
> c) a guilty conscience
> d) eased my conscience
> e) in all conscience
> f) an easy conscience / a clear conscience

Discussion (p 126)

1 Students work individually to decide which things would make them feel guilty and to add three more items to the list.

2 Pairwork. Students compare their lists. They discuss which three things make them feel guiltiest and what they would do to ease their conscience in each case.

3 Students discuss the questions in pairs or small groups and then report back to the class.

Optional activity

Students could rank the 12 things in 1 according to how guilty they would feel, giving one point to the one they would feel least guilty about and 12 points to the one they would feel most guilty about. The rankings could be pooled, either with the whole class or in groups, to produce a class / group ranking.

Test

Scoring: one point per correct answer unless otherwise indicated.

1 (2 points per question)

　1　I'd rather they got here a little earlier.

　2　It's high time we were leaving. / It's high time we left.

　3　If only I liked living here.

　4　I'd rather I didn't have to drive to work, / I'd rather I didn't drive to work, but there's no alternative.

　5　It's about time you started getting ready to go out.

2　1　It's rather a strange looking building. / It's a rather strange looking building.

　2　We'd rather go to Paris given the choice.

　3　It was rather late when we got home, so we went straight to bed.

　4　I rather wish you hadn't told me that.

　5　It was rather too expensive for me.

　6　He's angry, or rather I should say furious.

　7　I'd rather have gone last night if I'd been able to.

　8　She looks rather like her grandmother, don't you think?

3　1 e　2 g　3 a　4 b　5 d　6 c

4　1 clear　2 ease　3 all　4 on

5　1 sponsor　2 raise　3 door-to-door　4 donate　5 hungry　6 boycott　7 livelihoods　8 campaign　9 rights　10 issues　11 impact　12 habitats

Conscience Test

Name: _____   **Total:** _____ /40

1 Special uses of the past simple *10 points*

Rearrange the words in b) and then complete the sentence so the meaning is the same as a).

1 a) I'd prefer them to get here a little earlier.
   b) they rather I'd ...

   _____

2 a) We really should be leaving now.
   b) time it's we high ...

   _____

3 a) I really don't like living here.
   b) I if only ...

   _____

4 a) I'd prefer not to drive to work, but there's no alternative.
   b) I'd I rather ...

   _____

5 a) You ought to start getting ready to go out.
   b) time about you it's ...

   _____

.2 Lexis – *rather* *8 points*

Put *rather* into an appropriate place in each sentence.

1 It's a strange looking building.

2 We'd go to Paris given the choice.

3 It was late when we got home, so we went straight to bed.

4 I wish you hadn't told me that.

5 It was too expensive for me.

6 He's angry, or I should say furious.

7 I'd have gone last night if I'd been able to.

8 She looks like her grandmother, don't you think?

3 Sentence stress *6 points*

Which stressed word, a–g, would result in the following responses? Look at the example.

     a   b   c   d   e   f
Did you and Sue go shopping in London last Saturday

       g
with Sara?

Example: No, Sunday. *f*

1 No, the Saturday before last. _____

2 No, Sara couldn't make it. _____

3 No, not me. _____

4 No, me and Angela. _____

5 No, we went to Guildford. _____

6 No, we just went to the theatre. _____

4 Lexis – collocations with *conscience* *4 points*

Choose the correct alternative.

1 I've got a totally **empty / clear** conscience. I did nothing wrong at all.

2 Telling her what I'd done helped **ease / lighten** my conscience.

3 Are you in **every / all** conscience really happy to do that?

4 You'll have it **in / on** your conscience all the time if you don't tell him you've made a mistake.

5 Lexis – charities and causes *12 points*

Complete the sentences with words from the box.

> rights boycott campaign donate
> door-to-door habitats hungry impact
> issues livelihoods raise sponsor

1 Will you _____ me? I'm doing a walk for charity.

2 We've managed to _____ over ten thousand pounds.

3 How do you feel about _____ collections?

4 We're asking everyone to _____ a few pounds each.

5 Millions of people in this country alone go _____ every single day.

6 We're hoping the public will _____ all their products.

7 Many people's _____ depend on tourism.

8 Our latest _____ is to develop educational facilities.

9 We need to stop all human _____ abuses immediately.

10 There are many more _____ that need addressing.

11 The _____ of tourism here has been very positive.

12 Many unique _____ are being destroyed every day.

14 Review 2 *Teacher's notes*

Just a coincidence? (p 127)

Discourse markers

1 1 But   2 After all   3 however   4 as well
    5 Whereas   6 Not only   7 but also   8 however
    9 But incredibly

Words of wisdom (p 127)

Rather

1 a) We should not grieve, but rather find
       strength in what remains behind.

   b) Friendship is unnecessary as it has no
      survival value. It rather gives value to
      survival.

   c) I wish I had never read so much. It rather
      gives me an inferiority complex.

   d) The English are a rather foul-mouthed
      nation.

   e) Life is rather like a tin of sardines. We are all
      of us looking for the key.

   f) 'When I use a word,' Humpty Dumpty said
      in a rather scornful tone, 'it means just
      what I choose it to mean. Neither more nor
      less.'

   g) Given the choice, I'd rather be a failure at
      something I enjoy as opposed to a success
      at something I hate.

Word games (p 128)

Compound adjectives

1 a) 9 across: dressed, 4 down: haired,
      12 across: looking

   b) 5 down: educated, 1 down: informed,
      13 across: minded

   c) 3 across: mannered, 6 down: thinking,
      2 down: behaved

   d) 10 down: spoken, 6 across: tempered

   e) 11 across: loving, 7 across: faced

   f) 8 down: working

Internet lexis (p 128)

1 Words in the order they appear: attachment, server,
    inbox, log on, search engine, homepage, online,
    chatroom, newsgroup

The 21st century (p 129)

The future seen from the past

1 1 would be swallowing
    2 were on the verge of colonising
    3 were going to be delivering
    4 would be
    5 were going to be carrying
    6 were to last
    7 were supposed to crash

Greetings from Nepal (p 130)

Patterns with *have* & *get*

1 got him to agree
2 got to do
3 got a small truck to take / had a small truck take
4 got going
5 got a local guide to take / had a local guide take
6 have people running
7 get the photos developed / have the photos
   developed
8 get you packing / have you packing
9 get to meet
10 get you all teaching / have you all teaching

Strange but true (p 130)

Using modals to talk about the past

▭ **62 SB p 159**

1 a) A man decided to post himself to a friend in
      a large crate as a surprise birthday present.

b) A man on a commuter train's inflatable underpants were triggered to expand when someone splashed them with water. They were only supposed to inflate in the event of a tidal wave.

c) A man boarding a plane said 'Hi, Jack' to the pilot and air-traffic controllers called in armed police as they thought a hijack was taking place.

2 1 would bring
2 would post
3 should have arrived
4 might have rescued
5 can't have been thinking
6 would inflate
7 must have splashed
8 should have been able
9 couldn't move
10 could have been
11 can't have been paying
12 would notify

▭▭ 62

... And to finish tonight's programme, we said we'd bring you some amusing stories from this week's press from around the world, and here they are:

In the United States, John Franklin, a cleaner from Illinois, decided last month he would post himself to his best friend as a birthday surprise. He climbed into a large crate and got his wife to post him to his friend's house thirty miles away. He should have arrived the next morning, but unfortunately the crate went missing for six days before finally turning up in Malibu, California. Postal workers might have rescued him earlier, but they mistook his desperate banging for the ticking of a clock. Mr Franklin said he can't have been thinking clearly as it seemed like such a good idea at the time. An understatement if ever we've heard one.

Japan now, and Keita Ono's inflatable underpants caused chaos on a rush-hour train in Tokyo last week. Mr Ono, 43, designed the rubber pants so they would inflate to 30 times their normal size in the event of a tidal wave. He explained that he'd always been afraid of drowning and that he wore them 24 hours a day. Mr Ono thinks that somebody must have splashed some water on them, triggering the sensor and accidentally causing them to inflate. He admitted that he should have been able to deflate the pants, but he said he couldn't move at all and was firmly wedged in the middle of the carriage aisle. Things could have been much worse had it not been for a quick-thinking passenger who punctured the pants with a pen.

Finally, Detroit airport was last night put on red-alert when a man boarding a plane greeted the pilot, whom

he knew, with the words 'Hi Jack'. Air-traffic controllers, who can't have been paying too much attention to what was going on, ordered armed police to board the plane, before realising their mistake. A spokesman said that from now on, officials would notify air-traffic control whenever there was a pilot called Jack on duty. I don't know!

Word challenge (p 131)

Students play the game in groups of three: Students A, B and C. Student A is the referee and turns to page 138 to look at the answers. Students B and C take turns to choose a square for each other to complete. If Student B chooses a square for Student C which C cannot answer, B can win the point by giving the correct answer. The game then continues with Student C choosing a square for B, etc.

1 1 by 2 through / apart 3 up 4 In 5 up
6 up 7 off 8 of 9 into 10 against 11 in
12 on 13 at 14 by 15 for 16 in 17 of
18 up 19 for 20 up

Lexis (p 131)

1 a mind b take c herself d conscience
2 a 3 b 1 c 4 d 2
3 d sue
4 a to pull everything off
b a terrible mix up
c a slight technical hitch
d get their act together
5 a fiasco b armchair c graffiti d law-abiding
6 d dirty conscience
7 a 3 scratch card b 4 bad hair day c 1 gap year
d 2 GM food
8 c first and finish
9 Suggested answers
a homework b traffic c performance / result
d headache
10 word

End of Course Test

Scoring: one point per correct answer unless otherwise indicated.

1 (2 points each for 9–14)
1 'll be checking
2 is
3 'll have been going
4 goes

5 'll be

6 'll only just be going

7 won't mind

8 're

9 'll have landed / 'll land

10 'll be

11 will be living / will live

12 will have given birth

13 'll be

14 will have become / will become

2 1 whereas

2 not only

3 but more importantly

4 as well

5 This means that

6 however

3 1 h) 2 f) 3 b) 4 a) 5 g) 6 c) 7 d) 8 e)

4 (2 points each)

1 Local residents have neither been consulted on the issue, nor have they been informed of developments.

2 So awful was the congestion on the roads that the minister missed his flight.

3 Such were the measures taken by the police to control the crowds that trouble was avoided.

4 I can neither understand wanting to climb a mountain nor can I empathise with people who do.

5 (2 points each for 1–7)

1 It may / could / might have been Paul who took it.

2 You should have asked her first.

3 I'm afraid we couldn't find it.

4 It must have been him who took it.

5 We tried, but he wouldn't tell us.

6 You might / could have called me!

7 They might / may / could have seen you.

8 He can't have looked very hard. I found it easily.

9 She might / may / could have been there, but I'm not sure.

10 He could have told me, but I really can't remember.

11 He could talk when he was only 18 months old and he hasn't stopped since!

6 1 going 2 to help 3 broken into 4 to go out 5 to let 6 decorated

7 1 marvellous 2 agency 3 accommodation 4 conquer 5 dangerous 6 apparatus 7 motivation 8 volunteer 9 electrical 10 communication

8 1 The river was on the verge of flooding and people were asked to evacuate their houses.

2 She was going to do a sponsored swim for charity but she broke her leg.

3 The elections were due to take place in May but had to be postponed because of the fuel crisis.

4 I had expected we would experience some problems but it was a complete fiasco.

5 He was supposed to give evidence in court about the fraud but the charges were dropped.

6 The Mayor was to attend the opening ceremony but at the last minute it was cancelled.

9 1 teaching 2 come 3 crying 4 water

10 1 whenever 2 whoever 3 Wherever 4 Whichever 5 However 6 whatever

11 1 It's high time I thought about getting a new job.

2 I'd rather you didn't tell them for a few days. / I'd rather not tell them for a few days.

3 If only I could play the piano.

4 I'd rather not leave until 5.30.

5 I wish the rain would stop.

6 It's time you started considering others a little more.

12 1 I'd rather have white wine if you don't mind.

2 This soup is rather tasty actually.

3 I rather wish you hadn't done that.

4 He looks rather like the actor Tom Cruise, don't you think?

5 Try to look at it as a challenge rather than a problem.

6 It's rather too expensive for me, I'm afraid.

7 I'd rather have gone to Paris instead.

8 It seems rather a long way to go just for three days.

13 1 of 2 against 3 by 4 on 5 up 6 of 7 into 8 unto 9 in 10 up 11 to 12 up 13 up 14 through 15 for 16 of 17 into 18 in 19 on 20 to

14 1 turn 2 store 3 chat 4 search 5 attachment 6 suspended 7 solitary 8 trouble 9 against 10 details 11 high 12 light 13 at 14 spoken 15 consuming 16 broad 17 act 18 off 19 up 20 card 21 gap 22 mouth 23 sponsor 24 clear

Name: Total: _____ /150

1 *Will* for predictions and assumptions *20 points*

Choose the most natural alternative.

A: Do you know where John is?

B: Try his room. He (1) **'s checking / 'll be checking** his e-mails. He usually (2) **is / will be** at this time.

A: I saw Jim the other day, walking past the school.

B: Oh, right. He (3) **was going / 'll have been going** to the gym. I think he (4) **goes / will go** to the one over the road.

A: We (5) **'re / 'll be** late if we don't get a move on.

B: Don't worry. He (6) **'s only just going / 'll only just be going** through customs. Anyway, (7) **he doesn't mind / won't mind** if we (8) **'re / 'll be** a few minutes late.

Complete the predictions by putting the verb into an appropriate form using *will*.

9 We _____ (land) on Mars within the next fifty years.

10 There _____ (be) a World President by 2050.

11 Humans _____ (live) on nothing but pills by the end of the century.

12 A man _____ (give birth) by 2020.

13 It _____ (be) possible to have holidays on the moon in fifty years.

14 Cash _____ (become) obsolete within 30 years.

2 Discourse markers *6 points*

Put the discourse markers into the correct place in the text.

> as well   but more importantly   however
> not only   this means that   whereas

Research into storytelling skills reveals that deep male voices are preferred by both children and adults for reading aloud. Their soothing voices help you to fall asleep, (1) _____ women's voices are perceived as less likely to make you drop off. In the survey, storytellers were judged (2) _____ on the soothing quality of their voices, (3) _____ on their ability to make a story come alive and having

enough characterisation in their voices (4) _____ . Women tend to have a problem putting on deep voices. (5) _____ they often sound unconvincing in male roles.

Mothers, (6) _____ , are still regarded equally to fathers when it comes to singing children to sleep.

3 Formal and informal language *8 points*

Match the formal words on the left with their more informal equivalents on the right.

1	commence	a)	look / ask for
2	prominent	b)	before
3	prior to	c)	trick
4	seek	d)	later
5	depict	e)	very bad
6	deceive	f)	well-known
7	in due course	g)	show
8	severe	h)	start

4 Inversion after *neither*, *nor*, *so* and *such* *8 points*

Complete the sentences in b) so the meaning is the same as a).

1 a) Local residents haven't been consulted on the issue or informed of developments.

   b) Local residents have _____

   _____

2 a) The congestion on the roads was so awful that the minister missed his flight.

   b) So _____

   _____

3 a) The police had taken such measures to control the crowds that trouble was avoided.

   b) Such _____

   _____

4 a) I can't understand wanting to climb a mountain and I can't empathise with people who do.

   b) I can neither _____

   _____

5 Using modals to talk about the past *18 points*

Complete each sentence in b) so the meaning is the same as a), using each of the modals in the box once and the underlined verb.

> could couldn't may might ~~might~~ must
> should wouldn't

Example: It's possible that she <u>did</u> it.

> *She might have done it.*

1. a) It's possible that it <u>was</u> Paul who took it.
   b) It _____ Paul who took it.

2. a) It was a mistake not to <u>ask</u> her first.
   b) You _____ her first.

3. a) I'm afraid we didn't manage to <u>find</u> it.
   b) I'm afraid we _____ it.

4. a) I'm certain it <u>was</u> him who took it.
   b) It _____ him who took it.

5. a) We tried, but he refused to <u>tell</u> us.
   b) We tried, but he _____ us.

6. a) I'm annoyed you didn't <u>call</u> me.
   b) You _____ me!

7. a) Perhaps they <u>saw</u> you.
   b) They _____ you.

Correct the mistakes in these sentences.

8. He mustn't have looked very hard. I found it easily.

9. She can have been there, but I'm not sure.

10. He could tell me, but I really can't remember.

11. He could have talked when he was only 18 months old and he hasn't stopped since!

6 Patterns with *get* *6 points*

Put the verbs in brackets into the correct form.

1. The party really got _____ (go) just after you left. You should've stayed.

2. If you can't do it on your own, get one of your classmates _____ (help) you.

3. My car got _____ (break into) again last night.

4. I rarely get _____ (go out) these days.

5. I finally got my parents _____ (let) me have a party.

6. I got my flat _____ (decorate) last week.

7 Word stress *10 points*

<u>Underline</u> the main stress in these words.

1. marvellous
2. agency
3. accommodation
4. conquer
5. dangerous
6. apparatus
7. motivation
8. volunteer
9. electrical
10. communication

8 The future seen from the past *6 points*

Use the prompts below to write complete sentences in the past.

1. The river / on the verge of / flood / and / people / ask / evacuate / their houses.

   _____
   _____

2. She / be going to / do / a sponsored swim for charity / but / she / break / her leg.

   _____
   _____

3. The elections / due to / take place / May / but / have to / postpone / because of the fuel crisis.

   _____
   _____

4. I / expect / we / experience / some problems / but / it / be / a complete fiasco.

   _____
   _____

5. He / suppose to / give evidence in court / about the fraud / but / the charges / be / drop.

   _____
   _____

6. The Mayor / be / attend / the opening ceremony / but / at the last minute / it / cancel.

   _____
   _____

9 Patterns with *have* *4 points*

Put the verbs in brackets into the correct form.

1. He's desperate to learn English. He'll have you _____ (teach) him before you know it.

2   I'm having someone _____ (come) round tomorrow to fix the broken window.

3   The film will have you _____ (cry) with laughter.

4   We had the neighbours _____ (water) the plants while we were away.

10 -ever 6 points

Complete the sentences with words from the box. Use each word once.

> whichever   wherever   whatever   whoever   however   whenever

1   Come and see me _____ you like. Any time at all.

2   Could _____ has parked their car in front of the gates, please move it?

3   _____ you end up for dinner give me a call and I'll try to join you later.

4   _____ you choose, I'm sure you'll be happy with it.

5   _____ many times I see the film, it still always makes me cry.

6   You can wear _____ you like. It's quite informal.

11 Special uses of the past simple 6 points

Correct the mistakes in these sentences.

1   It's time high I thought about getting a new job.

2   I'd rather you tell them for a few days.

3   If only I can play the piano.

4   I'd rather not left until 5.30.

5   I wish the rain will stop.

6   It's time you start considering others a little more.

12 Lexis – rather 8 points

Put rather into the correct place in each sentence.

1   I'd have white wine if you don't mind.

2   This soup is tasty actually.

3   I wish you hadn't done that.

4   He looks like the actor Tom Cruise, don't you think?

5   Try to look at it as a challenge than a problem.

6   It's too expensive for me, I'm afraid.

7   I'd have gone to Paris instead.

8   It seems a long way to go just for three days.

13 Lexis – collocations 20 points

Complete the sentences by adding the missing words.

1   He's got a really good chance _____ getting the job.

2   She's always coming up _____ the problem of lack of funding.

3   He's _____ far the most generous person I know.

4   What's the password to log _____ to the Internet?

5   We should weigh _____ the options very carefully.

6   The jury returned a verdict _____ guilty.

7   He took the law _____ his own hands.

8   She's a law _____ herself – always unpredictable.

9   It's a once _____ a lifetime opportunity.

10 I finally plucked _____ the courage to tell him.

11 Nothing springs _____ mind at the moment.

12 We'll pick you _____ outside school at 7.30, OK?

13 It didn't really live _____ to our expectations.

14 Unfortunately, our plans fell _____ at the last minute.

15 I'll take your word _____ it, but you'd better be right.

16 He doesn't say much. He's a man _____ few words.

17 I can't put my feelings _____ words at the moment.

18 He's always putting words _____ my mouth.

19 She'll have it _____ her conscience all her life.

20 I could never be a door-_____ -door salesman.

14 Lexis – general 24 points

Choose the correct alternative.

1   It was found at the **turn / change** of the century.

2   They've got a lot in **store / keep** for us today.

3   Do you ever visit **chat / chatting** rooms on the Net?

4   Try looking for it through a **search / find** engine.

5   I can't open the **attaching / attachment** you sent.

6   He was given a **suspended / hanging** sentence.

7   He was in **solo / solitary** confinement for months.

8   He's always been in **problem / trouble** with the law.

9 It's **against / opposing** the law in this country.

10 Can you give me precise **particulars / details** about the accident?

11 We need a very **high / tall** profile campaign.

12 We got up at first **light / sun** this morning.

13 They were totally shocked **in / at** first.

14 He's very softly-**spoken / speaking**.

15 It's a very time-**eating / consuming** process.

16 He's pretty **broad / wide**-minded about most things.

17 They really need to get their **act / play** together.

18 I'm afraid we've had to call the party **off / out**.

19 There's been a mix-**down / up** over the tickets.

20 I won £50 on a scratch **ticket / card** the other day.

21 He went to India for his **gap / space** year.

22 Most of our business is by word of **ear / mouth**.

23 Will you **sponsor / donate** me for my charity walk?

24 I've got a totally **clear / clean** conscience about it.